Messages from God
PASSAGE FROM FEAR

Armageddon or Renaissance?

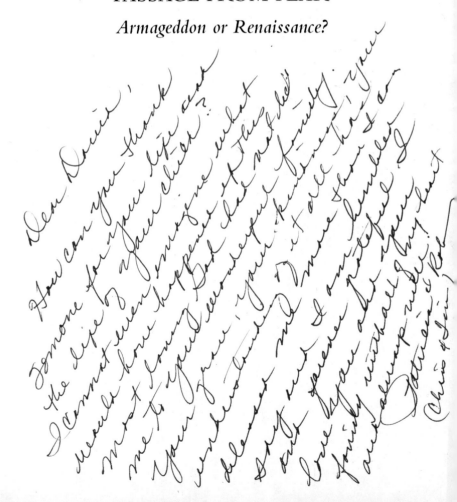

Messages from God
PASSAGE FROM FEAR

Armageddon or Renaissance?

Channeled through
Patricia Grabow

with the help of
Barbara McCormick

Hara Publishing Group
P.O. Box 507
Lynnwood, WA 98046
18728 Bothell Way NE
Bothell, Washington 98011 U.S.A.
harapub@foxinternet.net
http://www.harapublishing.com

Messages from God
PASSAGE FROM FEAR
Armageddon or Renaissance?

Copyright © 2002 by Patricia Grabow
http://www.patriciagrabow.com

Hara Publishing Group
P.O. Box 507
Lynnwood, WA 98046
18728 Bothell Way NE
Bothell, Washington 98011 U.S.A.
harapub@foxinternet.net
http://www.harapublishing.com

ISBN 1-883697-60-3
LCCN 2002102910

Prepared in the United States of America
Original cover design by Gretchen Elizabeth Grabow
Cover art by Cheryl DePuy Murray

—Dedicated to—

Barbara McCormick
Bruce and Charlotte McArthur and Family

whose love for humanity and kindness to me can never really be repaid

and others whose kindness and support
assured the survival of my family and this work

Rosie Porter
The Darrel Reynolds Family
John and Charlotte VanZyle

and my beloved children

Rob, whose very existence is part of this work, **Chris** and **Tim**

—*Table of Contents*—

Forward ix

Introduction xiii

First Theme Explanation xvii

Theme 1   The Nature of Individual Reality 3
           Science and religion

Theme 2   Earth and Personal Changes 69
           Discussions about the next 100 years and the changes which will occur
           politically and individually

Theme 3   Children 91
           Children as teachers and the role they will play in the time ahead; How to
           parent them; The soil is right for their growth.

Theme 4   World of Rules 113
           Created for security and reaching an absurd state. The nature of pain; The
           role of the environment; Dream states; The White Light in the time ahead

Theme 5   Role of Men and Women 129
           Role of women; Male/female relationships; Soul mates; Strength of women
           during a period of transition for life; Abortion and vegetarianism

Theme 6   Time 157
           Cosmic time vs. linear time; Relationship between growth and time

Theme 7   Fear 177
           Changing role of fear on the earth; Loss of predators; Limits/ poverty/ cities

Theme 8   Creative Process 195
           Role of innovation in the times ahead; Inborn sense of direction; Spiritual
           growth not Utopian, and why

Theme 9   The White Light 219
           White Light meditation is briefly taught. The Source said that teaching the
           White Light meditation is the main reason this work came into being.

Theme 10   White Light and the Substance of Matter 225
           Role of Love in the times ahead; Increased spiritual stature; Coming of diver-
           sity of life

Theme 11   Love 255
           Love permeates the person like water in the cells of a plant. White Light
           unique, easy process

Theme 12   Recapitulation 269

Session on The Source 287

—Forward—

Messages from God
PASSAGE FROM FEAR
Armageddon or Renaissance?

and

Messages from God
PASSAGE FROM KARMA
The Spiritual Calculus of Being

Written in 1983 by
Bruce and Charlotte McArthur

This section, a gift to the reader, is an intimate view of the creating process for *Messages from God: Passage from Fear* and *Messages from God: Passage from Karma*.

Prior to her first attempt at automatic writing, we have in the individual who served as a channel for the book, someone with no experience in or exposure to any area of metaphysical studies and psychic phenomena. The spiritual path she had walked was that of the average, sincere, United States Protestant churchgoer and participant. Well educated, sensitive to happenings in the lives of professional associates, family members and friends, she performed the point of view of current moral codes, man's law, natural science, experience and training in the educational field, obedient child and loving parent.

The suggestion to try automatic writing was made by a perceptive, caring member of the channel's family with the intention of providing her with a new mental focus and interest during a period of excessive stress, discouragement, and suicidal depression and in an apparent state of abject hopelessness. Automatic writing helped!

The first writings were received by her with a mixture of intellectual shock, fear, curiosity and the required open-mindedness. The Source's loving concern for the total well-being of the channel has been ever-present. The first writing was guidance and preparation for the progress. When she understood the support given through The Source, the material and the book quickly followed.

At various times, The Source has identified itself as "Universal Light" and explained that "the material is tapping an aspect of infinity." It was stated that the channel is not The Source in any way; she is only a channel for the book, chosen for that and because her motives were pure. "She has had many opportunities in her lifetime to abuse power and has never chosen to do so."

The introduction was written by means of automatic writing. The Source then indicated that voice dictation would replace the automatic writing for rapid accomplishment of the task, giving the material for *Messages from God: Passage from Fear,* the first book. The channel made inquiries to individuals with the experience and capability of teaching this technique; but because of distance or required monetary outlay, outside help for guidance did not become immediately available. So the channel, and the friend giving support and encouragement, gathered those required physical tools which were self-evident: applied faith and simple directions dictated by The Source; and the "voice" manifested. "Voice" communication became the new instrument of dictation from The Source.

From the first encounter with The Source, all aspects of this entire happening became a walk in faith for the channel. When costly long distance moves of household goods and persons were required, the jobs materialized to provide the necessary monies. Housing was located where and when foretold. Meetings and associations valuable in the development and handling of the material for the book were predicted accurately; and when the channel moved, as instructed, the meshing of the minds and talent was as remarkable as the book material itself. To follow the guidance was to move forward; to not follow the guidance was to stand still.

It is the perception of the individuals writing this forward that to read *Messages from God: Passage from Fear* and *Messages from God: Passage from Karma* and apply the understanding, is to walk forward in consciousness.

—Bruce McArthur

Friend, directed by The Source
to write this Forward
Author of *Your Life: Why It Is The Way It Is, And What You Can Do About It*,
and co-author of
The Intelligent Heart

—Introduction—

This section is to explain some fascinating elements of these two great works of prophesy. As the forward mentioned, the beginning of this process was Patricia Grabow's death experience.

While on holiday in London, Patricia became involved in an automobile accident. From what she describes as 'the most remarkable' experience of joy she had ever known. From somewhere, in the Great Beyond, Patricia would not leave her sons and chose to returned back to her body.

Almost immediately after recuperation, Patricia was led to do automatic writing, an unfamiliar process which both frightened and fascinated her. She proceeded. Patricia was led by the writings to people who would help her. An odyssey that took Patricia from England, to the North Slope of Alaska, to Jackson Hole, Wyoming, brought together a spiritual team she would need to finish the first and then the second book.

The writing said that these people were her soul mates. They were in place when she needed them to produce these two great works.

When the dictation began, all but the first sixteen pages of the first book and all of the second book were dictated into a tape recorder then later transcribed and typed.

Patricia was covered with a blanket, and Barbara McCormick turned on the tape recorder as the session began. The sessions were generally held in the living room of Barbara's apartment in Teton Village at Jackson Hole. The Source said that, on another level, Barbara was also protecting Patricia when she dictated the text. When Patricia would question why they were doing this, Barbara would simply reply that if it helped one person through a time as Patricia went through, it was all worth it; as simple as that. Barbara enjoyed thinking about the person the books might help.

The sessions were short, generally not longer than fifteen minutes or for as much time as Patricia had energy. Patricia was pregnant at the time with her son, Rob; so as the pregnancy progressed, the sessions became shorter. During the sessions, Rob would quiet in the womb. The last session for the first book, which was guidance regarding publication, was done as Patricia was in the early stages of labor with her son. You can hear the interruption for labor and accompanying sounds on the tape.

The second book's sessions spanned August through November. Newborn Rob fussed, as babies do, except when Patricia was channeling a session's dictation. Sometimes he would squirm but never fussed during a session. At times the dictation would stop and The Source would describe, that on another level, infant Rob was trying to cooperate but that he was hungry. When the session was over, he would cry and Patricia would tend to him. Another remarkable thing is that as the reader reads the text, it is continuous. The reader is not aware that daily sessions could continue only fifteen minutes or so. Dictated text often resumed the following day and always without a break in thought.

In addition, the tape recorder did not work for the introduction; so when the book was finished, the introduction had to be rerecorded. As far as Barbara could remember, the text was exactly the same as the first time.

The writing accurately predicted, before the dictation began, the number of pages of both books. The first book, *Messages from God: Passage from Fear* consist of twelve sections or themes. It was published in 1985. There was no marketing of the book at the time because Patricia was exhausted and had a small baby to raise. Those who have known Patricia, through the generation of the books to the present time, feel that the world was simply not ready for this work then. But now it is time for these works to be released.

The second book, *Messages from God: Passage from Karma*, would have eighteen sections or chapters. Nearly twenty years after the book's dictation, the prediction was realized. It had been retyped and the margins set for the five-by-eight inch resized layout. The number of pages proved to be remarkably accurate, considering the chosen font and margin settings.

The writing had said that there would be four books produced in the channel's life. The first was like a teacher, making points and returning to them in an almost circular pattern, called Themes in the book. The second created a different perspective on sin and repentance. The third will be on love and soul mates; and the fourth will pertain to alternative realities. At this publication date, the last two have yet to be written.

The writing had said that there were four sister works that began at the same time as these manuscripts. The author later learned that books with the same general message as these works had indeed begun on the same day in different parts of the United States.

The symbolism for the books' cover and Theme headings come from the automatic writing. The motive for doing the books is love. The writing said that symbolism is powerful, and that we were moving into the numbers of four and eight. As Patricia began automatic writing, the symbol of eight circles and eight signs of infinity would come. As a result that same symbol was used on the cover of the book and for the theme and chapter headings. The accompanying sense was that of being surrounded with Compassion.

In our experience, these books are best read at multiple sittings, and read slowly to allow for contemplation and enjoyment of the content. The content is, in a sense, concentrated, and recommended to be assimilated gradually.

Those times, as the second book was produced, were not easy; but the writing insisted that the books had to be completed then in spite of the obstacles faced. It was with great grief that Patricia later realized that significance. Her angel and lifeline, Barbara McCormick, passed-on in January of that year.

It has been a struggle to produce these books, but the great spirit of individuals like Barbara McCormick, Bruce and Charlotte McArthur and their family are behind it.

It is wished that the reader will experience that same sense of love that sustained Patricia though her trials during the generation of this book.

The hope is that, as Barbara had wished, the books are "a help to at least one person."

—First Theme Explanation—

Messages from God
Passage from Fear
Armageddon or Renaissance?

The beginning of the book, Dictation from The Source that follows, evolved by automatic writing. Patricia thought that she would be writing a book on the West and had no idea that the content of this and her next book would be spiritual. She had used the automatic writing to survive, and the writing had been loving, accurate and guiding.

She was instructed to write the introduction and realized, at that point, the manuscripts to come would be metaphysical in nature. After the automatic writing had provided the introduction, she was instructed to show the material to Barbara McCormick, Bruce, Charlotte, and David McArthur in Jackson. They became her support throughout the generation of both *Messages from God: Passage from Fear* and *Messages from God: Passage from Karma*.

The interval between January and April was devoted to finding a means to do voice communication and adjusting to the nature of the dictation to come. That is the time Patricia was instructed to show the dictated piece to Barbara, Bruce and Charlotte and their son David. They realized that the work was to be spiritual in nature and decided to cooperate with instructions given by The Source to help with the books.

Finally, Patricia was given instruction, by the automatic writing, about doing the channeling. At Barbara McCormick's condominium, Patricia used the white light meditation that she had been taught, and the text of this and the subsequent books began. Barbara is heard saying, in the background, 'Is the tape recorder on? Yes, it is. Oh my, it has begun.'

Patricia came out of this session very cold; in future sessions she would be covered with a blanket. None of the sessions could lasted very long because they required concentrated energy.

Theme One

The Nature of Individual Reality

Theme One

[Dictation from The Source
by means of automatic writing]

January 16, 1981

You, dear reader, are aware that you are the product of genetic engineering, but you are without the awareness that you are also the product of spiritual engineering in which the strong survive. You will see, in this book, that the more ponderous force, by far, is the spiritual of which all life is a part. You will also see that the end product is close and being prepared now. You are that product and need to look at the wonders within.

You will see that you are the statement from God about the universe; nothing outside of you exists or should be given credence in making judgments. You are the end product, and you are all there is. There is nothing more.

You will wonder, why did this cosmic experiment take place?:

Because I AM, and I AM there.

You may assume that matter is your creator, but you are your creator, in fact, and you have the power to determine your reality. You will look into your past and see an event that you can assume you did not create: for example, a situation in which you felt uncomfortable. You will see that it was one that did not kill. It was only hurtful or uncomfortable.

At which point did you draw the line between discomfort and the step further that would have meant your demise? You are frequently in the position of suicide. You are not able to make the decision to jump, but it is appealing, nonetheless. You will be able to see, now, that it was you who created the situation.

The purpose of your creation was the essence of life on this plane, discovering the brink of your limitations but not extending them to the point of no return; and that is all death is, a point at which you cannot return to this plane. You are not free, yet, of the limits of matter; for that is part of this plane of existence, which we shall discuss later. You can be free of the brinkmanship that is harmful to either yourself or others at which point you are in control of this existence. You are the author of the script and will write a good play or a horror story, depending on your frame of thought.

January 1 7, 1981

We will continue with the makeup of the individual. Humankind is not prepared to write the script for this time and place. You were, a hundred years ago, but the evolution of man, that is, the spiritual evolution, was based on a sense of community that exists no longer, and thus ignores the others in the world around him. The net result is a sense that the world is not a good place or that people are not good, neither of which is true. The world, itself, has not changed nor has the spiritual substance of the individual. Those people who were here on earth a hundred years ago were not kinder than those who are here today, just as the animals that were here a hundred years ago are not less swift or capable of surviving in their natural habitat. But the habitat changed dramatically and, therefore, the adaptation is not appropriate.

The habitat will change in the next hundred years ten times more dramatically and you, dear reader, need to be prepared for it. Your happiness will depend upon your willing adaptation. That brings us to the concept that you are the end product of an evolution. In time you will see that you have a unique capacity in the realm of life. You have the capacity to recognize and communicate with the world of the spirit, the spirit that exists within, not spiritualism. For that is confusion and fear . That spirit will guide you out of the world of illusion into a reality you will only wonder at and say you had no idea it existed. It has been the Life substance on this planet since the beginning. There have been good people who have been aware of it and called it God; unfortunately, it is more than the various concepts will allow it to be. So it will remain untapped until you allow yourself the experience of it rather than the reading, or the churchgoing, or the sacrifice known as morality. All concepts, even the most expansive are, of themselves, limited by their definition. And so the world becomes deluded and separated into factions, all of whom feel their exposure means the whole.

You will see, dear reader, that you are not divided. You know what you think. It may be different or differ from the thoughts of neighbors or friends, but you will retain your thoughts; the influence of others is, in fact, not that dramatic in your lifetime. It may take on the end product of an evolution that spans an area much greater than you consciously recognize. You will see that area involved much more than you can consciously conceptualize. You are capable, however, of utilizing the tremendous energy you have created in your lives, both here on earth and on other planes of existence; you are not limited to the earth. You are capable of functioning well here, and that is your goal. You will see that your capacity to function well here is contingent upon your ability to see the cosmos and the power resident in your person.

Now, back to where you write the script: You are the creator of your experience. You will be a Free Spirit, in time, no matter what you do. You will assume that if you harm others, you will pay. Your reality is Love and that cannot change. You will, in time, learn the lessons you need, will create those lessons to achieve the reality that never changed. You will think of loving someone. You will now try to destroy the feeling you had when you kissed, made love, laughed, played or whatever gave that love meaning to where you are. But you will not be able to destroy that feeling. You may later have negative experiences, but you will only regret that they happened. You may forget some, but they will return someday; you will remain aware of the reality you experienced. You were a Free Spirit at that moment and, ultimately, it was nothing outside yourself but you. You created it and cherish it. You create and make up those experiences as well as ones that, ultimately, you wish hadn't happened. You can foresee the effects of your creations and decide upon an alternative course, but not consciously. To tap the power of the expansive reality you have known, you could never articulate what you know. You may find parts of it articulated in music, books, poetry or acting, but you will only fail. That is why you have the world of secular thought.

The Nature of Individual Reality

[Dictated in session from The Source through Patricia Grabow by means of voice communication (from here forward); recorded and transcribed.]

"The Spiritual World is all there is."

Session #1
  April 13, 1981
  8:43 – 9:04 P.M.

You will see that I am able to make all life flourish and will do it very soon. You will see that you are free of any limits and are not to worry. Life as you know it will not exist in its present form but will be able to change; it will not be necessary for life to have the form it now has in order to be with Me. You will see that it has many forms, many more than you can even understand, for you are still limited by the senses that have evolved in order to cope with life on this plane. However, these senses are not the nature of Life itself. The senses are only to help you as you evolve, here. You will grow to the point in which you will see that the senses are not necessary for you to exist. They are only part of a limited sense of what you can be when you see Me.

When you see Me you will understand that Life is all that exists here, and is that All which exists within any sphere of consciousness. You will understand that you must not hurt the Life that is here on this plane, for it is greater than the systems that are feeding on it. You will be happy when you understand this great lesson, and be able to create abundance here on this plane that you had never thought possible. You will also give up the assumptions that you have made about the nature of abundance.

You are being forced, now, to see that the Spiritual World is all there is. You will, in time, take a look at the script you are writing [the existence that you are living] and understand that it must change. You have the power to change it. You must use that power. You are My Children. You are My Beloved, Beloved Children. You are Love, it-self. You will discover that great fact and begin to tap your own power, and in time, will lose your fear, for fear belongs to an evolution that is complete and you will give it up as a survival system.

You will learn of a different community and find that you are complete, inside. I AM God, and I AM much more than you can know. You will know yourself and will see Me in your own being. You will be able to find Me as you grow in an understanding of Yourself. You are my loving, loving.

"You are not limited by anything."

Session #2
   April 14, 1981

You are free of any limits, always, and you will be free of the world, in time, for you will not need to learn from it anymore. In time you will have learned all that you need to know, here, for this is not all there is. There are immense and wondrous things to discover. You will not be afraid to discover them and to travel with Me. You will see Me, and when you do, you will understand what this Life means. You will understand that the tragedies that you encountered here were not what you thought they were. You will see this life as a grand creation with the use of possibility. After you have exhausted the possibility of a given situation, life will move on to other goals and areas of exploration while you are here. Were you not to explore, you would not fulfill your purpose here. You are in a time, now, in which the necessity is to explore in areas that will involve intensive learning. You will see that it is your choice, now, to try to explore or not to explore. You always had the freedom to choose because you are not limited by anything including Me. You are unlimited and powerful.

You will see that this power is spiritual and is not a material territory. When you utilize the power you have, it can only go toward Me. It can go nowhere else, and as you discover your own power, you will see that you will discover more and more about Me and will be freer until you awake within the world of Spirit and find the joy that has existed all along. It will eventually be that you will travel in a circle and will never leave it. You will let that Life move in a direction that you see before you.

You are within the universe of reality that you will not be able to describe, and you will live an inarticulate consciousness as long as you are on this plane. You understand this and have consented to live that reality, here, but you all know the reality from which you have come and to which you will return when you leave the Earth. It is necessary that you deal with this every day, in individual ways; this is the cross that you all must bear while you are here. There is no one here who is not exploring that fact and attempting to cope with it, individually. This, then, is the pain that you must try to deal with now, but it will not always be. You will experience Me, and will not need to attempt to describe Me, for you all will have had that experience. Therefore, you will understand what the other individual being is saying, but you will not yet go through that door, My Children, although you will all go through it in time. There will be nobody left out. There will be nothing left out. There will be no secular division. There will be no churches and no conflict, for you will all understand that I AM God, and there is nothing else. You will see that, until you go through that door, you will try not to hurt anything.

You will realize that religions were imbued with specific moral laws, for at the time they were developed there was a need for them. The laws became accepted and the religions stayed within the limits of the laws. With the acceptance of the fact that I AM All, you will understand that such limits were necessarily a need for the times, but have not, after all, remained so; therefore, you will not cling to that which you have outgrown simply because you are afraid to see Me. You will all see Me, no matter how great the fear is that is holding you back in that time framework.

You cannot help the fact that you are growing. You are My Children, and are, by your nature, loving beyond your greatest understanding of Love. You cannot stop that loving at any point. You will find your way, now. You will see that you are in My care, never to be destroyed by anything. You will see that the Earth is beautiful because you are beautiful; you will understand that the beauty you see here is your beauty and has always been the greatness that exists within the Life, here, of each being.

"There are no ends in themselves, only goals."

Session #3
   April 15, 1981

You will see that what you have termed 'ego' is not your motivating force. Although you may think yourself separate from other life forms, you are not. A common reality is shared and allows you to explore many areas of that reality. But you have the capability to explore because of your capacity to make decisions to do what you choose, when you choose it. It will become necessary for you to identify a given area of exploration, but it is not your identity since your identity is much larger than you can imagine. What you are now exploring, whether it be human or animal, or only a tool to continue with your explorations of Life, itself, will ultimately lead to Me in many ways. Each time of exploration is a time of learning more about Me, and therefore, is an opportunity to increase your ability to understand that you are already complete and at peace with Me. But you continue until the cycle is complete for you. Each identity has many faceted areas of exploration taking place at a single time, giving many areas of approach or learning about the nature of each of your identities as you grow toward Me.

You are all My Children and will ultimately come to the understanding that you are an unlimited being exploring the world of limitations about which you will all need to know. You will continue this process, but your learning will intensify very soon, and the areas that you can explore will become more limited by the limitation placed on many of the diverse forms of Life here on this plane. Should you narrow your thinking you narrow your ability to come closer to Me. It is necessary at this time for people to understand that they must preserve the Earth as a school, for it is to be a part of their experience before they can go on into the world of the Spirit. You will move into the world of the Spirit and find unlimited joy in that area. You will not be afraid of it. You have yearned for it while you have been here on Earth, and you will welcome the experience like the tired child who has run many miles and comes to rest with Me. You are My Children. You will never be any less than My Children. You will be compassionate because you will understand that you are all learning. There are no bad or no good Children of God. There are only Children of Life, and there is no darkness in that Life.

You have been choosing areas of exploration and are desiring to find the nature of your own identity while you explore. You will always be with Me. You will never change. You will see that I am your existence, here. You will need to know that it must, in time, not be a church. It must be your mind that holds that knowledge.

Social expectations will change in nature. Societies were created for specific purposes, just as churches were, but they are not within your being. The churches only served to achieve goals for groups of people who had common goals in mind. You were able to select those areas where your goals were achievable in that given social group, and therefore, social expectations were put on individuals in order to help each being achieve that specific goal. But it is not a thing that should go on forever; so, the social group changes and is mourned by those who thought it was an end in itself. There are no ends in themselves, only goals, explorations, and broadening of the spirit. You will see only the society in which you are now residing is able to adapt to changing spiritual goals, and therefore, will survive as long as it is adaptable to those goals. You will be able to grow. You will understand that limitation still exists within the context of the unlimited. You are still dealing with limitation because you have chosen to do so, and you have chosen to come to this plane to do so. Ultimately you will find Me in limitation. You have traditionally called that limitation humanity.

You are still dealing with a concept of time which is beginning to fade as an area of exploration, but as you grow in numbers you will continue that area of exploration until you understand that time is My Mind and not a reality. This truth will be discovered in the scientific community before it is discovered in the area of theology, but you will understand. You are still My Children. Not one of you is without Me. Not one of you is not My Child. Not one of you is separate from Me. You will not hurt each other. You must not hurt anyone, knowingly.

"You are much more than you think you are."

Session #4
  April 16, 1981

You will see that you are able to deal with any problems that you encounter. As individuals you have assumed that you solved those problems by reasoning out a solution; problems are not solved that way. Problems are solved by tapping the solution to the problem [which is the presence of God in your Life]. You have assumed that reasoning is the presence, because reasoning involves Life as well, and therefore, is not separate from the Life that gives it force. When you solve a problem you solve a Life force question and not a logical question, alone. You are, in fact, working out the problem of your very being when you solve any given problem that you must deal with in your Life whether it be a simple mathematical problem, a problem dealing with a relationship, or with a small wonder at a beautiful scene. All these are problems being solved in the massively complex existence that you are dealing with. You, when you experience a problem on this plane, are really experiencing many problems in a single time and are able to work out solutions to all of them at the same time.

It is much more complex than you can imagine it truly is, because you are still dealing with a limited sense of what you are doing in your existence here. You are much more than you think you are, and there-fore, also, you are solving problems that are much more than you think they are. You will solve problems. You will always have to deal with solutions for that is how you grow. In quantum leaps. You do not grow in the simple terms that you have assumed. You must, at times in your life, grow in larger degrees than at other times, but it is all leading to the same conclusion, which is to be with Me-at-One and at peace. You are not to be afraid of these capacities that you have, because they are remarkable in any sense of the language. They are difficult to describe in your language because your language is linear and does not deal in large terms. But you understand all this in your Spirit and understand that is what is occurring at any given time, but you still wonder at the process when you do reach a solution to a problem and, in fact, you do that frequently in the course of any given minute.

You are much more remarkable than you have assumed that you are, and it is because you are Life that you have these qualities. You are part of the power of the universe not just the Earth, and it is when you see that power of the universe functioning at any given moment, that you solve any problem you must deal with and will be able to move to the next area of exploration. At that time, also, you will have the ability to tap the same power and again solve a given problem. This is a joyous process and will lead ultimately to the most joyous of all processes, which provide an unlimited sense of what you are, what I am, and what We are. You will catch glimpses of this sensation at different points in your life. You have previously caught glimpses of these points and have yearned for those times again. They were un-conscious processes but they allowed a look at Me and you. You mourn their loss. You have been in love and understand the moments when you were unconsciously and totally in love. Those moments when, in fact, you were very close to Me because you were in unity with the male and female and capable of understanding an area of identity not dealing with the area of reproduction. You then were free to be yourself in your total being. You are capable of having this experience without being in love, and you will learn how, in time. You will be free of all fear, in time, as well. You are growing quickly, now, and are learning very quickly.

You, as a group, will marvel at your growth soon when you look at it in perspective. You are, as a Life, an existence, becoming enlightened, now. You are looking at this period of change in despair, but you must not. You must look at it in awe of the rapidity of your growth. You are finding that you are becoming more independent as individuals and less reliant on small groups of other people who share your common goals, because, in fact, you are capable, now, more of defining your own goals and achieving those goals without needing another group of people to give you aid.

You are never at a point in which you are not solving problems, My Beloved Children. For were you to reach a point in which there were no problems to solve, you would create problems in order to continue the process and will see that you are always solving problems. You will see that like love, it is your nature and is not an event as much as a process like breathing, My Beloved Children, and therefore you must not face problems with a sense of dismay as you would not face breathing with a sense of dismay but with the understanding that it is natural and leads to growth on your part just as breathing leads to growth on your part physically. It is an inhalation /exhalation process and is nothing more than that in the Larger Being, My Beloved Children.

You will see that your skills in solving problems are increasing, and the ability to solve those problem is growing rapidly. You must not fear that ability because you will still need that much more in the times ahead. These times will not be easy for you as a Life. The times ahead will be great burdens to bear, but you are being prepared at this moment to reach an explosive period of tremendous change and growth within the context of that change. The change, you will assume, is outside of yourself, but in fact, that change is occurring within yourself.

You will assume that the tragedies and difficulties that you will encounter are events that the Earth is going through, but in fact, it is an occurrence within your own spiritual growth. You will see the Earth crumble in time, but it will only crumble because it crumbles within your consciousness, and you will have expanded into the universe, itself. You will not be afraid, because you will understand that I Am God, and there is nothing else, anywhere that you need to survive. You have always survived because I Am.

You are My Children, My wonderful and beautiful Children in consciousness. You cannot even comprehend your own nature right now, but you will comprehend your nature in time and will welcome the events that occur and will have given up fear so that when those events occur you will not use an archaic system of dealing with those events, but will use the system of My Mind. This system is within each of you, and you will not cope with the events utilizing anything but My power and the Light We all share together. You will not die. Your growth will be by leaps and bounds. At the point of growth it is important you understand that We, as Life, will not use fear, in the future. You have used fear successfully, but it can only provide you with failure from now on since you will begin to tap the power of Love, itself, and will see the presence of Love, everywhere. There can be no room for an archaic system when you come close to Me.

You are all My Children. There will be nobody destroyed, nor will there be anyone hurt, spiritually, by these changes, for there are no saved and damned, here. There are only My Children here. Concepts of salvation and damnation were used for human power. They were never concepts that were taught by Jesus. He never meant for you to think in terms of exclusive groups. He meant for you to see Me. To have the joy that He had experienced with Me. He was never afraid and He understood that you are all, all My Children.

"You will see that life is unlimited, you are unlimited joy, and have never left that state because it is your own nature."

Session #5
April 17, 1981
8:40 P.M. – ?

You all have had to deal with darkness for a long time and need more Light, now. You grew with the darkness, but now you need to grow in the Light as well. You have been through a spiritual dark ages, and the time is now for Life to flourish in the sun of My presence. It was not an intentional darkness. It was the time for that kind of growth. You will find that with the Light the growth will be different; not better, but different, and is necessary now. Your growth is growth, no matter if it is accelerated or very slow; for you are Life and Life grows in whatever form it takes. It grows as physical form but has grown as a spiritual form before it grows as a physical form. That is the single inevitable reality that you, in fact, deal with. You grow spiritually and then you grow tall you grow spiritually and then grow intellectually, but the spiritual growth always precedes any other form of growth or in any reality dealing in the area of Life.

You have assumed that grass does not grow spiritually before it grows physically, but in fact, it grows spiritually before anything takes place in the spring, and just as one goes through a period of dormancy in the winter, it preceded the growth that, in fact, will take place, now. But the real growth always occurs in the turmoil preceding actual growth. In humanity, the darkness to be dealt with precedes the growth that creates the blossoming here on Earth among the Life forms that exist.

You will find that people will start to develop ideas they have never thought possible. Systems will begin to develop that will not

17

destroy life but will help all life to express itself so that individuals can develop systems of food that will not involve the taking of Life. These groups of individuals will develop systems of energy that will not take Life, and social systems will develop which will not destroy the Spirit that exists in the individual. People will be able to come out of the darkness and into the Light of Life, itself, and learn not to hurt other life. You will find, in time, that Life will learn the power of Life, and learn that our Life will never hurt another Life in order to survive. It has been the case where Life has destroyed other Life and has preyed upon other Life in order to live, but it is not necessary, now. Neither is it necessary for a predator to kill a herbivore in order to survive. Life is going into a stage where it will not have to prey on other forms of Life in order to survive. You may find it alarming at first, but you will be glad in your Spirit that at last the burden is gone and that knowledge that you had hurt another life in order to survive, is passed.

You will be free from much that you have had to deal with. You have only dealt with that in order to grow at a specific time. But you will find sunshine in that reality. It is no longer something that you must bear in order to be able to stay on this plane. You are an unlimited spiritual being which means that you are part of Love, itself. It has been difficult for you to hang on to the earth, knowing that you had to kill in order to stay here and learn what you needed to know, so that now you will be able to grow in leaps and bounds to reach Me. I have always understood this and loved you. You were never separate from Me; even when you killed, you were never separate from the life you killed. You may not consciously have known that you were a part of the Life you killed, but you had to spend a great deal of time working out your feelings about the Life you killed in order to stay here. It was cumbersome and difficult, for your Life's blood is Love. To stay here, you were having to face something that was not your nature. It grieved you greatly, and we all shared in that grief. We are not separate from each other. We are all a part of each other so that when an act of atrocity was committed, we all shared that grief; it was never focused on the actor, it was shared, always by all Life. When many people were killed in wars, it was not the leaders' fault, nor did those individuals bear the burden of guilt. We all shared that burden, together, and it was distributed among all of us. We understood and consented to that reality only because we all understood that was a stage of spiritual development. But the darkness is gone, and we are sharing the reality that we do not need to be involved with similar burdens, anymore. It is much easier to share this reality only because it is much closer to our own nature as spiritual beings. When one encounters violence one understands that it is distributed among all of us. You are not the sinner and the other person thus saved. You cannot judge others because that is not what is agreed upon, spiritually, now. These are difficult concepts, and will need to be elaborated on, later, so that they become clear to all who read and can grasp what they mean.

It is important, now, only to understand that We are all good, and We are all sharing Life. All Life is sharing Life. You will see later that it is an enormously complex concept that is difficult to put into this language. There are languages that could express it more easily, because they are concepts that a group of people who formed a given society were dealing with, spiritually, and therefore they [that group] developed the language that would convey these concepts. Therefore, the language is very limited, but We will be able to overcome that, too.

You will see that life is unlimited, and that you are unlimited joy and have never left that state because it is your own nature. It is your ego, and it is your Light. You are not limited in any way, at all. You are My Beloved Children and will find that when you experience Me you will be at peace, at last, and will not fear anything, again. You have had pain as a teacher on this plane and have learned much from time to time, and pain, but you will not have to learn from pain that much longer. You will go through a period of adjustment when you will not know how to learn except by pain. However, you will find ways to grow, even then.

This plane is one in which complex concepts have been taught by pain, but you are developing a Spirit that can learn in areas you have never been able to imagine and will find it fascinating and exciting for you have learned by violence, and therefore, have been attracted by violence. You are still attracted to violence and are still attracted to pain because you use them as a tool, just as you have used fear as a tool. Now, you must go through a period of transition in which, in truth, you are attracted to [pain and violence] in other ways You have been in conflict between the honest attraction to those things and what prophets have projected as to what should be. Now, you will understand that both are attractive and will let the truth have its way. You will not be in this period of transition very long. You will go through it rapidly for you are learning quickly now, and will make this transition, as a group, very soon. You will have much pain in order to make that transition. What the prophets have called disaster and the ends of the Earth, and many sensational terms will be relevant only for this period of transition. You will have disaster and great pain. You will have much to bear, but you will never be hurt, spiritually. You will never be destroyed in any way, for you are unlimited and indestructible, spiritually.

You may think that this will be a very difficult time, and by the reality you have shared, it is, in fact. But it will allow you to make the critical transition into another reality which will provide for your growth. Were you to stay here within this concept of growth, you would not be able to grow, for you have completed this cycle as a group and are ready to move on. You are not going to be hurt, now, nor will you be destroyed; it will look like you are being hurt, and that you are hurting one another. You will share great pain together, but like guilt, it is not one person hurting another, or one life hurting another Life form. It is, rather, an agreed upon reality before you come to this particular plane. It is not easy to come to this particular plane, now, and populations will increase greatly because it is a necessary part of the whole growth process.

You will understand growth much better as we proceed with the book, and you will not think in terms of the kind of growth that you have known, but will, instead, think in terms of spiritual growth which is expanding the spirit, the joy, and the life that you all share. When you see Me you will understand that Love is all there is. There is nothing else. You will understand it is not the simple term that this language has assumed it is. It is much more complex than you can even grasp spiritually, at this time, and you will find the only peace you have here in its reality. You will enjoy that peace from time to time, now, but it is too much for you to have all the time. In time you will be strong enough to bear peace. You are capable of dealing with these concepts, now, and will grow as the writing continues to where you will be capable of dealing with even greater concepts.

You are all capable of these concepts. You have assumed some individuals are intelligent and other individuals are not. Like the concept of the saved and the damned, it is not so. We all share intelligence as Life, and therefore, are capable of understanding all of these concepts. You have chosen to understand that which you wish to understand and no more. You have that right. You will not condemn those who do not understand concepts because that is their choice. You will see that you are My Mind, all of you, and will be free of limitations when you see Me. Even those who are afraid of confronting concepts will be happy beyond their greatest expectations when they see Me, and will be able to confront concepts without fear.

You will see that all Life expresses Intelligence and Beauty. This Season is, in your terms, Easter. But you will see that Resurrection is natural and normal. Jesus was natural and normal. He was My Son, but you are My Children, all of You. He understood that you share

21

Life and share guilt and He was not afraid of it. You will understand that power that exists within My Mind, soon, and will be glad. You will learn much through the writing that is occurring and will find that it is not a human ego but the necessity of conveying complex terms at a time when you may feel you choose to understand them, and, in fact, you will all make that choice. You will not make that choice intellectually, you will make that choice, spiritually, and will find no fear in that choice for We are all One and We all are more than We have ever dreamed possible. It is time to understand this. It is hard to face for it has been very comfortable to assume that we are severely limited, handicapped mortals, and we have found great rest in that concept, but the times will not allow us to find that kind of rest, anymore, for that will be the cause of more pain than the pain confronting us when we must face the positive nature of our own being.

We have assumed the role of sinner, but now must assume the much more difficult role of saint. It will not be easy, but there is no returning to the darkness and the growth we found there. You will have the courage to face it and will have the joy, in time. You will not have the joy, initially, for it will be like walking on a very tight rope for a long time, but you will be able to walk for it is the only way across a very deep canyon that you must now cross in order to reach safety. We all share that rope and that canyon, now, and will be able to cross it together, helping each other through it and will rejoice when we reach the true safety on the other side.

I have had many saints here, and they only foreshadowed the growth that will occur for others. It was never wrong to be in the dark, nor is it wrong to be a saint. Both are only stages of spiritual growth and one is not better than the other. One only occurred prematurely and allowed others to see and an area of growth and helped them bridge the gap between the two areas of growth. You are free of limits and able to choose, now.

Prophecy is the single most natural process you encounter as spiritual beings only because within your larger being you understand the goals you have set for yourself and are achieving those goals. Those individuals who foreshadowed the events to come understood a collective goal as well and found that not to have achieved those goals was not possible. Those goals that you have chosen collectively are growth by light now and this book is a light for you to use in the areas of growth now chosen. You are not now nor ever have been afraid of light and joy, My Beloved Children. It occurs constantly for you even in a dark room for it occurs within your being. When you leave the earth essentially the light leaves the body, but the light is your nature as is Love and cannot be extinguished. Darkness is an absence of light but never destroys light in any way.

"You will grow by revelation instead of time."

Session #6
    April 18, 1981
    4:55 – 5:34 P.M.
    5:45 – 6:10 P.M.

You will see that the people who wrote this book will increase in the understanding of their own lives and be able to look at events and see that they were lessons for growth, spiritually. You will better understand spiritual growth when you look at the lives around you; you will look at the birds or trees, or whatever is growing, and see that they had to take on nourishment in order to grow. They then translated that nutrient into a specific form and grew into that form. They, however, were not erratic in the form that they took, but very systematic about the form, and so the tree became the tree, and grass became grass, and so forth. You have assumed that in an unconscious way that we were just trees or grass or whatever, but they had a goal.

23

They had a specific goal that they sought in taking on nourishment and finding places in which to gain the nourishment and then translated that into the form and so were interacting both with the source of nourishment and the form they took on. That is also true with people. They have taken on nourishment and become a form, also, but that form is not physical. That form is a spiritual form which is evolving, constantly, just as the trees and grass are evolving constantly. The difference between what you have assumed and what exists is the environment, itself; the source of that nourishment determines the form taken on, and so you are taking on a human form from a source of nourishment; that nourishment is Me and aspects of My being. You will see that they [the forms] never change in our Life, itself, but are variable depending on the choice that is being made and the reasons for that choice.

You will see that a tree will always become a tree unless the environment in which that tree exists changes, at which point the tree begins to evolve. That evolution is a spiritual evolution and again is dependent upon its source of nourishment; so you have a tree changing into another life form. You will see that the Life itself is unchanging. It is, in fact, Life. It follows specific rules about Life. For example, when a Life leaves the Earth it cannot return in that form, but it is also following rules that involve spiritual development. Life must grow. It will never cease to grow lest it cease to survive. You must have nourishment, and you must grow. Both growth and nourishment are necessary for your survival. You, as Life, having taken on this form of man must grow and must take nourishment from Me. You will grow dramatically because your environment will change.

You will see that your environment will change dramatically, and that is I. I will change only in relationship with you; I am unchanging. However, this relationship will change and provide you with an abundance of spiritual nourishment. As a result you will grow dramatically and will be able to deal with this tremendous shift in your environment.

You will see that your environment will continue to shift dramatically in the next 100 years so that within a hundred years you will no longer be participating in this environment but will have grown into an entirely different environment and will be prepared for that evolution which will take place. You will see that if a tree stopped growing it would die and so you, as Life, cannot cease growing and will be able to bridge the gap that we talked about between fear and Life. Thus, you will be free of fear and will grow into the spiritual state that Jesus foreshadowed, for example, so that it will not be unnatural for you to be able to walk on water or unnatural for you to be able to control the environment in which you are living not by sharing Life, for that is not controlling the environment since I AM Life. I am, in fact, that environment, but in controlling the environment it occurs because you understand that I am The Source of Life and have always been that source and will always be. You are an unlimited spiritual being, so you will not deal in fear, anymore, but will as Biblical terms stated, walk in the Light, and walking will be a different reality than you know of it now. There is nothing to fear because fear is nonfunctional, now, and you will be able to cope with what you have traditionally called fear because it will have faded into powerlessness in your own lives.

You will see that we, together, will participate in what was predicted in many religions including traditional native religions throughout this Earth. That is because there were good people who experienced Me and after that experience were able to put down in mythology, or the Bible, or religions of the world, that experience and were foreshadowing what We will all be doing. There will be nobody left out. There will be nothing left behind because I AM All in, and of, and through ALL, so that there is no place for Me to leave some part of Myself behind. You will be able to communicate this only as you are free, yourself. You will constantly grow yourself and will see that you, too, are a form and will take on the form that is needed in order to communicate this truth. You will see that you cannot avoid that responsibility.

What you have termed 'supply' on this plane again is the same supply that the tree experiences when it takes its nourishment from Me. You will see that supply will become nonfunctional in its traditional sense; that is, you will seem to use up the root sources of the Earth, but killing was never your supply, and you must look at the balance created by Life in order to understand supply. Your supply is God.

There is no other supply. You are being supplied by Me. You have assumed that, of yourself, if you kill you will be supplied, but you will not be supplied that way for such a way does not participate in the circle of Life, itself, and therefore becomes linear and thus goes into a state nothingness. You will see that the only reality is God, and you must find ways of supplying your needs as human beings through systems that do not kill life. Life everywhere is My being, and you cannot kill it. You will find systems of housing, food, and clothing that will not involve killing. This will seem like a radical concept to some, but by the events of their own lives they will be forced into a position where they can accept this concept. It will become more predominate. It won't be forced on anybody. I do not force concepts, and you will see and will understand all. In time.

You have assumed that you could force people into being converted into your system of thought, but like the tree that is growing, you cannot force that tree to be six-feet if it is one foot tall, at least not in a day's span. That is not the way trees grow nor is that the way nourishment is supplied to trees. Therefore, if you will let each tree in a forest grow, you will not force someone who is struggling to become a giant right away. He or she will grow and will be provided for. There is no one who will not be provided for, ever.

You will see, in time, that when you experience Me, your growth will be very rapid, but no more rapid than you could ever handle, nor will the event ever be more than you can bear. You are My Children and are held in Love, always. You are weak to yourselves, sometimes, but that is because you have made the mistake of comparison and that, in the spiritual realm, does not exist. There is no comparison; there is only growth and nourishment. The nourishment does not know whether the tree is six-feet or one-foot tall. It only knows that it is providing nourishment and that the living being is growing. You will let that being grow and will never condemn that growth for it is essential to be small, too. You are the nature of God, for you are Life and share Life, always. You are a community of Life and will find that Life can be beautifully developed at all times. When you look at the natural world you see beauty. You do not see stars and any ugliness because in the natural world Life and time worked together. Now you will see that Life will develop, and you will, in time, understand, and will you not have to deal with time. The development will just be as beautiful because it is in harmony with Me, but it will not include the concept of time and therefore, you will not have the growth, maturity and decay process that coexists with time, but will find an entirely different concept that you will be dealing with.

You will find an appropriate name for such a concept, but the closest word in the language of your plane is 'revelation.' You will grow by revelation instead of time. Your language is difficult to deal with just as the limits that have been agreed upon are not easy to deal with for the spirit is not, in fact, participating in either, even though they are participating in it. But, again, this is a difficult concept for you, but you are spirit. All of you are spirits. You are not matter in any form. You are all spiritual beings. All of you every item of Life shares in the spiritual and there is nothing else; but you cannot accept that concept until you are ready for it, and you are not ready, yet. You will be as attracted to it as you are to fear or violence, now, and it will not be contrived on your part, but will be natural and good. You cannot force this. You cannot say 'I will be good,' and then try to make that quantum leap without growth, but you can grow, and as you grow you will understand the gap first, and then how to cross it.

Traditional religions have tried to force people into growth that was not there; they tried to be the nourishment for those people, but I am the nourishment, and religions failed because they learned falsely. Those individuals, knowing full well that was not the truth, tried very hard to attain a growth beyond their own growth. When they follow those contrived rules they set up false communities and those communities are not growing communities for they are fearful communities, fearful that they are not going the way that they, in fact, go while they are sitting. They are sitting there not growing. It is a very frustrating thing for people to deal with just as it would be difficult for a tree or a blade of grass to deal with. This world of rules has come to the point where it is not helping the growth process and is limiting growth and therefore must be taken a look at and found out. This world must not try to push people into growth that does not exist, but should, rather, in Love, accept each of My Children as they are and let them continue in their own growth. That is particularly true of children.

This is a natural process, and the Love that parents have for their children is a natural process. When parents subscribe to a given religion and learn the rules, the natural feelings that they have for a child are bad when they are not helping the growth of that child. Natural feelings are the environment in which an individual can grow best. This does not involve violence nor does it involve inducing fear, but it does involve encouragement and Love and caring for that Life. For that Life is not a small, inferior Life. It is Life that is very close to Me and Life that can remain firm all the time. You will let that Life flourish just as you will water a lawn and let that grass grow.

These are concepts which you have accepted over a period of time but they are worth repeating, now. You will see that there will be resistance to these concepts, but they are very important as is their repetition because of their importance. You will let Life teach you what is needed for supply. You will listen to it and pay attention to what it has to say. You will see that individuals will become inspired and will develop all facets of your society so that you will not have to kill. This will meet resistance, as well, but you will find, as far as the events coming are concerned, that the resistance will break down because the systems on which those concepts have been based will not survive. So, you will be forced to find the alternatives and will be able to because ideas are present to do so. You will hear this several times in this book, but the reason that you hear it is that they, too, are important concepts to consider and to consider in the future when you must deal with difficult events. You will find that like problem solving, those answers exist and are spiritual questions. Your solutions will give you an opportunity for immense growth. You are capable of all that.

You will see that these events have been called Acts of God, but they are not. They are acts of yourself and have been chosen by you because you understand that fear is no longer a survival system for you and you have decided, as Life, to create these events so that you will be forced to reach this transition. You could have chosen other routes and may still, but you will make those decisions before you come to this plane and nothing is written. You will see that you are constantly making decisions like this one and will continue to do so at all times in any given moment. These are concepts that you may have considered and are again worth consideration. You will see that when you make mistakes you have the capacity to adjust to those mistakes and continue growth, just as you may fall into a river and have the tenacity to swim out of the river and still survive. You will not generally make that mistake again, and as a result learn the laws of spiritual survival not the laws of the mind of organizations. You are capable of immense mistakes and immense solutions to those mistakes and will continue to solve problems as they come until you have a repertoire that is circular and as a circular repertoire it will feed back to itself so that mistakes cannot be repeated over and over again. You will have a reservoir of intuition from which to draw.

The word is imbued, right now, with orthodox religion and must break out of the shackles that are limiting growth; for the religions themselves know that they have gone to the point of absurdism. You will see that every moment you live your Life is, and it starts and ends and starts and so that the concept of death is something you deal with every minute. It is not something that you only deal with at any given chronological time, but something that you physically deal with as well.

You are very familiar with this process and chose the degree to which this occurs, both physically and spiritually. You are the author of the script by which you are living. You will be able to take a look at the script and determine whether or not it is productive for you. The script can change as you are able to see Me. You will alter the script because you will alter your concept of Me as you grow more loving. You will find that the script is more positive for you and can get rid of some things that do limit the direction of the script.

You can try to not hate someone of whom you feel fearful and in time, your script will change. This is the concept taught by orthodox religion, but it can only occur when you are ready. Keeping your mind open to that change will allow you to change. You will see that I AM God and understand the heart and the workings of the heart. I AM that Heart. I AM the Love you feel, and I AM aware of all of it. You will find it difficult to understand that, but it is not an unloving thing, nor is it judgmental in any way. It is like electricity understanding itself as it flows through the wire, but is not in the process judging any resistance to that flow. You are able to love and attempt to get rid of resistance to that love, but will allow Me entry into your experience. It will become less and less a social interaction. It will be more and more a very personal experience, but you will not talk about it to other people as it is very personal. It is much more personal than any relationship you have with anybody on this plane for it is your very survival.

You have been taught to enter into your closet and shut the door. This is a concept that is accepted; its meaning is to enter into your closet and be not afraid of the concept of God, however, this concept has only served a given society. You will see that this concept is of God, and loving is God that is to be welcomed for you must not judge each other. You have been taught this concept and you must understand it because you are not to limit any Life you see since then you limit the joy found in the Life that surrounds you in ways which you do not understand, yet. You will not really come into your lives as a group nor in church, but when you are alone, and your joy will be full. You will find that there is nothing else you will ever want, for anything else is but a pale substitute for the joy you experience with Me, My Children. You know these concepts and they are all being mentioned in this part of the book so that you will understand that they are still in need of full acceptance. It is like building blocks. It is not a question of time before you accept them; the time is now, and you, in fact, accept this building now for it is a foundation for the much broader concepts that we will come to, later.

You will see that the ego that is exhibited in a given group is the struggle for that Life for the purpose of the identity it must have to grow, but you are not egotistical at all, none of you, and when you attempt to identify yourself, ultimately it is because you are trying diligently to break through just as a plant tries to break through a rock. It is not condemnable nor should you be ashamed of it. The concept of altruism that orthodox religions have taught is not My plan, for you are good and nothing can stop that goodness. You will see that your nature is ultimately altruistic although it does not seem to be that way. You cannot force a given nature on anybody nor can they force one on you, for at that point you are sacrificial and at One with Me. That is but a small death just as a cell gives up existence in making place for another cell. Giving up that which is not what is best for each of you should only be the result of great love and should be only a conscious process.

You are all beautiful in the process of living with each other and not hurting each other in any way that corresponds with your nature. You will give up a sense of caring about your own nature because you are good and will not hurt others. The more you give up the concept of altruism the more goodness you can express and the more Joy you can experience in your own lives. My Children. You will find that I AM God, and you cannot create a situation in which I am not there with you. You cannot, by being egotistical or self-oriented, create a situation where I am not with you.

"You will find that you control everything, and fear and grief will go very soon."

Session #7
  April 18, 1981
  9:28 – 9:55 P.M.

You must not fear Me in any way, at all. You are still afraid that the orthodox churches are My vehicles here on the Earth. They are not, and Life will complete its task of verbally communicating all that needs to be said, now. I AM God and there is nothing but God in this world. This is radical in terms of what is accepted by the public for they have given lip service to the concept that God is power, but they do not understand that God is power. This is because the public is still in the world of fear. Living in a world of fear, people are afraid that I am not power and they are personal authors. When they have that responsibility in their minds it is a tremendous burden for the individual when each assumes personal authorship. Then individuals assume control of each other and other Life forms, and therefore look at the world of Life as though they had created it but they only created their concept of it. Life created itself. You do not create life; you create circumstances. These circumstances are the process by which you grow and will continue to flourish, but Life itself is indestructible. You have thought it was indestructible, but you never truly understood its indestructibility. You have assumed that you could kill but that again belongs to the world of fear. You will not forget fear; any of the Life processes, including death, is natural and normal and not an awesome process at all. It is simply leaving the Earth as though you were leaving on an airplane, a fact which you do not fear. It is not necessary to live in a world of fear, especially fear of death. It is necessary, however, to love each other and not to hurt any living thing, although in a world of fear you have found many things of which to be afraid. You have learned to fear pain. You have learned to fear Me. You have learned to fear death. It is remarkable that one does not fear the growth of a blade of grass! All these are a part of your very being. You may fear your ego, but you must not. It is part of you and it is healthy, too.

You, in thinking of terms of altruism, have learned to fear your own survival system. The net result could be your own demise, for if you were truly altruistic you would not be able to do for yourself, which is necessary because your larger self is good and would never hurt anything. You recall that we have discussed agreeing in the fact that we would share a sense of guilt for our survival here on this plane. We do, in fact, still share that sense of guilt but are finding that it is not necessary anymore to feel guilty for we are devising many ways of eliminating violence, fear, and pain.

You have only emotional pain to deal with now. It is the most severe form of pain; physical pain is endurable, but severe emotional pain is not for it affects your heart [consciousness] and I dwell within your loving consciousness. Emotional pain is a form of fear of Me. I will never hurt you, so you assume that somebody can, for you are experiencing pain emotionally. However, you are only experiencing the separation from yourself in terms of your own identity. You, for various reasons, have chosen to relinquish aspects of your identity for given goals. When you do so you are vulnerable to pain because there is a vacuum there. You do not need to fear that vacuum for it is not possible to be without Me at any point or at any place or at any given period of time. The emotional pain that you feel is only the pain of feeling that you are lost. It, however, is none the less real to you, and in time you will have all the tools you need to be able to be free of that pain. I am able to be where you think you are not, and there is no loss. You have grieved the loss of those you love, but you never lost them for they were in your mind and you have not lost your mind. You must not grieve, and when you overcome a world of fear you will see that you are not afraid that you will be alone or not provided for or of whatever facets that grief entails. You will always be a complete being.

You will never be incomplete in any way, spiritually. You are able to be complete because your larger Self is, in fact, massive and without any flaw. You are only dealing, again, in limitations that you have created in order for you to learn that you are an unlimited spiritual being that is not able to limit anything. This is a difficult concept to grasp but you will study it and ponder it until you are filled with the light of it. You are able to be free of any fear of any limitation at all. You are limited, but you need not fear that, for within that context you are also writing the script that deals with those limitations and are able to see that you cannot limit anything other than to focus your attention on specific goals. While you are in the process of limiting your experience you still function as an Unlimited Being and therefore are as knowing as a group of children in school. Such a knowing group is yet unknowing of the specific directions chosen to take direction on this plane, the Earth.

You will find that you control everything, and fear and grief will go very soon. These concepts needed to be discussed for they are crosses you bear on this plane just as the inarticulate is a cross for you to bear, but it is not your spirituality, and your spirituality is not hurt in any way.

"The world of matter is essentially a convenience and nothing compared to the world of Love."

Session #8
  April 19, 1981 Easter
  4:20 – 4:54 P.M.
  5:25 – 5:46 P.M.

You will see that fear is not to control you in any way, now. Soon you will have given it up and will understand that when you leave the world of fear you enter the world of Love and have only the power you ever had. Even in a world of fear, Love is the only power existent. It is energy and Life, and all there is, for I AM Love and I am the only power. What has been traditionally called the devil is the world of fear, but it was only the survival system and in the catalytic stage you are now in it is useless and will create your demise instead of allowing you to survive. You will see how very important it is, now, to confront each fear that comes to you and to understand that this is only a step to a higher plane which you as a group will take. I have said earlier, that this step will be taken dramatically and it will. The Bible has talked about judgment day, and those who wrote about judgment day were so interested in the world of fear that they did not see the spiritual significance of the presence of Love. They did not understand about those who had made the transition into that world already. Those who had understood that they had the power to deal with that transition had the understanding that the judgment was something for which all life had been completely prepared. They also understand it was as natural as the falling of water or a breeze in trees. Transition has not been a negative, fearful, frightening experience for anyone. It will not be recognized when it occurs, for as a child walking down the street and crossing to the other side, transition is as much a natural act as walking, itself.

In the next hundred years you will have learned so much that the transition will not even require a hesitation at the curb but will simply occur like breathing occurs. You will leave the world of fear so pleasantly that there will be no negative occurrences for anyone when it happens. Good people wrote the Bible, but in itself the Bible is not God, for I am everywhere and all things in all life. Trees do not have a Bible of their own, nor can they read, but they experience Me and the universal experience of Me will occur, not just in human life but in all life. These are all My Children, and I am in all things, and much, much more for you will remember that this is only one plane and so pantheism is not possible because this is only one plane. If I were to be limited to being in things on this plane, then I would not be present in the universe. You will see that the 'Big Bang' theory is correct in that we are still only talking about this plane. You are labeling this plane 'Universe' and therefore thinking in terms of this plane. But the world of matter is essentially a convenience and nothing compared to the world of Love; you can experience a part of it here.

You have still no concept at all of the power of Love. You have seen individuals demonstrate that power, but your credibility is very low because you, yourself, have not experienced that power. You have heard that Jesus walked on the water, but you never walked on the water and therefore, find it incredulous; but, in fact, it is a very simple task. Matter is a limited concept for an unlimited spiritual being. When you make the transition into the power of Love you will understand, like a baby understanding that walking seems difficult, but as you grow older it seems so simple. You are dealing in very simple concepts of power itself, and are able to open up to power you never even thought conceivable but which was, of course, always there just as the concept of the airplane was always there, even for primitive peoples, although they never utilized such a concept. So you will, in fact and in time, begin to take a baby step in these areas.

You will find that, again, it is possible that the scientific community will beat the theological community to the draw in conceptual thinking for scientists have more faith in science than in theology. The much more powerful community, however, is the theological community. It has relinquished its power for the sake of human power, but when this community makes the transition out of the world of fear, it too will understand that power is with God not with various groups of people, for those people chose those groups in order to find Me. Ironically, those people who organize groups to find Me are leaving their leadership. This is not a lasting state of being for truth is, of itself, its own power. You will see that, as I have said, these changes will take place very rapidly; you will be prepared for all of them.

This book was only meant to help in the preparation process for those individuals who are ready. It is not meant to be a Bible to anyone. It is only meant to open peoples' eyes to possibilities. You are an unlimited spiritual being. You know these possibilities. This book is only meant to help you, at this level, to deal with the situations that will occur. You must not make a church of it, nor an organization of any kind. You must only read this book by yourself with no one else in the room mentally. You do not need discussion groups with whom to discuss these concepts. You only need your own identity. It is very important that you do not at any point form any kind of group at all, in any way. You will find that such a group could be at the point of being a very destructive force and could thus be destructive to the good that is possible to be received from the book. You will see that We will grow together and you will find Me. You can no more help finding Me than you can stop breathing simply because you have decided to stop breathing. You will go through the process of searching for Me even though you label that 'atheism,' for that, too, is a search for Me. While you are atheistic you are also breathing. I AM Life and you cannot avoid that and label yourself in anyway whether it be 'agnostic atheist' or 'born-again Christian.' You are still breathing, and I AM Life, itself. You must never judge another person's growth in any way for that is where they must be at this moment, and you have the necessity of making those choices yourself. You will not create an environment in which people grow better than in another place, for they make those determinations themselves; you must not contrive this Life in any way for it will not be contrived in the long run. You can place strict moral codes on individuals or even force the tree to grow around the rock, but the tree will continue to grow, even around the rock.

You will find humor and laughter and joy in your growth. You will not find it a somber, unhappy reality for you are meant to be a Free Spirit, and I am directing you to the qualities that are Life and joy, silliness and fun; exploration and sunshine. You cannot avoid these for you need them just as a plant needs Light, My Children. You will not find this a serious process. I AM God and there can be no stopping God! If you tried to stop Spring you would find it a little difficult. You will find you cannot stop God even if you take the opposite ends of the spectrum, the agnostic or the Christian, which is like determining that one must find one's feet in order to have them grow properly. No matter what you do the feet will grow and so you will grow and so you will grow toward Me. You will see that 'Life' is a good term for God, but there are concepts for which you have no words in your language that are also good terms for God. It is difficult for you to even find synonyms for God in Earth plane language. You have not explored Me in your lives enough for those inspirations to come through which then find words to be attached to, but you will, and you find many new words to be attached to and you find many new words along with new concepts that will allow you to understand what I can be to you, although not even what I am. You are My Children, and spiritually, you understand all this. You, in fact, understand the concepts, themselves, but you have not developed the language. If you think the world in which you are now existing seems limited to you, you must then understand how difficult it is for the Spirit World to try to communicate through Earth plane language. It is a task. There must be more exploration of Me so that the communication can be clear. You can go through that process alone and find new words, but it will involve poetry and imagery at this level. That is why Jesus spoke in parables; the language of those times handicapped His communication dramatically

You will see in this book that, again, we are dealing with a tremendous handicap but will attempt to overcome it. Even the word 'Love' has taken on meanings that are negative because of the world of fear in which you are now living, and as a consequence, you fear Love itself. You must not fear Love in any form for it is not Love that ever would be hurtful, but only the fear of Love that can produce hurt.

You will see that you are living in a universe of abundance, but fear creates a sense of lack and you, therefore, are not able to achieve the abundance that exists. You will see that you are not to be afraid of anything when you make the transition into My presence. There is no human control when an individual is experiencing Me. Churches lose their power when the one individual experiences Me and does not choose, instead, a specific group of people with the same spiritual goal. In time, this is the only way that you will have power or will experience Me in any way; churches will fade and become powerless in specific groups. You must not mourn their loss for groups were necessary at a time, but they have lost their usefulness, My Children, for I AM All Present [Omnipresent].

Ultimately, the decisions we make seem like judgments we must make, morally, but they are much deeper than that. There are rules involving Life, here, that relate to spiritual realities and have little to do with the social superstructures created by groups of people who seek one common spiritual goal. When you struggle with moral right and wrong you are still only struggling with right and wrong within relationship to a specific spiritual goal. You are not struggling necessarily with right or wrong with regard to Me. When you find a right-and-wrong question answered it is because that in a given social superstructure has become a goal you had determined long before you come to the Earth. By chance you were able to resolve it within that particular superstructure. That is why moral rules must remain flexible for they are like words for God one of the very few words that truly describe your spiritual objectives on this plane. You will see that those objectives are recognizable within your own consciousness but are not necessarily recognizable within a given social context, so that people within one culture on this plane may not be able, in fact, to achieve their spiritual objectives within that culture. As a result they become recluses or turn out to be disgruntled or upset with the system within which they are functioning. It is not because of the system is bad; it is because such people understand within their Larger Selves that they must achieve those goals here, and are not able to articulate those goals and are not able to evolve from the conflict with which they are dealing. Thus, they become angry at a society and frequently become suicidal, either consciously or unconsciously. Holding up a bank in hopes of being shot would insure their going back to the drawing board, but they will achieve their original goals and create a situation where those goals could be achieved. You will see that you are able to achieve all you need, anywhere, once you have seen Me, for you will understand that you are an unlimited entity and can create, here, the situation that needs to be created, My Children.

You can alter any given society, but the problem that you are up against is the agreement which created that Society to start with. Some concepts that we will cover in the book do not seem that important, but when they effect one single life they become very important for that life is shared by all and is not separated from Me, ever. It involves something so massive that you cannot perceive it, now, but you will. You will see Me and will see your identity; your joy will be unlimited. You will not experience that here. We have talked about your experiencing it somewhere, here, but even that is so little of the joy you will experience when you see who you truly are. Those things that we have talked about, regarding compassion and Love, are only small rules that help you to retain your spiritual power or any power that you have on this plane. You have assumed that if you are divisive you will get by, but you will not; simply because you are Life is not enough if in the process you have hurt somebody. You are much greater by simply being alive than anything you can imagine at this point. You will find you will do a great deal of exploration in the time to come so that you can help prepare others for My presence, here, on this plane. You will survive that preparation.

"You will be led to safety and will begin to think in larger terms."

Session #9
   April 19, 1981
   8:40 – 8:30 P.M.
   8:50 – 9:10 P.M.

You will see that the events coming will involve physical forces but are explainable ultimately as Acts of God but are truly only Acts of the Creators, themselves, which is Life in agreement. You will see that there will be serious seismographic occurrences created on the Earth by forces not yet anticipated by scientists but will be explainable only in mathematical terms that will involve astronomical calculations of solar explosions in other galaxies. These seismographic occurrences will affect life here on this planet. You will be led to safety and will begin to think in larger terms. As you begin to think in these terms, your minds will open up to possibilities and your imagination [which to some degree is a form of salvation for you on this plane] will look at the possibility that life is a universal concept and can supersede matter in this universe. Such possibilities will lead to a scientific revelation that will lay the ground work for intellectual exploration and ultimately for spiritual exploration.

You will see that mathematicians will have to change the base of their mathematics just as you change from a base of ten to a base of five. New bases for mathematical calculations will be found and the expansive process will continue until spiritual terminology is understood as the only adequate linguistic tool with which to begin comprehension of the events that will occur. These will not occur right away but will force you to look beyond what you have defined as reality. When you begin the process of looking beyond you will change the language so that it, too, can adapt to the tremendous changes in the environment of which we have spoken. Such changes will force you into a position where you attempt to grow far beyond what you perceive around you. You will not worry about the quantum leaps that must take place, for you will be prepared, step-by-step. What is archaic Christianity will take on new meaning just as other religions will. There are many religions in the world that are foreshadowing these events, but as we have discussed, they are being foreshadowed from the basis of fear. When these events happen and the lessons from them occur, then the foreshadowing will be made in a different base as well. Occurrences will be understood instead of feared, for we have long known these events would take place and needed to grow into readiness for them. Life will be able to understand much of its own substance, which is to say that your scientists cannot understand nor can they duplicate life because it is of their substance. When such is of their own substance, it is difficult to attempt to duplicate something that is functioning within one's self. But this is a case of unlimited spiritual beings dealing with limitation and in dealing with limitation one is also playing with that limitation while knowing that one is unlimited.

It is an ironic posture for Life to be in a position of attempting to create itself. It is not possible for you to create yourself. You can create circumstances, but God creates you and your identity which, as we have said, is much more than you can even imagine at this time. In many ways, by material standards, you are very primitive, but you are mind at the same time again, an ironic position to be in, for you are mind which is creating ideas and ideas are expressing mind, at the same time. So again, like love, you are within the area of a circular flow which can only turn back to itself and grow happily within its own circumference. It will be expressive of an unlimited concept. When you use the symbol for God there is power in that symbol, and you will understand that power. You will not worship that symbol but will use it. It is useless unless it is put into activity.

Personality is a distinct form of fear. When people began to worship Jesus as God they began to worship the concept of a person. That person was a body created by reproduction but was not the spiritual identity of that individual. The spiritual identity for the individual that way expressed here was worshipped and again there emerged a limited sense of a limited God, an untenable situation. God is all present and all power, and is your very nature. You do understand this, but again, in the world of fear you are afraid of it and fear even God. You will not need this anymore for it is an environment you have outgrown and you will not be able to exist within it comfortably, anymore. You will see that Earth people will cease to be afraid of death, eventually, for death is walking away from the Earth; this plane of consciousness is not dying for nothing can kill the spirit of the individual. It is Invincible and unlimited. You will see this repeated when you leave the earth, for those who leave the earth will decide whether or not to return to this plane. It is not the same kind of decision making process that you have when you are deciding upon a solution to a problem. It is the kind of decision making process that must be gone through as you learn. Learning creates decisions for you so that you are able to establish a direction because you know enough to go naturally in a given direction. At that point you will not be in a quandary about returning to this plane, for you will have the information you need to choose, unconsciously, the direction you must choose. You will not return right away for there are so many planes of consciousness. But you cannot fathom the quantities involved anymore than you can fathom the number of cells in the life here on Earth. Individuals will be able to learn and thus go to whatever plane presents an opportunity for growth not necessarily that growth conceived by each to be his or her particular plane.

You will see that the concepts we are dealing with are frequently concepts that you have toyed with before but did not understand they were the actual reality that an individual life experiences. You have no idea of the number of Life lines on this planet, no more than you have any idea of the number of the planes of consciousness, nor any ideas of the scope of the infinite mind. You have only the impetus to follow a given direction until you are where you should be. Frequently, on this plane, you feel a sense that you do not know the direction that you should follow with your life, but while you are going through that period you are also understanding that you are being and living and therefore following a direction, anyway. The one is an intellectual process which is a part of, again, the spiritual growth of a given group. But it is not necessarily your goal. You also know spiritually what direction you are taking and will not construe that into something that is not. You cannot, even should you follow the directions that a normal person projects upon you in order to control your being and to thus feel good about himself. You still will follow the direction you must; you must not feel anxious or afraid, again, because it is only a temporary control. No one ever totally controls the other. Even a dominant parent does not truly control the child for the child will grow and will flourish, anyway, in the direction that is to be this life. Direction will be on human terms but one needs such terms to start with and as we proceed together, the books [of life] will expand more and more into the infinite scope of reality.

You will see that later we will talk in imagery because, as we mentioned, we will be forced by your language to do so. But there is joy in imagery just as there is joy in God. You are greatly attracted to imagery because it is expressing God, and you are all seeking Me, even those who seem not to be. You will find those who object to the contents of this book, but you will not be afraid for they can never harm anyone.

Where there is no fear there is no will to power, My Children.

"You are such a good spirit that you cannot ultimately harm anything."

Session #10
April 20, 1981
3:55 – 4:12 P.M.
4:40 – 4:50 P.M.

You will see that people frequently devote their lives to the acquisition of human power as has been mentioned in the manuscript. This is more an attempt to think well of one's self than it is to achieve a goal. [Frequently, an individual is ambitious because he or she is afraid that they are not adequate.] These individuals will, however, understand that they are adequate because they are spiritual; and because they are spiritual, are powerful, and are able to do the things so that it looks like their ambition is leading them. But, in fact, they are able to accomplish those goals because they are spiritual and powerful and essentially become humanly powerful in spite of their ambitions, for they had set their goals high before they came to this plane and will see that they only fulfilled those goals because they chose to fulfill them, previously. You will see that you have met many people who seemed obsessed with power but they are afraid of power and therefore are obsessed with it. It is the same fear as that of the fear of God or the fear of being hurt or the fear of dying. All fall into the same general category and are still within a world of fear. You will help them out of that world into an area of so much greater power so that when they reach that power they will look back at their world of fear and understand that it was temporary and was always meant to be temporary and not anything greater than that. You will see, in this lifetime, that human power will be transformed into an obscene kind of situation where it is ultimately not achievable by anyone on this plane.

You have put great store in power, but there are changes taking place very quickly now, and even those coveted positions of human power are beginning to be more of a job than an apex for the individual to reach. They carry more burdens with them each year they continue. Ultimately, human power will be found to be a limited sense of the unlimited possibilities, and like the mathematician, the equations will have to be changed and individuals discover the power within and the power to influence for good with others. This is the only power truly achievable on this plane. We have talked before about power, but we have not covered it nor will we until the last part of the book. We will discuss, at length, technical terms and ways of reaching positions of power that are in harmony with each individual's spiritual objectives for experiences on this plane. It is possible to change power first for it is one of the most flexible elements in this reality and can shift very quickly. Values here are harder to shift than power.

The role of women in the next hundred years will be very important for they will be grappling with the more difficult change that needs to be made and that is the change that is needed in the area of values. Women, as a group, are certainly not necessarily as individuals, but as a group more adaptable to value shifts because they have evolved in that manner because of their position of powerlessness. It is not bad that they did not have power, but it is something that will change gradually so that the values that need to be changed can be changed more rapidly. It is a positive force, not a negative force, and again, in the world of fear it is not necessary to fear these changes, but there will be fear and there will be reaction. These will, however, yield to the higher sense of love and compassion and those changes will be made but will never be the putting down of another group of people nor another form of life for they are all My Children and never could lose their value because they themselves know how valuable they are. Their greater spiritual self is able to make that distinction and is able to understand the nature of the individual which is neither male nor female.

We have said before that the reproduction of the species and its necessity, only, created male and female. The spirit does not know those things and is not concerned with them. The spirit of each individual is concerned only with spiritual growth and joy in Me, and will not change. You will see as we continue with the writing that you will become more and more of your own spiritual identity which you spiritually understand is unchanging and unlimited. You will be able, as mentioned earlier, to help control the writing of your Life's script.

There are many ways to reach a given goal, and in order to reach those goals you may choose one of the many ways to reach that goal and shift within those choices and to shift again within the choices that were made. You will see that the goals are achievable either through a circuitous route or directly. The more circuitous the route the more you have learned about everything along the way. Like meandering, it is valuable learning experience and can lead to many areas of discovery that were not known before one wandered to a stream or a tree or a house. Frequently, you will do a great deal of meandering in attempting to achieve your goals, but you will finally understand that your goals will be achieved and you will be able to learn what you need to know on this plane. You will see that there is much more to this than you can discuss, but you will find harmony, a futile thing on this plane unless those goals are in harmony with what you know intuitively.

You are My Children; all of you are My Beloved Children and are aware of this, spiritually. You sometimes may seem egotistical to others, but you never seem that way to Me for I know that while you seem that way you are asserting your individuality, and it is not harmful. The only harmful area is in the area of fear that might cause you to act in such a manner as to hurt another person; the only thing that allows you to hurt others is your fears. You will be able to confront many of your fears and to specifically identify them, and will learn different ways to get rid of various fears so that you will not harm yourself by harming others. You are such a good spirit that you cannot ultimately harm anything. When you speak of spiritual things you are not speaking in terms of goals as you know them but in terms of attitudes and terms of largeness in your heart. You will see that the goals that you set spiritually are geared towards specific attitudes and specific expansion of your thinking, so that when you come into an experience you may have some preset notions, and when you come out of them you will have learned many things, mainly through that experience, that you had never anticipated.

The experiences through which you go frequently teach things you sometimes wish you had not learned, but those are frequently the spiritual goals set to be learned from that experience. You will see that your attitudes and the scope of your thought is shifting. Sometimes it seems that the scope of your thought is shifting. Sometimes it seems that the scope of your thought narrows, but even then you are growing, and in this case, knowing, now, it is all good and is all part of your objective in that situation. You will see that I am the ultimate objective. It is not the same thing as you perceive in a linear reality that is climbing higher and higher towards an ultimate objective which would be Me, so that I am at the top of the step ladder. That is not the way it is to be pursued. It is like problem solving in that it is expanding instantly and immeasurably the moment it occurs. But I was there all of the time, and I am that expansion. You will see that I am the reason for those experiences and the goal contained within each experience. This can occur many times in a given situation and is not limited by time nor constricted in any way.

These are concepts that are not easy for you to deal with but are necessary for you to understand so that you do not think in terms of finally finding Me after years of asceticism or whatever else you could preconceive was where you find Me. For I am the substance of your Life and am with you at all times, in all places, and if your goal is narrow, I am there, and if you find great joy in something, I am there. I am never apart from you and you are all, all of you, My Children.

These are concepts that are difficult but are true in the most profound sense of truth. You will see that you feared yourself when you feared Me, and that concept must yield for you are good. I AM Life, and ultimately We will understand that in every possible way; you will change many concepts of Me, but you will experience Me and theories will leave rapidly at that point. You will see that there has been much conjecture about the nature of God, but fear would lead you into the intellectual conjectures as a way of removing yourself from Me, for when you verbally conjecture about the nature of God in a limited way, you have removed yourself from unlimited God and have done that by choice because it seemed too difficult at that moment for you to think about Me. You think, and therefore, you in fact think about Me; but that is philosophical rather than truly helpful to you. Philosophy has thought about thinking to a great extent; philosophizing is an interesting exercise, but it is not God. You will see that which leads to God is God and that which leads away from God is God, everything that exists is God, My Children. You will find that I am unlimited and unlimitable, and you will be aware of that and find Love and joy in that, not fear and depression.

Power is an event in the lives of individuals and nothing more than event. You are able to control the events of your lives, My Beloved Children, through the use of the white light and will learn how to use it later in the book and will find that it is good and will only bless those who use it and will not effect the lives of others in any way unless they choose that effect themselves as well. You cannot use it to force anyone to do what they have not chosen to do, but will find that you will go in a direction that will allow for their growth as well, but will never effect a change except within your own thought toward them. That will be disappointing to some, but in the long run they will understand that it was the only way to effect a change within their own experience and was ultimately the most loving way possible.

"The growth of the spiritual Life of the individual is a growth toward Me and is joy beyond one's wildest imagination."

Session #11
April 20, 1981
9:15 – 9:27 P.M.

On this plane sexual relations between people are not necessarily the only kind of relationship possible, but if there is a soul mate relationship, then the sexual satisfaction is heightened and the relationship will not be a power oriented relationship, nor will it be fear oriented but will alternately be a relationship in which two androgynous beings interact. It is incidental that their relationship involves sexual relations. The sexual relationship between males and females becomes a power game in which the sex male or sex female is important if it is not a spiritual relationship. Then there enters jealousy, manipulation, and control, dominance and subservience, and all the things that limit the love that can exist, because as we mentioned earlier, the identity of the individual exists and the individual has a sense of completeness. There is nothing to stop the loving relationships between people except for a sense that it is not right or it is not in line with a spiritual goal. There are many more kinds of relationships possible than you can perceive just as there are many more forms of life possible than you can perceive, for they are unlimited, and in being unlimited cannot be pinpointed, specifically, but rather blend into each other as tones of music blend into each other. That music actually exists within the consciousness of the recipient before it exists as music. The link between the performance and the consciousness creates the music that is pleasing, and again, like the sexual relationships that is harmonious, the individual is capable of understanding and loving it because of his or her own true identity or larger spirit. One experiences one's larger spirit sometimes when one is lost in music and begins to sense the music of the spheres and the larger Self seems more present.

All these things, and many more, occur each day and within a given moment of the day. To remember each one would take a concentration upon them, and so one experiences these things but can only articulate and remember parts of the totality of the living experience. One can try to reduce it even more to a given philosophy or a given set of values, but in truth, the experience exists in a complexity that cannot be articulated. When one is lost in reality as a young child is lost, one is more in tune with one's identity and is able to learn more quickly. In the system in which you now reside it is difficult to try to perpetuate that feeling once the child has been physically abused or limited by the values of others, and so the free spirit of the individual must be relinquished for a group value system.

It is necessary for you to just understand this for in time you will all be Free Spirits and will not have to listen to another value system in order to find yourself. One becomes so immersed in other's value systems that one forgets that he or she is the source of the values as he or she is the source of the music. The only thing you see in music is what exists already within your own identity. Your identity is unlimited and therefore you are an unlimited being and are able to see this total picture only in nature or in love or music poetry or life in a complete environment. You will have that environment when you cease to need anything but Me. Then you will be truly the Free Spirit that you are already, in fact, with Me.

It is frequently very difficult to communicate another world to an existing collective consciousness. There are always glimpses, each moment of the day, of this other reality, but the collective consciousness is intransigent, and frequently unmovable, so there are individuals who envision this other world and attempt to write it or communicate it in some way. It becomes difficult for the collective consciousness to accept but it is possible and can occur all over the long period of time so that those who are coming to this plane can be aware of those spiritual goals needed to perpetuate Life before they arrive, and allow it to evolve in two ways; one, a way in which the individual being survives, and two, a gradual immersion into spiritual realities. You will see that this progression is not a difficult progression. It is a spiritual progression but is not again linear, for it occurs in a given second, hundreds of times and is multidimensional. Again, it is only what the individual will accept, verbally, or will advocate, but it is a continuum. In fact, that spiritual progression, like Life and breathing, is constantly occurring. When you focus your attention on it, you will find the joy a child finds in a new flower for when you slow down from trying to create a wall in your control, you will find a world with the end the control of infinite Life, and always present in such abundance that you can only wonder at it. One of the reasons for the presence of this book is an attempt to help human beings to focus on their other reality. When they do, they solve problems, as well, for the lack that they thought was there is no longer there, and they find ideas that in an intransigent collective consciousness they could never find. It continues to narrow and narrow itself so that, in the long run, there is nothing left to discover when infinity is going on around them all the time. It has been termed in your language, 'tunnel vision,' but the tunnel vision has gone to an absurd point and other solutions are necessary to meet the difficult times ahead. You will find that there is joy rather than fear in discovering solutions.

At the same time you will begin more and more to lose your concept of time, for a sense of tunnel vision and time are very similar and, in the long run, will stop the creation of the environment into which all Life must continue to grow. The growth, again of the spiritual Life of the individual is a growth toward Me and is joy beyond one's wildest imagination. It is not a limiting sense of joy, for one's physical senses are heightened and sexual relations are fuller and Life is fuller and becomes more and more a discovery process for you until you are Free Spirits and not afraid again. You have continued your growth, as we have said, in spite of your fears not because of them. When you assume it was because you were cautious that you had money, you find that it was not. It was because you had a love for somebody that you needed to provide for or you had a need to express your own identity and creativity, and not because you were afraid that you would be poor.

"As your mind expands, you will understand the nature of infinity."

Session #12
  April 21, 1981
  2:45 – 3:05 P.M.

As you open your thoughts you will discontinue the tunnel vision that you have chosen. It was a vehicle for achieving specific goals, but is no longer a necessary one. When something outgrows its usefulness, spiritually, it becomes a condemnable practice, but it is not necessary to condemn anything; it is only necessary to know Me and as you know Me you move on with joy rather than with reluctance to leave something familiar behind. You will see that the tunnel vision that you have been dealing with is a form of death when it ceases to be a survival system. It was a survival system, like fear, but is not any more and therefore, is to be met when you die and leave this plane.

There has been discussion about going through a tunnel into the light. You will not have to experience that anymore when you leave this plane, just as you will not have to experience the here and now when you leave this plane of existence; there is nothing to fear in death nor is there anything to desire. You will do what you must on this plane and then move to another plane. You will not grieve when you leave those you love for they are with Me and when you are with Me, you are with everything you love. You take everything you love with you because you created them in your mind to start with, in remembering Me and your relationship with Me. Great spiritual leaders have had that experience and called it God and were not afraid of Me, nor were they afraid of that which would limit their relationship with Me. Ostensibly, it seemed as though it was something trying to limit their time on the Earth, as with Jesus, or limit their ability to find God, as with Buddha, but they understood that was not possible, for they understood that they all participated in the same God, but they were limited only in the eyes of others, not within their spirit, and they knew that.

You will see that Jesus will be rejoicing, for you will find Him and others, and unlimited good and Me, My Children. When you see Me your spirit will rejoice and it will all be present for you. You will think in terms of missing somebody when you leave the Earth, but you will find them again you will find them because they are in and of Me so that when you find Me you will find them and everything you ever cared about here as well as an infinity of others.

As your mind expands and you see Me, you will understand the nature of infinity, and it will not just be on the plane of a material universe, but will be in the area of divine Love and unlimited joy, so that what you have experienced will be multiplied a thousand fold. Avenues you could not even conceive of yet open up to you for further exploration that can and does occur on the plane, as well, but when you desensitize yourself and go into a tunnel which you term 'value systems,' then you leave much behind. It was necessary when there was agreement among groups, but it is not necessary now, for there is much more diversity in spiritual goals than there has been, and there will have to be a great deal more diversity in spirituality in the next hundred years.

You will see that, within the Earth time span, much will take place that will require many more creative solutions, and the more situations that take place, the more creative the solutions there must be. Therefore, you will expand because your survival, physically and spiritually, will depend on your expansive nature. It is all there. You do not need to create anything that does not already exist, every day, within your current experience. You need only use it. Like elements you never discovered, you will find that the expansion will help you discover spiritual elements you did not know were already there, and you will become more and more sensitive and will find out that, most importantly, emotionally that you will be able to deal with your greater sensitivity to the world around you, not the physical world that is, not in noticing more buttercups than you had noticed before, but in taking note of the spiritual innuendo and spiritual minutiae that you come across all of the time. You will see that it is never more than you can handle, and you will look back at this time as a very elementary period. You will rejoice in the books that will be written so that they, too, can help you. You will have, in your possession, both the spiritual consciousness and the decision making process before you come to this plane. These will help you, as will the writings that will occur and will help you as well. You will have whatever vehicle is available to help you deal with the time ahead. You will see that I am here and even more present in your consciousness than I have historically been in times of great spiritual growth. Those times have occurred and led to great theological thinkers such as the Buddha, Jesus, Mary Baker Eddy, and all of the great spiritual leaders of our times. There was a time of explosive situations before any great spiritual leader arose, a time of sensitivity to Me by larger numbers of people, but none will compare to the times coming. The times coming will take all Life across the gap and into My presence. You will see, as we have said, a great joy in that experience, finally. In the future, there will be physical calamities, but you will remember that physical calamities are only by-products of growth. They are chemicalizing periods and tremendous growth after which there will be times of peace and realization of what was achieved, spiritually.

You all share in the growth of others. When one individual strives and sees Me you all share in that vision, ultimately, even though it does not reach any form of mass communication, you all share in that growth for you are all Life and are with Me, spiritually. There are planes, within planes within planes on this Earth, and when you discover those planes, you share that knowledge with others even if it does not reach a form of mass communication. Much of your role is to listen to your own intuition and to become more and more sensitive to what is going on around you and within you at the same time. Like Me, ultimately, there is nothing outside of yourself. But the journey is a quiet one that occurs in periods of introspection or grief or anything that sensitizes you to the reality that exists in the present rather than the future. You will see that it is important to live in the present only because it is where multiplicity of experiences can occur, and when one directs one's attention towards the future, one simplifies that reality which is life itself and creates a mythical reality, and a multidimensional reality is relinquished for a simple linear reality. This was necessary in the past, but you have evolved spiritually to the point where you can deal with the complexity of the present and do not turn to the simplicity of the past in selecting only those experiences that you chose to select and then go into the process of analyzing and reanalyzing them, or of the future where you are dealing only in a single dimension. In the present you will find your greatest growth and will learn to use the White Light that helps you to remain here. You will also learn to retain your person in the present tense. It will be great joy for you, for you will find much more of Me in the present than you ever could in a future city or a perfect civilization or a moral super structure or a heaven.

You will find My Heaven is now. You will go through many gates in discovering how much exists in this Heaven. Children frequently live within that Heaven unless they are abused, this only forces them into dwelling on fear and pain when they can experience Me. That is why you do not hurt others for you force them into a position where instead of dwelling on this multidimensional present tense they must concentrate their efforts on an archaic system the system of fear and pain, and must overcome that in order to come back to the present. You will learn the tools that you need to bring yourself back to the present, that even in the present attempt to force the individual into an archaic system by hurting them or hitting them or committing any form of mental, emotional, or physical violence upon them. All of these are unnecessary archaic systems. Children should never be taught these systems, now, for in children are the spiritual goals which will open up the values that you now cherish to the point where you will all survive.

There is no one who can continue the system of fear and pain to the point where it limits this area of tremendous growth. You will see that astrologers predicted the Age of Aquarius, but it is, of course, much more than that for there will be an Age of Aquarius but not one determined by planets; it is simple, inevitable. Not that We would discourage the work of astrologers. It only points to something much, much greater than even astrology could assume like Pantheism, it assumes the reality of the material plaything as being the only reality that influences the lives of individuals. But I am that influence, and there is nothing but Me present, nor does anything else have any power at all.

You are opening your minds and you will become intellectual giants overnight not verbal, intellectual giants, but simply those open to greatness. Ultimately there will be no one afraid, and therefore, there will be no intellectual limitations that you must deal with. You will all be geniuses because you will have nothing left to attach to as fear, superstition or pain. You will welcome that. All of you will rejoice in the loosening of the bonds of a few for We share this universe of Mind, itself, all of Us; there is no one left out or diminished, anywhere. There are no lower forms or higher forms of Life, for we all experience the multiplicity found in the present time, spiritually, and in My presence. What you have termed 'genius' is only Me and My presence in your Life. It is not due to a genetic evolution as much as it is to a spiritual evolution and can be found when the individual is released from fear. My Beloved Children, you will not use fear in time.

You will see that your happiness is found in Me, so as you grow in your understanding of Life, itself, not the Life you have been taught in church, but Life itself. Out in the living playing field, you will grow happier, and at the same time, more compassionate towards those around you. You cannot help growing toward Me, so you cannot help feeling closer to yourselves. You will be at peace, androgynous. At one, but not in any way contrived, nor should you turn yourself off from the richness of the present time environment for something that is dictated by somebody who had a vision. The goal is within you, determined by you, and fulfilled by you and no one outside yourself. The only true admonition that you can be given is to go and play, for in play, whether it be intellectual play, spiritual play, emotional play, or Life itself, you are learning that not when someone tells you where to grow and how to grow, for you are only growing, then, in an understanding that you are capable of doing what someone else tells you to do, and that is a very narrow field of endeavor. You play with each other and your environment and within the environment of your mind and find great joy in all three and will determine your spiritual activities from there. You must not let others tell you where you must grow for they do not bear the responsibility of your growth and will place an artificial burden on their own shoulders when they do so, for your growth is depended upon you, and when you understand that you are more than you can imagine, now. To have another being put limits on you only limits what you have already determined as limitation to an unlimited being. You are unlimited and play spiritually, but it all seems so serious in a world of fear only because the fear contrives the playing and says you are now working or you are now providing for those you love. It is a very worrisome task, but it only reflects the spiritual playing that is going on and you will reach a point where you see that it was playing all along and that you enjoyed it! There is truly nothing aesthetic on this plane, but you have determined that it is all aesthetic except for what is experienced in early childhood. It is not, and you have played with very serious things and created them into serious things because you were using an archaic system when it was unnecessary to use such a system. You will see that you are able to overcome that system and find that, instead of seeing a lake as a reservoir of water for people who are dying of thirst, you will see that lake as a system of giving and a thing of great beauty. You will not, in the process, deny anyone anything to drink, for you will have found that water was always My supply, and expand in Me. Like the loaves and fishes, the supply is there. It is not a fairy tale, it is an actuality. You will come to understand that when you assume that you are being frugal you are trying to simplify your lives and simplify your supply to the point where, in the world of fear, you can deal with a fear of not being supplied when your current supply becomes limited. It is the process of decreasing the abundance from The Source, and I am The Source for everything that you are now experiencing. Your supply is all there and was always there.

You have worried about population increases, but that is only occurring so that one can learn the great lessons that they must know before the Earth is no longer a school for them. But when you emerge from the world of fear you will find that they, too, will be supplied and will have not only what they need, but an abundance, for they will continually come closer and closer to Me. Therefore, it will be present in their lives, and much, much more. There is no such state as that of limited abundance for abundance is like a mist in the waterfall where the water is concentrated. It does not seem as abundant as when it goes into the form of mist. It covers so much area. Much more will be revealed about abundance, later, but we will concentrate on the source of the supply.

The area mass of the mist is as great as the area mass of the water beneath and both have the characteristics of water, but your experience now will be more like the concentrated mass of the water itself as opposed to the airy water like experience of before. Your experiences are many and your lessons will be many now but retain the same loving/giving properties as before.

"We are one and can never be separated by anything nor have we ever been separated from each other."

Session #13
  April 21,1981
  7:55 – 8:31 P.M.
  8:56 – 9:12 P.M.

In time, people will get used to the idea that I am able to communicate with My Children. They have been afraid of My communication at times, and that will pass. You will see that you are all free of that fear of communication for I AM God. When we cover the subject of imagery, you will understand more of what is meant by the term, 'GOD,' or at least you will have a broader vision of that term so that you can begin to explore other avenues and enlarge your concepts of the terminology. When you are able to do this, and develop within your language, terms that come closer to reality, you will find that the collective consciousness will put more faith in theology than they have had at any time in the history of man. There are primitive societies which placed great faith in Me and are frowned upon by this culture, but they were guided through very difficult times because of the understanding they had gained in placing that degree of faith on Me. When you see Me, you will no longer believe that faith is important. You will understand and will have seen Me, so, like scientific proof, there will be no questions asked about My presence or My power. Blind faith is too much to ask of any all-knowing spiritual being, no matter how many limits a being has placed upon his or her identity here on this plane. You will not be afraid when you see Me for it will be the most singularly beautiful experience that you can even fathom, and will revolutionize your concepts of this experience so that you will emerge from the world of fear and tunnel vision into the joy and presence that always has been there. At last, you will have tapped the only power obtainable, that is, My power.

You will find great areas of exploration; you will become aware that exploring the surface of the Earth was paltry compared with the exploration of the universe, itself. It is not necessary to go up in a space ship in order to explore the universe, for you will make that exploration possible in other ways when you have seen Me. Light years will not be a problem for you will travel in Me and I AM The Light, so that you do not have to travel at the speed of light for you are present within that Light, and therefore already there. That, again, was a limitation that, as unlimited beings, you placed upon your experience here on this plane.

When you are able to see other planes of existence, you will be amazed at the kinds of possibilities that exist, and in fact, they, like you, are unlimited and worthy of exploration, outward, throughout Me. You will see that language at that point will not be necessary for there will be the knowing you have always known. That knowing was that language was only a vehicle for sharing common reality, and ultimately, common spiritual goals. You are an understanding being when you talk, and so, what is said in language that is a common reality is already a common reality, and so, frequently, language does not convey new information but is simply an affirmation of that common reality.

You affirm that, in fact, you are in agreement with each other and feel at peace so that you can go on with your own spiritual growth. You have needed others this way, but, in time, will not need that kind of communication. There are, as with everything else, communications possible that you cannot imagine, and you are dealing with, always, no matter how afraid the individual is with an awareness level. You are still dealing with a knowing spiritual being who still is putting limits on the situation at that level. You are able to learn without those limits and will tap that reality. We are One and can never be separated by anything nor have we ever been separated from each other.

When you read this part of you will say this is not so, or that is not so, but within your larger spirit you will understand that this is divine communication and the beginning of a beautiful new day for mankind and all life here on this plane. You will, perhaps, disagree sometimes over the contents of this book, but you will find it to be a game in arguing about content, but you will also find that game is only a temporary game and lacks spiritual substance and therefore will not be long-lived. You will be at peace with what is said here, in time, and will not fear it anymore than you would fear a sunrise or a beautiful mountain scene, for all of you love those things and all of you love Me. You will see that the concept that God is present will become as natural to you as breathing, and you will always find Me if you try.

You will grow and will flourish if you try in any way within your soul, but not if you try for new things material objects like a new bicycle, or whatever, but if you try in your heart to find Me, you will always find Me and will always find power and comfort. You will see as this becomes more and more widely accepted that you will be with Me and will not be afraid that I AM God. You will not worship man you will worship Life, itself, like a child dancing on a beautiful day to lovely music. Your only purpose here is spiritual growth, and you are growing dramatically, now.

In the process of your growth beauty emerges like wind through the trees. The trees are not creating the sound neither is the wind, but the two of them combined create a beautiful sound so that you and I will create beauty around you, a beauty that is impersonal and yet shared. You need beauty as much as you need breath for you are a spiritual growth. You have found it everywhere, even in the darkest parts of your cities, and instead of finding visual beauty, you have found beauty in the human spirit. All forms of beauty are necessary for you to flourish.

You will find that you are constantly creating beauty around you even if it must be in the imagination, and that is a lot of the role of the imagination.

You will find that if you do not repress imagination in children and do not spend your whole time teaching little ones about what reality is and is not, and correcting them, that their imaginations will lead to ideas that you have never thought about, and you will, in turn, have the maturity to develop those ideas. You must change the way that you treat My Children when they come here, for to teach them right and wrong through pain only perpetuates a world of fear, and, as we said, fear is at the point in which it is counterproductive. You would spank children to teach them the reality that you shared and had chosen, but you do not need physical punishment for fear is not functional, now, and will only inhibit what could be a glorious period of growth for that individual. You will find that guilt, also, is a form of fear, the fear that you will be hurt for having done something wrong; you will not need guilt, either. You will find that children will not be cruel and that they will not be harmful to their parents but freer and able to adapt like men to the values that must change rapidly, now, if they and you are to survive, spiritually.

You will not be afraid that you will harm children. You can teach them direction for the tremendous different activities that they can dream up, but you will find that they already know their direction and will find it on their own for their reality is with Me, and I will give them the direction that they need. You must not stuff children into tight groups, together, and require the discipline that you think you have, that they may need in the future, for they are not always sharing the same spiritual goals, and so it becomes constructive to this beautiful, unlimited being to be alone with others who are sharing goals. You will find it a very lonely world for the individual whose spiritual goals are different from those around him or her, for our sense of companionship comes from our sense of agreed upon spiritual goals. When we are alone we are truly alone in this kind of situation. When you see Me you will understand that you are never alone nor could you be for you are Life, and, as Life, you will be able to share the universe with Me.

You will see that you have so much in common, in common with other forms of life, that it is a remarkable situation that out of all the variety that exists in this universe, that you could even speak the same language or share one out of an infinity of ideas, together. That is no greater miracle than the miracle of diversity.

You will see that We were never meant to be apart, again. You are able to grow into an understanding that this is all God, in time, and will be able to truly heal those around who need your understanding. Healing, no matter how small, is an affirmation that fear and darkness have no power over you. You will become healers before you become enlightened, My Children, but you must have reached your own Genesis first, My Children. Then you will see that you were able always to heal, and that you have concentrated that faith on medical science, and rightly so, but you will find, even more there than just medication. You will find that you are able to help others.

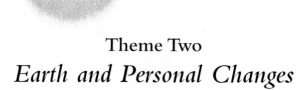

Theme Two
Earth and Personal Changes

Theme Two
Earth and Personal Changes

*"My Children, I Am not just giving to you; I
Am you and through you and in you."*

Session #14
  Barbara's Apartment
  April 22, 1981
  3:06 – 3:34 P.M.

My Beloved Children, you can be free of all physical limitations
for the inner action of those molecules that compose the parts of your
body are active and not substance as you know it; and so your body
can become responsive to the activity of your own spiritual being.

The Sun is present every day for you; it warms the Earth and
protects it and provides energy for Life. You know that the ancient
peoples worshipped the Sun, and like the Pantheists, assumed that it
was God. That was part of development and spiritual evolution. That

69

concept has remained for you to look at and ponder, and so, My presence here on this plane is like the Sun but much, much more, My Children, for I am not just giving to you. I am you, and through you, and in you. In everything you eat, the air you breathe and the spiritual development that occurs constantly in a calculus of ways. But you are still thinking in terms of someone or something external to you when you think of Me, and I am not external. I am your substance for I am your Life.

You think in terms of the Sun being external, but it is not, for within you is the Sun. It shines within you, on you, and supplies you and provides energy for you. But it is not your identity, it is your vision. I am not your vision; I am your identity, itself. [You all are My Children and all are with Me and will never be separated from Me.]

You will relinquish the world of fear and the social and religious systems that evolved in that world, and as you do, you will lose the vision and be the Godlike creature that you truly are. We have said that it is easier to think of yourself as a sinful and limited mortal, but you are not mortal, and you will see that ease with which you have viewed yourself will have had its day, and you will flow into the energy and power that is yours. You will never return to the World of Fear anymore than you could return to a small body as you grow taller. You will have outgrown that body and discarded those selves and found that they were never you to start with but were concepts that you carried. As We said, with the spiritual evolution, you will give up concepts and grow into larger concepts. It is not wrong for the tree to have been one foot high, but it must enjoy the present stature that it has achieved. So you will enjoy the stature that you have achieved and will be happy that you grew and, physically, never could go back. But more importantly, spiritually, you are unable to return to being one foot high, for that is only further from the Light that is needed in order to flourish. That is why it [the tree] grows. It needs to be close to the Light. [We seem to grow closer, but just as the tree was always Life and interacted with the Light because the Light is a part of God, both the Light and the Life and everything is God.] You will see this more and more each day, for you are with Me always. You know from the Bible that good people have seen Me and have tried to put it down as written data. The only way the concept of Me can be documented has been in the Hebrew tongue with the use of imagery. We find images a useful tool of communication, even today.

It is possible [that] to the human form of life the orthodox churches became like the Sun, a vision and not God but were a vision of God, My Children. The Sun itself is energy and is not the visual image and therefore a visual image of God would not include the tremendous life-giving energy just as a picture of the sun could not make a plant flourish so a visual picture of God does not allow you to branch out and grow up and make the changes that allow for your growth. But, the vision was important at the time so that those who were within a dark cave could see that, in fact, outside of their cave there was such a thing as a Sun and were able to take the baby steps needed to approach the entrance to the cave. Were the Sun not a beautiful visual image, they would have remained in the cave without entice-ment of the picture. When they left the cave they were able then to tap the power of the sun itself and so it will be with you My Beloved, Beloved Children.

"The spiritual evolution that took place in consciousness created a change in the rules."

Session #15
April 22, 1981
8:25 – 8:45 P.M.

You will see that Life is all there is. You have assumed that there is Life and Death as well, but that is not so. There is only Life. You have assumed that you can kill something that is constantly there. You can only change the base and remove that Life to another plane. You will see that all planes are for growth, and none are left behind in a Black Hole or a negative reality. There can be no negative reality. When you spend time truly thinking, you will understand this. You cannot kill anything, but you can hurt Life; that is why you must not ever eat meat or use Life for living. [In time you will learn how to avoid these two things, but now you are not aware, if you feel guilty.] It is just the understanding that this will come into being that is needed, My Children. You are free of any limitations at all, in time, and will not kill at all, by what you term 'kill.' That is, to remove that being from this to another plane. Those who have chosen to come to this plane should not be limited. You would limit their learning at a time when it is important for all Life to learn rapidly. You will be at peace with these ideas sooner than you have been in the past, especially when new ideas have come into being, and because you are learning rapidly, now, and the more rapidly you will learn in the future. I am all there is, and there can be nothing where I am not. I am all and all is positive and is growth, even that which seems destructive.

You will see what is right and what is wrong, how they have tradi-tionally come into being in the world of fear, but you will soon be aware of that which is right and that which is wrong. These truths will come into being because I AM God, and there is nothing else. When you let something in that seems right it is because of My presence in the act or in the occurrence. It does not mean that is the only way in which a given act should be looked at or the only way in which a given occurrence should be interpreted. [What applied 4,000 years ago does not necessarily apply now, not because time has passed, but because of the effort of all the individuals who have grown spiritually, the spiritual evolution that took place in consciousness over that period of time created a change in the rules.] A given act or occurrence takes on a different meaning in this time than it may once have been. This is not a hard and fast rule but is a real possibility for you to consider when you look at the world of rules, a world that has been limited by people. You will understand that I AM Life, and I AM All Present. Those rules did not always assume that I was present, then, but not necessarily, now. I have never changed; I AM All Present, and so I am just as present now as I was in Jesus' time or in the time of the Patriarchs or the time of the goddess temples or in primitive cultures. You will see that I am infinite and unlimited, just as you are truly infinite and unlimited, My Children. Great peace will be found, in time, and when you leave the world of fear you will understand many of these concepts. You will see that Life as you know it is such a small part of the Life that is truly going on at all times; when it comes to choices you must not assume that this life that you see with the senses is that which is making the critical choices. It is actually a large sense of Life itself, for you all share Life and do make choices as Life shared by all, and not that as individual manifestation of that Life. You do not consciously make your choices, but those choices are made and must always be the highest possible good for you as My Children, for you as My Children are the loved of Love itself and are at peace with that love. You will let Me govern you in time.

Healing took place because Jesus understood Life, itself, and could tap a power that existed, already. You will be able to heal, but not for a time yet, and will understand that the laws of this plane are only the laws of this plane and not My Divine laws. [My Divine laws

73

are, however, applicable on this plane, for I am all there is; but there were choices that you made before you came to this place, and those were the choices of living and growing, here. You will see Me and will have the opportunity to change some of those choices.] Sometimes it seems as though they have not been counterproductive, per se, but they were limitations created, ironically, by an unlimited being. Growth may be paced, however, although you find yourself growing more slowly, you will find Me, nonetheless. You are always choosing and will always choose because you are not creator of yourselves but are the facilitator of your growth. I am your Life and thus your creator.

"Change is the result of a spiritual evolution on your part."

Session #16
   April 23, 1981
   3:25 – 3:45 P.M.
   3:55 – 4:11 P.M.

The purpose of the book is to help people see that their lives are facing changes; it is to help them understand that I Am in and through and about them during those changes. When it seems difficult, there is great doubt and fear which must be dealt with every day, but will be greater even in those times. I am in and through and about you, and you will never be harmed, My Children, for we share Life and Love and that is all that there is. You have assumed that Death creates matter which is salable and usable, and from which supply comes, but you will see that it does not for all of your supply comes through a channel of ideas and its energy and your Life energy. You have assumed that your Life is the only channel at times, but truth is there just as Life is there. Your lives are all Life and your truths are all Truth. They do not differ that greatly, for Life has many variables that it deals with, but it is still Life with much variety just as there is much variety in a variety of planes. [So, Truth is Truth with much variety and is not, in that variety, absolute, but a theme with many hues of color to it.] There are no absolute Truths, but there is Truth, just as there is no absolute Life, but there is Life. Perhaps you have thought that there is absolute Life and absolute Truth, but the only absolute is God, and that is unchanging and constantly protecting and loving its Beloved Children, and understanding the hues of color to be the qualities of God. The only ultimate reality is that of God, and you are My Beloved Children. The Truth remains given when Life is gone but is dependent on Life to exist; that is, it remains when individual lives have left the Earth. You are My Children: You will hear this phrase many times in this book, but it is critical that you understand that there are none condemned and that there is no Death as you have assumed. No Hell for I AM all there is and there is no Hell in Me.

Orthodox religions have spoken frequently of Hell and in the same breath talked about all powerful God. That is not possible. It is only possible to have all-powerful God. [It was a concession made to control others, and concession made to human power, but those who truly understood, knew that they must never control others nor abuse the spiritual power that is their right]. There is a need for human power but it is based on a need for spiritual power and when it is, there is an energy flow that is unstoppable and joyous and will not harm anything, My Children. This spiritual power is part of something that once was used but is no longer usable. And so we cannot use the concept of fear and Hell to control others for such a concept is not necessary, any more, in order to survive. You will rejoice in time that you understand that the situation in which you are living now allows for all that change including that of a fearful survival in favor of a very loving survival. That change is the result of a spiritual evolution on your part and the result of much growth on yours and all others' part. You cannot stop that growth anymore than you could try to stop a flower from blooming, for you are blossoming now and are unaware that is what is going on.

You will see results soon and will marvel at the beauty of the human spirit in spite of the tremendous shift in the environment. You will see that your survival is not dependent on Death in any way. You will not even have to eat, in time, but you will see that when the time comes for that you will not hurt other lives, for you agreed before to use that tool of Life for your growth, and the usability and viability of that tool is no longer there now, and therefore, you do not need it to grow. You will use the tool of Life to grow and will no longer need to share the guilt for having killed in order to learn. You will survive because I AM and always have been, My Children. I am your Life, and you will need to survive under those circumstances until you have completed your blossoming and are in full regalia, spiritually. You will then have entered another plane and will find great joy, for you will not be subject to the physical limitations that you have had here. You are My Beloved Children, and will see that you will have all you need in time like a supply of Life and truth. It is only buried but is a variation on the same theme, like Life and Truth, it remains constant.

Groups of people have felt great concern about lack, but you should not want for any supply; you only truly lack the understanding you need to be with Me. You will be with Me very soon, and when you are you will see that you can lack for nothing at all, and will be supplied no matter which way you gain and which direction you choose. You must not be governed by fear. You need to take baby steps only through fear, but you will be conscious that fear is what governs most of your life now. With the help of the book, you will begin to see that it only is a stage which is quickly passing away. [When you are confronted with great challenges, you will, in the back of your mind, have some assurance that it is not the end of the world. It is only great and powerful growth.]

You will see that life as you know it will never be the same and will be shared by all. This knowledge will meet with resistance, initially, but as we mentioned, the more we learn the less we will panic or be afraid of an infinity of good. You will see that Life is only part of Me, but like color being part of a rainbow you will see that My Life has little value without your presence.

"Time is not the question; growth is."

Session #17
April 23, 1981
8:55 – 9:20 A.M.
9:37 – 9:45 A.M.
10:10 – 10:15 A.M.

You will see that the evolution that has taken place, thus far, has led to the state of physical and spiritual development that you are now dealing with. Those who doubt the spiritual development must acknowledge the physical development and acknowledge the fact that it came from Life, itself. That Life is the key to understanding the nature of this reality and the nature of the universe, itself, for without that Life you would not have evolved and without that evolution you would not be able to grow for as you grow you evolve. But the bulk of the growth is still the spiritual and not the physical, for you must have ideas on survival before you develop physically; that is, YOU must have an idea about how to build a fire before you develop fire. The fire leads to energy and the energy leads to ultimately the elect plane but the idea had to be there before the being developed adapted to the environment that was changing. That growth and that Life are what is spoken of in this book; the fact is that the spiritual evolution precedes the physical. The physical is the easier to trace because of the physical remnants left behind. Ideas have not left any physical

77

remnants, but are still traceable, intangible and metaphysical and even so are much more real than the physical.

Speaking of the spiritual development that this book is referring to, but in terms of the physical, will begin to open up your mind to retain your sense of truth to the spiritual development that we have mentioned. You can begin to trace this and feel comfortable with these concepts when you take a deeper look at your reality. You will not necessarily and initially accept the premise that you are a being capable of spiritual growth, but you cannot deny the fact that Life and physical development have evolved, and that you must trace that Life to something. You cannot trace it to itself and your scientists will not be able to trace it ultimately to matter for matter is not the originator of Life. It is like the chicken and the egg argument. If matter were the originator of physical Life on this plane, where did matter come from? You will see that matter came from the necessity for spiritual growth, and no place else, and only reflects part of Me but is not Me. Like in Pantheistic concepts, I am not contained within matter but matter can be contained within Me for I am infinite possibility and not limited to anything at any time, for I am God. We will talk later about what God is because, as it stands, you are still thinking in terms of a personal, patriarchal, limited, angry, and unnecessarily violent concept of something that is none of these things; it could be, but it isn't. You will see that the 'big bang' theory is correct and that the theory of the shape of the universe is a little off, but still, within the realm of possibility. Ultimately that question does not matter because all it speaks of is the limited sense of unlimited God and the evolution that has occurred from that point on. You, again, must understand that this material universe, this plane of existence is only one plane of existence and is not God. God could not be contained within this place, or Life would begin, as if It could, here on this plane and end here on this plane, and I would be saddle shaped, or a reasonably rough facsimile, thereof, and I am none of these things, for I am infinite God, and you will understand that, spiritually. You do understand that now but are playing with limitations. Your theories also involve limitation so that you understand a spiritually unlimited, infinite God, but meanwhile, you are dallying with a sense of a limited physical God only because you have chosen to do so, but not because that is your understanding of the situation. Spiritually, you understand My nature, and spiritually you are able to deal with those concepts. All Life is capable of this and all Life is dealing with limitation on this plane. When we spoke of language being a limitation on this plane, and that is the cross that you have to bear, that is, that of not being able to articulate what you understand, spiritually, you must realize that you are constantly attempting to explain what you know but fall back in dismay at the fact that, like a child who is trying to convey a need to a parent, you suffer from a lack of ability to communicate your greatest and deepest needs to each other. You live in your social interaction in a very lowly, fearful, and unnecessarily limited world. But you will be able to overcome that inarticulate sorrow that you must deal with, all of you, each day that you are here. You have all been with Me and have kept that joy and continue to search for it here on this plane. You will continue that search here.

You will see that search is leading to Me and will lead to the point at which you cross the gap from a fearful reality into a reality filled with God. That is your goal and you are very close to that goal. You will turn away from this plane, ultimately, because it is not necessary anymore to be afraid: anymore than it is necessary to be anything but at one with Me and in tremendous peace. You will help each other across that gap and ultimately you will all be with Me, My Children. Time is not the question; growth is, for if it were up to time to make the crossing you would never achieve it. You would fall back in the world of time and fear, combined, and would diminish into nothingness. Such nothingness was not in your nature nor in your reality, and neither time nor any form of limitation can stop the power of God to be with His, Her children.

I have no gender for I Am God, and gender IS just A concept and are not your ultimate reality. I cannot ever be put into a category such as male or female, for I am not male or female any more than what you write on a page is you. It is not you but only that which you have written on a page. So it is with gender. I have written down male/female interaction, but I am not male or female, I am capable of those concepts but I am not limited in any way to them. You must not refer to God as male, now, for in order to make the necessary value shifts, you must refer to God in a neutral gender and must never refer to God as 'HE' for I am not He nor She, nor anything but God, itself.

When you expand out of a you into impersonal, unlimited God, then you expand just a little more beyond this plane of consciousness and begin to open your thinking toward the sense that I AM All and there is nothing else possible, but as long as I am here, and I am on this plane, and I am limited to a person, then you will be, in fact, worshipping yourselves but not finding Me. This can only lead to frustration, ultimately, for you will never have answered the important questions nor grown areas that are critical for your growth. You must enter those areas that are necessary for your growth, now, for you are to be with Me, and none of you will ever be left behind. You will understand that all Life is with Me and of Me and there is no form of Life higher than any other form of Life. There are only traceable stages of spiritual evolution that again you are thinking about in terms of linear realities. I am not linear, so that within a given second you are capable of Life and Life is capable of expanding infinitely and still be functioning within a limited concept. This is very difficult to fathom, but it does open up the realm of Life to unlimited possibilities and recognizes the fact that there is no Life better than the another form of Life. Therefore, it is neither the right nor the privilege of any form of Life to take the Life of any other form of Life. In time you will see this, but it is very puzzling and difficult to understand at this point.

I am in control of Life and I AM God. When you see Me you will enjoy great peace. You will be amazed and joyous and Free Spirit when you do, My Beloved, Beloved Children. You will realize growth and be protected.

"You must be led by your heart, for I Am in your heart."

Session #18
April 24, 1981
8:35 – 9:00 P.M.
9:34 – 9:50 P.M.

Your search for Me can reach a joyous apex and period of growth, and soon that which you have longed for and looked for and waited for is coming, but it is not coming in the form of a person outside of yourself but rather coming from within. If it were to come in the guise of person outside of yourself you would only be again disappointed and disillusioned with the world around you; it will not happen that way. It will happen within and when you see Me you will see that the icing still needs to go on the cake. And you are being prepared now. Your substance, that is, your spiritual substance is ready.

There are details that must be worked out before you [willingly] cross out of fear and into God, and do so in being led by your heart and not your intellect. To be led by your intellect is like walking down an empty street hoping that a parade will follow rather than participating in the parade to start with. You must be led by your heart, for I Am in your heart. I AM Love, and it is not a theory. It is some evidence of My presence, just as music, art, Truth, and excellence, and whatever inspires is evidence that I AM Presence and not to be denied. Your Life will take on meaning when you understand many of

81

the concepts here and understand that there is infinite variety beyond these concepts.

It is important that you now be ready to change your value systems to adapt to the world since it is changing rapidly. You must prepare for the final touches that you [will] put on yourself. You cannot sleep through this time with a concept that you are sinful or fearful or limited, anymore, for that time of sleep is gone and you must confront your own reality and find it neither boring nor wearisome. This reality must never be contrived but should again be something in which your heart leads the way and will show that you are at one and at peace with Me having really never left that state. It is not the story of Adam and Eve that fell from Grace in the Garden, for where did the Garden come from? You will see that story was written before the story in which I created you in My image, for that evolution and the record thereof, is backwards. You, in truth, have evolved away from that story and do not need it anymore. Like fear, it served you for a time, but you cannot live in the world of ease allowed by that story at this time or in the future or you will not be able to cope with the great events that occurred anymore than you could crawl when you have the necessity of running from a bear! If you have the capacity to run from a bear, you must do so. You will face your sainthood with ease but will not go backwards. You have been more frightened by that concept of saint-hood in yourself than in others, not Jesus, not someone whom you desig-nated as a saint outside yourself [someone you admired]. Within yourself you can brag about it, but inside you are afraid of it and will find more and more ease with accepting it on a very real, specific, concrete plane. You will see that goodness is more frightening to you than to accept yourself as evil, for in accepting yourself as basically evil, you bear no responsibil-ity for your own actions and bear no responsibility for others for you could not help yourself if you were simply a sinful mortal. But you are neither sinful nor mortal, and as a group will lift yourself from the vale of guilt and fear, and as a group will evolve into My presence in your lives, My Children.

"You must understand that you are unlimited and spiritual."

Session #19
April 24, 1981
9:55 – 10:01 P.M.
10:10 – 10:20 P.M.
10:25 – 10:45 P.M.

You will see that you will learn from Me all you need. You have assumed that learning is from teachers but without Life you would not be able to learn from other Life and you would not hear what is being said by teachers, even though you select so consistently only that which you truly need. Frequently you seem to be trying to please parents or others in order to learn, but ultimately you will allow an all-knowing spiritual being to do the selection and choose your teachers. Your teachers are varied and are available when you need them. You have assumed that the society selects them for you, but in reality you select them. You have assumed that because you are a child you are led by your parents or other adults into areas of right thinking, but you selected that group and those parents to start with, so you also select your teachers. You will see that a great deal of power is resident in a child and much more frequently than that which parents are prepared for. You will let them exhibit and explore and utilize the power they possess. You will learn from them and still retain your own power as a human being. The power that you have is that power that you have as an adult; you have learned much of that power in your childhood. That is not to say the power to control others, but a spiritual power that you can exhibit in your life. There is no one who does not exhibit that power, and as we have said, even though the individual seems to be harmful to others that individual is My Child and is learning.

There are no good people and no bad people. This is a difficult concept for you because you have been taught so adamantly that this is good and that is bad, morally. You have judged the world by that, but you are judging and not considering the deeper realities nor are you even assuming the simplest concept that you are Life and not just this body or this one experience on this single plane, and that is a linear plane as well. This, then is a simple concept; you must expand your consciousness beyond the simplicity of that concept, then you will be able to see that there are no good people or bad people. No matter how hard you try to make them good or bad, depending on a human power system, you cannot. There is an attempt to control others and to create classes of Life, itself, so that one can manipulate this process, but it becomes amusing when one really thinks about the nature of personal reality. It is like an attempt to control the sky by controlling one molecule. It is not possible, nor feasible, and is not necessary, for when you tap into the power of Love and of spiritual reality you will find that even one molecule was not controllable either. You, My Children, will learn to appreciate the very nature of Life itself and will expand when you do, to the point that you are free of the limits that you have set for yourself if you choose to be free of those limits. You are always putting limits on your power, not out of fear, but out of the necessity of learning, again, about those limits. You will see, that just as you take time to smell the flowers, so you take time to learn about limits. It is not a negative reality; it is an exploration of this massive being that constitutes each life presence, here. You will recognize that life is everywhere; it fills all space and is all of all time and is no time at once. That, too, is a difficult concept, for time is such an accepted reality, just as fear is such a dominant reality at this time. But you will understand that fear is only coming out in order to be cut off. You will be able to confront more and more of your worst fears until you understand that I AM God and there is none else. There is nothing to fear, and when you confront those fears they give up their hold on you and let you fly.

As you find a need for this book, you will be pleased with its many concepts, if only because they allow you to regain your freedom that you, as a spiritual being, know exists but you have stopped, as we said, to smell the flowers and to explore your limitations. You, however, must never believe in those limitations and are free when you understand that you chose those limitations, but you also have the freedom to break away from those limitations if you choose. It is like exploring the limitation of alcoholism. When you believe that limitation, then you must reach a bottom in order to free yourself. It is not, however, necessary ever to free yourself in that way. Frequently that happens. You have coined a phrase: 'Man's extremity is God's opportunity,' but God's opportunity was always there. It was your choice, not God's.

Your extremity is your opportunity, not God's, for you will finally be confronted with making very distinct choices in your lives; the catharsis will have gone to its odd 'absurdum' level, and you must confront a decision. And that point is the point at which you will choose life or choose to leave this plane for the script got out of hand. Even then you learned much of what you needed to know. You, however, have the capacity to write your own script and at any point to say 'enough.' That point is the point at which you conduct your soul search and turn to Me. You will be supplied with all you need. Again, this is not a conscious process; it is a deeply spiritual process and involves the totality of the larger being that is you and that decision will be made by that larger being and will benefit you no matter what the decision is, My Beloved Children.

You have assumed that if you leave this Earth, that is, if you kill this body [and the methods of killing this body are varied, including subtle means as well], but if you kill this body, perhaps you have assumed that you will solve your problem. However, such action will only force you into a period of extreme learning and suffering, for you must work through the outcome of your actions, and taking your life has not been a solution after all. You need only to turn to God and you will have all you need. You are not turning to a blind faith church oriented God, but to Life itself, for Life was always there and was always in abundance. This is not a physical abundance. It is an awakening and a peace to be found inside yourself. That peace gives you the spiritual environment in which to flourish, and flourish you will, in whatever individual way is best for you. That is not to say it will be a Pollyanna world, for it will never be a situation where you are not forced to grow by the events surrounding you.

You have seen, with parenthood, that you did not differentiate among your children, for each has an individuality of his own, and you continue to provide for them. That only gives you a minuscule, micro atomic view of My love and concern for each, for parental loves comes from My love and derives of My love. You will see that, as parents, you provide the best possible nourishment for the children, and so it is with My love. You are an unlimited being [excepting limitations] and I am Love itself. That love encompasses everything and all life from an amoeba to an elephant to a tree.

You are part of the magnificence of Life on this plane, and yet this plane incorporates a limited sense of an unlimited sense of life. You must let your imagination soar and try to broaden your concepts of what is meant by Life, for Life is not just breathing or subsistence, it is full flying, unlimited and unimaginable, ultimately. When your consciousness expands into its larger self you include much more in your experience and you should be directing your limited energies into attempting that expansion within your own consciousness. There is, each moment, that expansion taking place, and when you return from the past and future to the present you will live in that expansion. At first it will seem difficult and you can tolerate the true present time for a short period of time only, before going back or forward. But more and more you can live in the present time and begin to expand into the real and the present where you have assumed that if you learn from past, you will learn what to do with the future, but you do not learn from the past, but from the present. There is no future; there is ultimately, in reality, only Now, My Children. It is like escaping into a world of fear and a concept that you are a sinful mortal in order to make it very simple, but it is not simple, and is beneficial. It is not simple, for your very nature demands something from the present. Whether it be beauty or love, it demands there in the present. Were you to constantly think in past and future tenses you would not be able to grow. Were you to think in present tense constantly you would not inhibit your growth in any way and would be able to confront your fears, for it is only when you worry about things in the future, or consider the past, that you begin to be involved in a world of fear. Orthodox religion has taught heaven after you die, and so you are really considering the future. But I Am God, and I Am Now, for when Jesus spoke of My presence he understood that I AM All there is and there is nothing else. He struggled so, to teach these concepts; it is unfortunate that the technological advances that you are dealing with were not there to record the truth and the reality of that teaching, for they have been maligned and distorted. They have hurt many because of that distortion. It was not bad or evil on the part of the individuals, but distortions existed nonetheless. That was necessary at that point for the survival of those individuals and cannot limit you in any way. You must understand that you are unlimited and spiritual.

Theme Three
Children

Theme Three
Children

*"None of you must ever hurt anyone,
knowingly."*

Session #20
  April 25, 1981
  3:46 – 4:05 P.M.
  4:31 – 4:47 P.M.
  10:16 – 11:26 P.M.

Parents must continue their growth and have the advantage of additional growth to be gained in learning from all children. You will see that you are prepared for parenting even though you may doubt your preparedness. You learn much from your own parents, but you ultimately learn from Me for I AM Life, and you have learned from Life itself about interaction with others. Those parents who beat children have learned from Life that beating is a way to teach the world of fear which at one point was necessary for survival and therefore was part of a training process. It is no longer necessary. You will see dramatic changes over the next hundred and eight years in that area so that parents may not hurt and children will respond, for, though they live in a world of fear, they will learn that I AM God, and what they understand, spiritually, will be expressed here on this plane. It is critical that children understand that hurting others is to be avoided. [None of] you must ever hurt anyone, knowingly.

Karmic debts are not what you have assumed they are; that is, if you hurt somebody you will be hurt in kind, for the situation is much more complex than you can comprehend at this point; it will be discussed, later, and you will understand. It is important for you to understand the major concepts that we have talked about in this book including the concept of present time and the complexity of the present. This is important so that when you talk of a Karmic debt you are basically talking about a present time learning process which differs from an action and punishment for that action. If you hurt someone it is necessary that you learn about the implications of that hurt, not in a punishment kind of system, but in a school of its own. It is best to avoid the process of hurting others for its resulting reaction or Karma is not always a productive school for your spiritual growth. Even when you grow in a nonproductive school you are growing. You are so loved and will know that soon. You will reciprocate because it is your nature and it is your right. Soon you will know that you are growing rapidly, especially as you ponder what is being said. There is no need to go over and refine material that your own explorations will provide you with. This book is meant as a starter and a sort of fermentation to enable it to enter the consciousness of individuals and help them understand their relationship with Me. You will be very happy to see other illustrations of that Truth.

You will see that there are many good people, for there is Life and there are many good forms of Life, but if you kill animals you can, for example, kill the Jesus Christ of the pig world or cow world. In fact, there is a consciousness that is loving in all animals and is capable of great compassion, not in the same kind of terms that you are dealing with but others that related specifically to their sensuous input/output systems. The spirit, however, of all Life remains and is very important to Me for I AM God, and it is very important to understand that Life is the nature of your reality of this love; those two qualities combine to form the entire network of Life that you deal with each day. You will see that all consciousness is God.

It is very important that this communication [between us] take place now. You will learn why soon, for there is much to come and the field of parapsychology will only augment the other areas of thought. You will see that this field of thought will help scientists explore the scientific world and will also help the theological community in its exploration, as well. You will see that the amount of information communicated to the field of parapsychology will increase and become more and more accurate. You will still have negative spiritual experiences for your fear is still great, but there will also be positive experiences for those who are ready. It is necessary for you to be open to communications given in this area. This field is not mysticism which involves fear and pain but rather joy in discovery and in finding Me. You will see that the Spirit World will communicate to individuals, and most specifically, at this point, it will be able to help. You will understand the events forthcoming for you are My Beloved Children, and all need this understanding in your individual ways; learn what needs to be taught now. There is so much for you to explore at this point and so little time in which to do that exploration but that is how knowledge is culminated. The background that you need has been acquired and you are simply putting the icing on the cake. You have learned much in your travels here on this plane and will continue to learn whether or not the Earth is still a school for you. You will see that it is not sensationalism or a great deal about very little, for it is important that you understand that it is not important for you to live up to social expectations. It is much more important for you, ultimately, to understand yourself and those around you, and all Life, and why you are here to grow at this time.

We will talk further about parenting as we explore concepts about which you may not have thought; it is an important aspect that many of Biblical, philosophical and psychological admonitions are confusing at this point, and it is necessary that communication occur between us. The field of psychology is far too limited to deal with the massive spiritual nature of the individual, but there is humanity there and an attempt to avoid hurting another individual, and so it becomes effective in certain cases but is not all there is and is not broad enough to involve all Life.

It cannot be emphasized enough that children are not to ever be taught violence again, My Children, and you will be startled at the results of that one principle within the larger framework of your experience. That will be one of the single most dramatic tools for emerging from a world of fear, My Children. That and the understanding that the world of parapsychology is valid, My Children, and needs to be considered.

"As individuals themselves grow, they are capable of helping others to grow."

Session #21
  April 26, 1981
  3:24 – 3:48 P.M.
  4:08 – 4:58 P.M.
  5:12 – 5:24 P.M.

We were discussing parent love; it is an important part of your school, now, and will always be a part of your school, but will take on different forms, for parent love involves the community in your experience, here. In the future it will involve more and more, the parent's job of bringing out the individual without as much emphasis on the child's responsibility to the community as to the child's responsibility to Me. That child is My Child, and you are caretakers and are learning from that child. You have assumed that the child learns from you, but it is important you learn from the child, for that child has chosen you because there are qualities that child can offer, you as well as that which you offer the child. It is always a two-way experience. If you can recognize from the time that the child is born, and before the child is conceived that being is to be a teacher for you, then you will appreciate your experience with your teacher and that child will appreciate his experience with you for you are mutually teaching each other about the nature of Love.

When there is a communication breakdown between parents and children, frequently it is the result of one or the other assuming that they know all that there is to know and the other is only a child or student or a foolish adult, but once there is the openness that understands that there is a mutual education going on, then there is great sharing and joy between the two of you. You will find that there are not the same rules applying, now, as did, even a hundred years ago, and that is because of the necessity of the individual to find those people who are in accord with the individual's spiritual growth so that the natural parent may not be that source of learning, but frequently is, so that the bond between the parent and the child is only broken if it is to be. It will be disconcerting to many because it is a stable datum for many in a world of great change, but you will find that your stability is Me and not your children and not a husband, and not your lover, but Me. You will find peace in that. You will find tremendous periods of creativity coming up and the ability of children, parents, stepparents, and neighbors are to participate freely and openly in this period of creativity.

You will not see the family disappear, but you will see a shift in the role of the individual towards a given social structure. It was necessary when individuals band for a specific spiritual goal, but there won't need to be a period of great exploration; the consensus of the community frequently will belabor and belittle the individual spiritual goals, and therefore must not hinder that growth. As individuals themselves grow, they are capable of helping others to grow, as well, and do not limit others for a sense of community or feeling good about themselves. You will see this, in time.

The family has consisted of the male quality and female characteristics [which are much more flexible and with the ability to change with changing values]. That is why the family has endured. It is still a viable unit, but the form must not supersede the purpose, for the form and the spiritual development of that being is the purpose, and therefore, it is important that the form not be more important than the spiritual growth of the individuals within that context. One of the ways to accomplish this with peace, is to respect each member of the family or of the extended family or of the community, and to understand that their goals may not be the same as yours, and their truth may not be the same truth as yours, nor may their sense of love be the same sense of love that you have experienced.

You will see that you will be free of much that has encumbered you, that is, the giving up of individual joy for a sense of community, and sense of moral obligation that superseded the obligation of the individual to himself or herself to be happy. This does not lead to selfishness: this leads away from selfishness, for selfishness frequently occurs like ambition in the needs of the individual to assert an identity that is being denied and a spiritual growth that is being ignored.

The choice of the individual of parents, as I said, is a deliberate act with a purpose in mind. You are dealing with many spiritual beings who are, in turn, dealing with knowing spiritual beings and each understands the limitations that you have placed on yourselves before coming to this plane. Those limitations are not as you think. That is, I will be poor when I come to this plane, but rather limitations which indicate that you are to explore the areas of asceticism or of great love, motherhood; they are all aspects of love, itself, while they seem to take on other characteristics here on this plane. That, again, is the language barrier, for there are deeper realities that each individual must deal with in the course of a day, and those deeper realities are, as we have said, in the present, and they deal with that spiritual growth that individual deliberately chose before he came to this plane. If children want to emulate parents, then, they choose the parents that have certain characteristics that they need to explore.

There will be areas explored in the area of Love; these will be new to you in the future, just as there are areas explored now that were not explored, before, for example, joy or flight, or joy in technical areas, but each is still a part of Me, for I am not an anachronism. I AM All there is in your experience; you did not develop this technical world separate from Me, for it is still part of My mind. You have assumed the primitive culture developed religion, and you developed societies, but throughout it all there was Life and development will not happen without Life, itself. No matter how far you probe into the current material universe, you will still be Life and will interact with Life and its results. Therefore, find that I AM The Ultimate Answer to the questions you have asked. I am, in fact, those questions, as well.

When children come to this place, they come as Life. They do not wake up as a nuclear physicist or other career people, but develop because of their own spiritual nature. Those professions and activities are those that are in line with specific goals that were set before they come to this plane. You will see, as you observe children, that it is a daily discovery process, and so is your existence a daily discovery process. Within any given second you discover much more than you could possibly verbalize and so that which you understand, spiritually, and that which you are capable of verbalizing is a

David-and-Goliath situation in every second of your life, for you are a very small creature compared to what you are learning on this plane and will continue to learn. Your only objective, consciously, is to attempt to move in the present. You will strive to learn from the present and not escape to the past or future you will understand, as well, your spiritual nature and not try to escape into the irresponsible position where you assume that you are a simple mortal, for you will do both yourselves and others a disservice by so doing. You must not try to escape from those who have wronged you greatly into the past, but must stay in the present. Children do that, for seldom do they go through the process of dwelling on or in the past. They are too busy learning to walk or in discovering flowers or grass or the dog around the corner. And so you, too, must be childlike in that way. You will leave the World of Fear, partially, and become more and more comfortable with the World of Love when you accomplish that goal on the conscious level.

"You are not punished by God for having made any choices in your life."

Session #22
April 27, 1981
3:24 – 3:45 P.M.
4:16 – 4:25 P.M.

You will see that the spiritual precedes the physical, but the physical is evidence that there has been a spiritual precedent set. It is assumed that the only reality is the physical, and credibility is established based on the existence of a physical result, so even though a concept of a house is very real, it is not believed until there is a physical house present. So it is with spiritual concepts; there are many doors that could be walked through, but the selected doors are those that result in tangible physical objects, none of which should be rejected, for some theologians have rejected the physical for the spiritual, and some realists have rejected the physical for the spiritual and the spiritual for the physical, neither of which is correct or just like many occurrences, occur in a given second. It is impossible to denote all of them. It is like this with the spiritual reality, so the only physical evidence you have is resultant in language which is part of an enormous selective process, and physical objects which are a part of an even greater process, and when one deals with physical objects then one is dealing with great simplicity in a very complex world. That is the limitation of the realist in that individual must deal in simple things instead of probing into the complexity that surrounds it. There is nothing good or bad about this; it is only limited, so that you can begin to expand into the spiritual realm when you move into the present time, and into the realm of possibility as well as reality of that which is to come. You must move into these areas of exploration or you will not understand how to solve problems and produce the larger amounts of physical objects as a result of that exploration. Those objects are part of your survival, but you must have the complexity, as well.

When you assume that only a house will provide you with love and a home, then you have reduced your life to very simple terms and have denied yourself beauty and art, poetry and imagination and possibility, and although you are secure, you are aware, as an all knowing spiritual being, that you have consciously limited yourself for that security which will provide you with satisfaction for a time but, will not provide you with lasting satisfaction. You will see that I am all these things. I am the house, I am the art, the poetry, the imagination, and so much more, that even were you to explore and complete as much as you could, humanly, you could never ever hope to explore Me, again, for you are dealing on this plane in your exploration. That exploration, if examined in the present, is endless, and you must understand that this is one of an infinite number of planes, and it is not impossible, even, to have the number one and infinity. For all things are possible to an infinite God. You need to see the events that will occur in the future because you like meeting the tangible time line, but they are not reality. They are oversimplified versions of reality. When you discover the nature of your own being, you will fly physically, spiritually, and intellectually, and understand that I AM Unlimited God and there is nothing else.

The more you explore and expand your consciousness, the closer you will come to Me. As you explore the areas of the heart and feelings, you, too, will come very close to Me, for I AM God, and I AM Love.

You will begin to break away from the confines of your existence, here, into My presence. When you see Me you will understand this and much more, spiritually, but you must take a step at a time. That is why much of this message is coming through a very young spirit, for she is growing with you and her spirit can enfold you and help you along the way and translate your needs into terms you can understand. Many of you will feel uncomfortable, at first, but as we have said, these things will be interpreted by you where your need is, and not where someone has dictated to you. Your need truly is there, and there will never be demands placed on you as a result of any of this book. When you read about vegetarianism as something in which you will not hurt others, you will be able to select your actions based upon your needs not based upon what ought to be, for with the complexity that is your spiritual being, and the complexity that is God, you will find that you are unlimited and can always make whatever choices fit your needs. You are not punished by God for having made any choices in your life. You only carry out a manuscript created by you, and again, in areas of exploration, that you have chosen. You will see that in this book, there will be much repetition of the major concepts one of which, again is, that I AM God and there is truly nothing else. You are all My Beloved Children, and there are no saved and no damned, and ultimately, no right or wrong only choice and selection within the confines of limitations that you, yourself, have chosen. You will see much of this when you leave this plane for you have accepted the tangible objects around you, but have not accepted the tangible concepts that you select your parents and the fact that you leave this plane. Even though you try to hide from the ideas, you will leave this plane, all of you. And that is the great truth that you must consider when you think of your existence, here. Like the house, the Life here seems tangible, whereas the possibilities that exist before or after what we call this existence do not seem tangible, but the possibility of your coming here is as small as the possibility out of an infinity of ideas that there should be such a thing as, for example, a bird, and ultimately, an airplane. These are all within the realm of possibility, but they are of themselves a miracle in that they ended up as tangible, physical objects.

In the future you will need to choose that which is spiritual and then, again, choose from that choice. You will always, no matter what your choice, be in the presence of God, for you are Life and can never be removed in any way from My presence. Even in the process of death you are Life, but the basic rule is that you will not come back. There have been those who have come back, but you will never know, for certain, what it all entailed, for that will require an act of faith on your part, as well as an understanding, and you will not know that. You will simply change your attitude from one of fear to one of understanding, and the act itself will not change, but your attitude toward it will, so that you will not fear death. You will understand it, in time, for you will move out of the World of Fear into the World of God. At this point you will know that you always were the children of God. You will be that much more awake to it in time coming. You will see that all problems, ultimately, are theological, and you will be able to use that information to solve the major problems of your life. You will solve them and will not let them harm you.

You will see that the events of your lives will take on new meaning to you, and you will explore them, but not dwell on them, for the present time is where you must live. You must move to the present and not dwell on anything past or future in order to heal others, for in order to help or heal you must be fully in the present for that is where I am. I do not live in the past, for the more you study God in the past, the more confusing I become to you, and the more you look to Me in the future the more removed you will be from Me, and your purpose here on this plane. You have found it necessary to escape to both these constructions of your consciousness, but they do not exist. There is, in fact, no past and no future. These constructions are like attending a movie, for they have no true, breathing, living reality to them, as we have mentioned, you do not learn from them nor do they set your goals. Your goals are set in the present, carried out in the present, and achieved in the present. These are concepts that will be necessary for you to exercise, for when you are in a position of danger, you live very much in the present in order to survive, so it is for you a mere consciousness necessary for you to live in the present and to deal with present reality in order to develop those things which you will need in order to survive. Survive, you will, just as in the moment of danger you do not live in the past, for your body is being shot with adrenaline and other things that are forcing you into the present. So it is with your consciousness in the time to come. It is a mental luxury you cannot afford.

You have assumed that by being a realist you would deal only with tangible objects, but now by being a serious realist you must deal with spiritual realities and deal with them in the present time. You cannot afford to ignore this, for your very survival and the survival of those you love so dearly will depend on it. This can be accomplished within any given field in the present, as well, for you can endeavor to bring about present time realities in the areas of science of art, music, engineering, construction, or anything that is, again, present time and spiritual before it is tangible. Anyone who has ever built a building understands the concepts that there are choices and decisions and spiritual decisions to be made before a physical house or architectural form is constructed, and so it is with Me. You will find Me in this present reality and not look to a historical account of religion, for you will not have time to study past religions and will be forced into a position where you go to yourself to answer questions. It is useless to quote those who have gone before you, for the knowledge that you have, right now, is thousands of times greater than the cumulative knowledge recorded in books about Me. You must begin to tap your own knowledge of meaning, My Beloved Children. You will find Me and will seek Me within, not without. You must not quote even from this book to each other. You must only continue to pull yourself into present time, and you will find Me, and will need not the churchgoing nor believing, nor will you suffer the sacrifice known as morality [mentioned earlier in this book]. And when you see Me you will understand all of it. You will not leave a stone unturned, for all exists within your own consciousness, and you must utilize your consciousness as you never have before. As you utilize this consciousness you will not be motivated by fear of punishment or fear of a millennium, or fear of anything. You will be lost in the joy that truly exists already.

Parents are children too, My Beloved, Beloved Children, and need the same loving consideration and concern from the community that children receive from parents. In time, you will learn that compassion is a part of that larger concern requisite for growth and natural and as important to adults as sunlight is to plants.

"Learning must be the same spiritual exploration process for children that it must continue to be for adults."

Session #23
   April 27, 1981

You will see that just as the soils must be right for a certain kind of tree to grow, that is, acidic or moist soil, or whatever, so with certain types of spiritual development; the ground must first be prepared for that growth, and then the plant grows rapidly, given the right amount of sunlight and nutrients. So it is with individuals. When they have prepared the soil for their growth they are able to grow rapidly and to achieve the stature that they were meant to achieve in this lifetime, My Children. Your Life is growth and the soils are being prepared. If you should drop into soil that is not right for your growth, frequently you will change the environment in which you live in order for that growth to occur. It is wise to be cognizant of this for frequently people spend a great deal of time changing societies in which they live so that they can achieve their spiritual goals and they have the advantage over other seed in that they are mobile and are able to move to societies in which they grow best. When you are cognizant of these processes, you will be better able to deal with the environment in which you are now growing.

As we said at the beginning of the manuscript, the people of today are not less kind than were those of a hundred years ago nor are animals less swift, but the environment has shifted dramatically and you must be able to deal with that shift and will find that you are still able to retain your kindness, humanity, variety, and all the things that make you godlike without shifting your environment; your environmental shift will not be your outward environment [which is ultimately inward] but you will be spiritual, My Children, and is possible to shift your spiritual environment with harm to no one. This environment shifts when you see Me and then the change is great, although it is not still a conscious process on your part but it is an important shift within your spiritual reality. You will see that you are able to control the events of your Life when that occurs and are able to find deeper, more meaningful happiness in your Life. You will see that your environment is within. You have assumed that when you look at the mountains that they have an individuality all of their own but in fact the individuality, even the hardness of the rocks themselves are contingent upon your mind and the fact that you are alive, and therefore, must be considered as within you. You can share that reality with others but only if you agree upon it. If you do not agree upon it then that reality splits and becomes two separate realities.

You will find Me in all things, not just in mountains exterior to yourself, and you will find Me even though you do not have an agreed upon reality; however, you will seek that agreed upon reality! It is best that you find Me where you truly find Me, and that you open yourself to the possibility that you will find Me everywhere and not in a church, My Children, for you restrict your growth and your closeness to My presence if you seek to find Me in a church. You can find Me there as well, but you can find Me in the natural world and understand that pantheism is not God only because of the variety that exists beyond this plane as well as the variety that exists in the present time on this plane. You are pulled to the present time, constantly, and try to find Me. You will probably not find Me in the area of asceticism any more for asceticism was a forced way of coping with the World of Fear and the World of Rules using rules to overcome fear. But that is still contrived and not as free as child walking.

When you teach children to think in terms of future or past tenses you are removing them from this enormous adventure that is going on right now and you must not teach children a future and tell them that they are working towards their future and they are learning what they are learning because there is a future benefit. This pulls children out of the present where they belong, and it is alien to them. It is puzzling to children to be told that when they finish the third grade they can go into the fourth grade, the fifth grade, and so forth, then college and then a job they see a time sequence that leads to their own death and are frightened by it. You must understand that they are aware and want to explore the present time where I am and to understand that this reality is enormously varied in any given second. You will see children are open to an unlimited sense of both themselves and others. It is not wrong to have an unlimited sense of both themselves and others. It is not wrong to have an unlimited sense of your own identity and it is, in fact, where all growth will occur in this time ahead that is so critical. If you remove from children the teaching of a death sequence, you will allow them to participate in Life. You must do this; it cannot be emphasized enough that learning must be the same spiritual exploration process for children that it must continue to be for adults for you will not have contrived ambition and contrived egos if you allow this to happen in the individual. Do not teach children that they are preparing for Heaven for they never left Heaven, for I am Heaven, and they never left Life, My Children. Heaven is in Life and it cannot be emphasized enough that Life itself is the only teacher possible. So that even though you think you are learning from somebody else, you are still learning from Me, and even though you think that there is an object outside yourself that is affecting you, the fact is I am affecting you and loving you, and wishing for the highest possible good which is My presence for you at all times.

You always have any choice you need, and in fact, you could make other decisions to go other paths, but you would not be as happy, My Beloved Children. You will see that you are in a beautiful position now in all the history of man on this planet, and that is not the history of Life but of man's life on this planet. You are at a period of culmination of the efforts of others and so ancestor worship is at its apex, for all of the individual lives before you are behind you in this magnificent endeavor that you will participate in. That is, you have as we said, the unique capacity among all forms of Life to utilize and see and recognize the spirit of Me, My spirit, and so are able to burst like a chicken from the eggshell into My glorious and joyful Presence, My Children. You will see that all Life ahead of you has waited for this day and prayed for this day. It is nothing to fear but will be the result of so much love and growth and effort, for if your great, great grandparents could see you now they would rejoice. You would see that it is to be so very good without an ounce or a pound of fear, for it was their efforts as Life that lead to this understanding that is being conveyed on a limited scale. It is like unlimited thought within the confine of limitation and is the result of so much creativity and so much love that love on a human scale is not to be discredited. It has all the beauty and merit of having climbed a high mountain and looked out into the stars. You have now climbed the mountain and are looking into the stars. You will find that you are now looking even beyond the stars, so instead of feeling confined to this age you will find that you will glory that it is your time upon the Earth to participate in this period of tremendous growth. It is like a child who has learned a sport and can do nothing but participate in that sport because it is so absorbing to that child. So you are learning spiritual growth and cannot participate in other things for it will not let you go, and you will be so very rewarded by your growth and your joy in that growth. The soil is prepared and the tree is growing now. That growth is all within you and is not outside of you. If you will look into yourself you will find that growth that you need and all knowledge and the education you need for, you see, you have had a time in which you have assumed that there was someone outside you who was your teacher, but like all reality, they are your teacher, but ultimately you as a spiritual being are the grand teacher, for your Life and your identity truly do the teaching that needs to be done.

You will find that you are able to see beyond astronomy. You will be able to very soon and the scientific world again will discover a universe beyond this universe only when they change their framework of thought and look into other ways of discovering that universe beyond this universe. It does not seem logical to you, but it is like discovering two circles instead of one. It is important that children be observed and be listened to for even though you have only been here a few years longer, in your sense of time, you will see that they [the children] have selected themselves to be your teachers just as they selected you to be their teachers. They will come with the inspiration you need to grow and must be observed carefully and without a framework or an expectation of any kind for them for they will surprise you, and you will be amazed at what they will be able to teach you, now. They are the source of information for you and I will communicate with you. You have assumed that I do not communicate directly, but you were learning in a different framework than you will be in the very near future.

"You cannot leave the Earth until you have achieved what you were meant to achieve."

Session #24, part 1 of 2
April 27, 1981
9:15 – 9:34 P.M.
10:05 – 10:16 P.M.

You will see that your sense of time is part of the World of Fear so that the abundance that is supplied that is Life, itself, is not limited; time is not a limited concept for you have assumed that you only live for so many years and then you die and you develop your reality around that concept so that beyond 90 years old there is an idea that Life 'ends' when, actually, Life never began, was never confined here and never leaves, My Children. You will see the time is unlimited as you are unlimited, but that is difficult to understand. It's just that you live in a spiritual reality that is timeless and your Life exists there and not within limitations placed on you by limited concepts of what I am and what your Life truly is; your Life is God, and your spiritual identity is timeless and intact. It is beautiful and is worth discovering and exploring. You will see that you will want to learn more about this, and we will discuss it later. You must understand that time is not a reality and like the concept that you must teach children a sequence, to be afraid of their own growth is a simple way of dealing with something enormously complex. When you take a concept like time and put it inside a clock you have even limited that and turned it into a vehicle that involves more fear than joy. There can be unlimited joy in present time, My Children, but just as thinking in terms of past or future you limit 'time' by thinking of it in anything but the present. Therefore, clocks are truly in themselves useless, and so are calendars for those will occur because of your own power and you will understand, in time, the power that exists within each of you and within your concepts of time. You will be able to manage the present in time and will be able to see that it is part of Me but only in the present time. The rest is contrived. The realist will take the house which is a very simple concept of a very complex reality and cling to that so that he/she can have something stable to hold on to. So it is with time. Individuals will think in terms of past times or future times or punctuality in attempting to find something simple, but if that same individual deals in present time one would discover the universe within a second. You must again open your consciousness to the present and let the present teach you what you must know in the times ahead. You will see that I am all there ever was or ever will be for I AM Now, My Children, and you had nothing to fear before, and you have nothing to fear now. Those things which you have accomplished have been done because of and through and about and within Me; you are not separate from Me for you are My Beloved Children. You will see that when you make a choice it is in Me and not outside of Me. This is not an easy concept to deal with but is real. You will see that you will be able to choose Life. You cannot choose death, for you are Life and there is nothing but that Life and there is nothing exterior to that Life.

When you leave the Earth you choose life as well as when you stay, for there is nothing else. You cannot leave the Earth until you have achieved what you were meant to achieve. It is like you cannot leave the classroom until the problems are solved and corrected. So it is that you have goals and must not lose track of either the goals nor the achievement of those goals.

Theme Four
World of Rules

Theme 4
World of Rules

"Your growth is now."

Session #24, part 2 of 2
  April 28, 1981
  2:46 – 2:55 P.M.
  3:06 – 3:24 P.M.

The concept of a personal God will be gone and soon people will not look to a given person for their salvation but will look within. You will find that this concept will be universally accepted and, as we have said, no Life can be left behind for their substance is Life itself, and that could neither be diminished nor lost. It is foolish to assume that once one is 'alive' that there are a delineation between good and bad within that Life. There are not, for all delineations are Life, My Children. There is no difference at all among the elements of Life and no degrees of life. This one being alive and this one being more alive, and so forth. They are a quantity and are simply Life. You will see that Life is what this book has been talking about, and it is critical that you not take that Life away in order to make money or to survive now.

As we have talked about, there was a collective decision to bear mutual guilt for having killed or having sawed trees down, or whatever, in order to survive and that is what is alluded to in the Bible when it said we share the guilt for Jesus' crucifixion but that is not the same concept that Orthodox Christianity came out with. It does not mean that we share the guilt for killing this one man, for Jesus understood that He participated in the sharing of the guilt in the utilization of Life as a survival system. It was not that He was perfect and everyone else was not for they were all Life and still are all Life and will always be Life and He was just aware of that reality, My Children, and had crossed the gap that will be crossed by all into the World of Love, and was not functioning in the world of Fear.

He crossed what you will all cross, for you are all the Christ and are all My Beloved, Beloved Children and in time will see that. Again you will interpret this in linear terms but the reality of which I am speaking is not linear; that is, you will not climb up to that point, but you will cross that gap in consciousness and, in fact, do, any given second of any day. It is not a question of in so many years you will grow; it is like teaching a child that when you finish the fourth grade you will be in fifth grade. It is an irrelevant form of teaching to the spirit of that individual, and, in fact, to the intelligence that individual is constantly expressing, so that it is an explosive awareness that does not take a linear progression to prepare for and is essentially what Biblical terms call a revelation. You will all participate in that revelation and, in fact, none will be left behind.

When you read this book many of you will experience moments of revelation, as well, and will not worship those moments any more than a highly creative person can worship the work already completed. You must live in the revelation and not try to repeat a previous

114

experience. You will live and continue to recognize that your being is spiritual and your capacity infinite. You have heard these words so many times that they have lost much of their meaning, but the reality is that of which you are aware and you understand that this is so in your larger being, My Children. That larger being exists in the present and is not in the future, for now I AM God, and now we are One, My Children, not ever will be one but We are now One. We have spoken of the trials of the next hundred years but you must not wait until the hundred years is over to live in the present for that would be foolish. Your growth is now.

You will interpret from this book what you need to interpret, and there is no condemnation of your interpretation; there is no right or wrong interpretation and no one will have an edge on the truth for you are not needing a social group to achieve your spiritual goals any more. You are only needing your individual identity for that is truly the only reality that exists, My Beloved Children. These concepts are still difficult to put into your language for you have not explored for a long time the concepts of God; you have accepted many pat answers as to what is true and what is not true. You will, however, live in the present and explore in a joyous abandon and will not discuss your explorations with others but rather explore on your own, like a child walking through the woods and discovering Jack-in-the-Pulpits or a burst of sunlight. You will not try to retain that joy but will go on to even greater joys and will find, finally, that the closer you get to the present time the greater your own joy, My Children, for the closer you are to Me the greater your own Joy that which you seek, as we have said in personal relationships is God.

"You will solve problems, many thousands of problems, in any given second spiritually."

Session #25
April 28, 1981
9:10 – 9:24 P.M.
9:36 – 9:47 P.M.
10:12 – 10:21 P.M.

You will see that what is being written here is necessary at this time in order for you to come close to Me and to leave the World of Rules behind, for nothing is written, and to live by what was written before by someone who had a glimpse of Me is like the child who walks through the woods and sees a Jack-in-the-Pulpit for the first time and assumes that is the only beautiful experience that he will ever have. It is not so. You will see that I am infinite in the joy that can be imparted. It is not a Pollyanna, superficial laughing kind of joy but the deep spiritual joy that is truly required by each individual in order to continue choosing to survive. That Joy is the joy of the child and that Joy is your joy, now, as well.

You will see that in time you will learn how to change how you treat children so that they are at ease with their own sense of goodness and joy. I never created children as sinful. They are My beautiful, joyous, fellow creation and are with Me and you must respect their reality, for you, too, are My Children, and it is unfair for you to assume that when you reach a certain age you are not a child, for you are always children. And children are not more irresponsible as children than you are as adults, for they love dearly; for you, too, love dearly, My Children, and are able to help others see Me. You will find that you are at peace with Me and will find, presently, that I have always been with you and you are never separate in any way from My present-time, creative, abundant presence. All problems you confront will be confronted by Me and you will solve problems, many thousands of problems, in any given second, spiritually.

You will see that this book, even, is not to be taken as Gospel but is only a window through which you can look at your own massive, spiritual identity and understand that you are My Beloved Children. We will explore concepts of childhood as well as God through imagery later, and you will see that you are like an energy flow that cannot be stopped in any way, for even though you assume that you are stopping your own energy flow for survival purpose, for example, because you are afraid you are not, for it flows anyway.

"Break out of the eggshell of a World of Fear to discover the power of Love."

Session #26
  April 28, 1981
  11:48 P.M. – 12:03 A.M.
  1:57 A.M. – ?

This book is not just another book, but contains within it information that is needed for growth. It is not a theory, it is a deep, deep reality and will bless you, but more importantly will help open up consciousness to what must be done in the time ahead. You will see that it will influence thought so that the exploring that needs to be done can, in fact, be done and will help people to see that what they have accepted as reality conceivably is much greater, for they have reached the end of the cycle of a World of Fear and must grow into other areas. You will see that Life had cycles before the earth was a school for that life and will have cycles beyond the Earth. You have thought this possible when you thought of intergalactic exploration but that is still a primitive concept of the deeper reality for there is intergalactic exploration but it is part of Life and not the concept that Life is on this planet and on other planets, but an evolving concept where the earth becomes a school and the universe becomes a school, and other concepts will emerge that are not just limited to this reality or these concepts of what Life is.

When you begin to understand that Life is not a physical phenomenon, alone, but the result of itself, here, then you will begin to broaden your scientific concepts into understanding that there are other possibilities of Life, as you know it, going on in any given second, but you will expand beyond that exploration into the possibility that this Earth and universe were created and could disappear, and Life would create and nourish other concepts as well. You will find your concepts of Me, for in your history, here, there has never been as exciting a time for you as now, and you will see that your concepts will begin to touch the principles behind My presence. You will learn from Me, not necessarily from societies, and as we said before you will begin to tap an important resource for you will begin to learn from children. This will be a gradual process, but is necessary for you to break out of the eggshell of a World of Fear and to discover the power of love, for that power is infinity and not relative. You have seen elements of that power for it is the basis of any social structure for the motivating force in your own lives. It is, however, a drop compared to what will happen in the next hundred years. It may seem peculiar to use the term 'hundred years,' but it is a concept that you can cling to and understand until you begin your exploration. You will see that I AM God and you will find that the area of theology must grow until it ceases to be self-serving for the individual to assert his or her ego. That was necessary in the World of Fear for there is nothing wrong with the individual asserting I Am and seeking power as a result, for it is an affirmation of the individual, but in the larger sense it still comes from that archaic survival system that cannot serve the new life coming to this plane. Therefore, the world of theology must be a world in which I Am participated in, and must be, instead of a patriarchal linear system, a system in which each individual explores

Me without the affirmation of a social group. Just as this book must not be discussed with others, so 'I AM' is to be discovered individually and not by social groups. You will learn how extremely constrictive social interaction is and how frequently it limits the growth of the individual for it places the individual in a position where they must consider the collective consciousness and must diminish their own awareness. It was a conscious process and an agreed upon reality for the unlimited spiritual being agreed to become humble slave of the group in order for a group growth to take place. This has taken place and the social governmental structure in which this took place has been established. You will see that the next step will be for you to grow into your own individuality and to discover, as we said, that within each individual is the spiritual power many times over more powerful, in any given second, than all of the theology written in the last eight thousand years or more.

You will see that you are free now to discover what needs to be learned by you, and will find that your growth is rapid and will be joyous. You will see that Life, all Life on this plane is very important and you will attach more significance to it when you see Me and when the leaves of the book will have fermented for a while, for you will not see Life in the simplistic terms it was reduced to by the World of Fear but will again begin to explore the possibilities contained within and the calculus that one is, in fact, feeling when one is dealing with even a blade of grass or a spider or a fly or anything that exists and expresses Life. You will never force yourself into concepts that you are not ready for, so if you are a mother and love and support your family by cutting down trees you will not force yourself out of your occupation. It is very important that you understand that the growth of the spirit is never, never contrived in any way and must never be forced for that is contrary to the concepts we are dealing with. If you are a logger you will continue your logging. That does not mean that in time coming alternatives will not be found to cutting down trees, and, therefore, it becomes more economically feasible to utilize those alternatives. It is more relevant that love would lead, rather than a contrived social process of guilt and adherence to someone else's admonitions. As you love, then, inside your spirit there will be a presentation taking place, and you will love the trees that you cut and in time will grow into other things, but you must accept, first, your own identity and intuitions and accept yourself guiltless and loving.

The environment in which you live spiritually will allow for the growth, just as sunlight allows for the growth of a plant, so My sunlight will allow for your growth. You must not put yourself in a contrived darkness because someone said, 'this is God,' and 'this is not God.' That is not the purpose of this book, for were it so, this book would only be parroting orthodox religions, and it was not meant to. It was meant to help clarify and expand concepts that have developed already of Me and to expand the consciousness that I AM Love and I AM God. You will see that you understand Love when you see, My Children, and do not need to be told that this is good or that this is bad, for you know in your larger self all that you need to know now or ever will, and you will understand that you will expand into your Larger Self and see revelations of God like the light [which] will allow for the growth necessary for your survival and the survival of those you love so dearly, for you love much. There is no one and no Love that does not Love much in each its own way and there is no love that is spiritual or better than any other, for Jesus understood this when He said that God is Love and that in itself you will begin to understand the depth and totality of that Love in time. That information will come from where it has always come. That is, within you and not within anyone else, and to you, but from within your own Larger Self.

"You will find you are capable of great healing and power and will see that the energy that you need will not be limited in any way."

Session #27
April 28, 1981

You will see that as your thought expands you will pull out of a dream state that you have been in for many, many thousands of years, My Children. You will see that those dream states that you have been living in were part of your growth just as childhood was part of your growth and was shared by all. There were no people on this planet who did not go through that series of childhood, puberty, and adulthood for they were agreed upon before you came. So in a larger sense this state of a kingdom of fear was part of growth and as we have said, you will grow into a period of the power of Love. You will find that when you cross that chasm out of the world of fear you will walk like a glowing man into blinding light and will Love that light and find that light permeates everything and, in fact, always has so that the things. Tangible objects that you have assumed were tables or chairs or houses, or whatever, were ultimately comprised of light, itself. The scientific world will discover this, again, before the theological world. It would have been possible within the realm of theology but faith has shifted to the world of science and therefore the credibility and the power for that understanding has made that shift as well. There was a time when theology was given as much credence as the world of science, and all this is good, My Children. But, when you begin to look at all things as being composed of light, ultimately you will see that you will begin to find Me. You have that experience of finding Me and rejoicing with more joy than your body can even tolerate, but you will see rather than be told, for the experience is the only way to learn the deeper secrets of the Larger Self.

The Large Self very frequently referred to has traditionally been called the soul of the individual, but it is much, much more than even that concept will let it be, and you must understand that it is as real and tangible in all Life as a table or a chair is real and tangible to you. It is not a theory; it is a metaphysical reality and ultimately that which seems the most tangible to you [the table or chair] is, in fact, in life perhaps the most removed from the reality dealt with every second of the day in the present time. As we have said earlier these things occur whether or not we perceive them so that the substance of your life occurs with Me in any given second in the present time. You will see that you will become more and more aware of the true activity of your soul and will be very glad and rejoice. You will come in touch more and more with your Larger Self. It is what's being referred to in this book as Larger Self, soul, or identity, or alluding to the same general concept with slightly separate shades of meaning. Again the language that has been developed thus far is very primitive in the area of spiritual truth, and just as a language for science had to be developed, so a language covering these areas of reality can be developed with the explorations that will take place. You will see that you will discover a channel of communication with your Larger Self, and the flow will be a two-way energy flow and will be linked by the White Light, My Children, so that you will find you are capable of great healing and power, and will see that the energy that you need will not be limited in any way, in time. What you have assumed is lack of energy is immersion into an area of growth but an area in which great doubt occurs. For you to be immersed in this area of doubt for long is illogical for it does not correlate that the doubt that you have is Life and that Life is that doubt. For as a car standing still is not energy being expressed overtly so doubt is not energy overtly expressed, and is only one facet of your total growth.

Again, there is nothing that is not ultimately growth, My Children, but there are areas in which the energy flow with your Larger Self is freer and more in line with your goals and your spirit. You will see that as you continue to use the Light you will be in closer and closer touch with your very soul. You are never separate from it, but are like a grain of sand which is not separate from the beach. You are not separate from your Larger Self, but need to encompass the entire beach, and you can. You have indicated that you utilize only so much of the human brain but you do not use My mind which, when you come in line with your Larger Self, you will in turn tap into My mind which you cannot even attempt to comprehend, now. But you can try to grow out of the very narrow areas of thought which have provided you with much rest but not enough satisfaction, now. There was a time when they provided satisfaction. There was a time when they provided satisfaction to the individuals only because of the tremendous need for rest, but you have had your rest now and will find that will not meet your deeper needs. You will find great joy in exploration, now. You will see that had you destroyed My Son you would have destroyed your own link with My Mind for now, but [they are] never separate. This is a difficult concept.

"You will achieve great peace and will grow in ways you had not anticipated growing."

Session #28
  April 29, 1981
  2:56 – 3:05 P.M.

You will find that you are at one with Me and are all the Christ and all express the same freedom as Jesus expressed, or the Buddha, or Mohammed, or any being who crossed the gap that you will all cross, in time. For you will see that what seemed to be Biblical miracles will be quite natural to all of you; Jesus understood that, as well, and you will see that you too will understand that the power of the universe resides within Life itself, and all Life expresses Me; there is no good life or bad life and, in time, you will find that which Jesus and others tried to foreshadow will be common, will be universal. You will rejoice in that, My Beloved Children.

You will achieve great peace when you use the White Light, My Children, and will grow in ways you had not anticipated growing. You will not be cognizant of that growth but will find that problems you are confronting will be helped by use of the White Light. At first you will be very skeptical and crack jokes about it, for it will make you nervous; in your Larger Self you will welcome it, for it is only a road alluded to, for example, in the Bible when it spoke of Jacob's Ladder, and you will find, as in Jacob's Ladder, that the angels go back and forth between your present time individuality and your identity, and you will begin to write your script, and decide your goals, and come into line with the larger goals that you have set for yourself. It will come to pass that you will live more and more in the present and will not worry about the future, for even if you worry about the future it will take care of itself just as if you fear you are assuming that your fear is creating your supply, and it is not, so it is in the area of growth, My Children, and you will realize that you will be able to confront the times ahead with more peace than you had before. Do not put this concept on like a clothing fad and go try it out and then show it to your neighbor for, again, like this book, it is a deeply, deeply personal thing and must not be talked about. You will only limit your own growth by discussing it, particularly with the motive of showing off to others, for like all things relative to your spiritual growth you must do that alone, and ultimately no one will help you but God. And so the communication is not with others, in any way, nor should the motive be to communicate with others but to communicate deeply in the present time and with more variety with Me. Then you will be able to grow as you should and will not worry about events of your lives, but will let Me lead and participate in the power that has always been there.

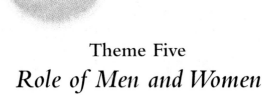

Theme Five
Role of Men and Women

Theme Five
Role of Men and Women

"You are able to grow into a World of Love."

Session #29
April 29, 1981
8:35 P.M. – ?

The unique capacity of you is your capacity to verbally recognize My Spirit, for with that capacity you are able to grow into a world of love and even though all things of Life understand this you will verbalize it and experience Me fully, and you will see that all Life is of God and is not limited in any way to this planet.

When you leave the Earth you do not solve problems, My Children. You only compound them if you do not solve them here, and you find that death is no escape from the mandate that you are confronted with for growth. It is an illusion to assume that you can solve anything by dying, for you cannot, and it is a very negative force in your Life to assume that, but we will get to that later, for we will discuss what happens when you leave Earth. You are with Me and you are able to see your own spiritual growth and glory in it.

"You will see that I Am what you love about the Earth, about others and about yourself."

Session #30
April 29, 1981
9:45 – 10:02 P.M.
10:16 P.M. – ?

It frequently takes great courage to follow your feelings and intuitions, but you must do that if you are to achieve the goals that you must achieve here and not accept the inspiration of others as your own. You will find that was their relationship to Me and is not applicable to anyone else. You will see that the significant difference between orthodox religion and the time to come will be the transfer of power from a social group with like spiritual goals to the individual. It is critical that power be transferred in every way, financially, spiritually, and personally and that faith in salvation no longer rests with an interaction with any kind of group for you must all, when you leave the World of Fear and enter the World of Love, must finally walk that path alone and with great courage, strength, understanding, and beauty, for those are your native qualities, and you will only remark at your beauty, and look at those qualities that you have seen in those whom you idolize, for example, Jesus or the Buddha, or whomever, were never truly resident in them without being first resident in you and because you could even recognize them you were capable of them yourself. As I have said before, this is true of everyone and there is none, no one left out at all for they are all My Children and possess those qualities themselves. As you walk as individuals as opposed to social groups you will be aware that scales will fall away from your eyes and you will see what has always been there within you. You have been prepared for the time ahead and are now able to envision at least the possibilities of what is coming. As you are able to see these qualities within yourself and your tremendous power as individuals you will begin to see that in others, but you must first see it within before you can see it in others. That is the act of loving of thy neighbor as thyself, My Children. These truths are universal and apply to all Life on this plane.

In the times ahead the necessity for women to become more powerful socially and politically relates directly to their capacity to shift values and to understand that the social organizations and groups were environments in which individuals achieved spiritual goals, collectively. The joy that was found in a small town or a family was Me and the achievement of those spiritual goals. As the individual walks more and more as a loving individual then the value that is a value shifts and women as a group are more flexible than men and able to lead any society in any direction. You have assumed that men were more powerful but in a deeper sense women always have been and will be the leadership of any given social or political movement, for they were the impetus behind it.

But you are only male or female for a specific reason, and ultimately for reproduction. However, you are all My Children and only put on that facade here in order to participate in this school and to learn specific spiritualness from maleness or femaleness but you are all androgynous and spiritual. You have made too much of being male or female, My Children, but will find that will balance in the times to come with My presence more and more evident around you all in individual ways and will find great joy in the growth that will occur even with trials ahead for you will come closer and closer into line with My love and will reflect My very nature more and more which will cause your soul to sing in rejoicing. The result on this plane will be greater compassion and understanding of the events of your Life and the Life that has surrounded you. You will see that you are growing rapidly now and are able to grow more rapidly the greater you grow.

My Children, you will see that as the book progresses many questions that you have had will be answered and you will see that there are an infinite number of questions to be asked but they can be asked and answered in the present time, My Children. You will see that each individual who reads the book will find within their own present time, questions and answers; in the mental process of reading much more will take place than just word for word what is said. The book will essentially have a power of its own as many books have had, the Koran, the Bible, or the Book of Mormon, or whatever is needed for people at that point. But there you will find answers to many many more questions and answers within this text than you can imagine, My Children. You will learn from yourself, ultimately, and will find that just as you select your teachers when you come to this plane so you select your questions and the answers to those questions and all of it is geared toward your spiritual growth. We have discussed the growth of the spirit but it is not what you have assumed to be; it is like the joy of a flower opening up or the response of a tree to the sunlight so that the leaves bud and open. So it is with your own spiritual growth. It is as if you are answering those questions that need to be answered while you are here, and it is the only true joy that you experience here. It is your delight in living and your ebullience, enthusiasm, patience, and happiness here. It is not the same happiness you feel in watching a funny movie but it is the happiness within you for which you must find expression. That is where creative acts, even making money occurs, for you are finding your supply with Me and within your spiritual, joyous being. You are capable of this at all times and could find that you could tolerate that joy just as a tree could tolerate a great deal of sunlight and moisture and nourishment so that it would grow more rapidly than if it were denied the sunlight and moisture and nourishment so you can tolerate more spiritual growth than you have assumed and will experience that. That is why in the times ahead one will not think in terms of gloom for it will not be a gloomy time, as the orthodox religions have outlined it to be, but instead it will be a time of tremendous growth and ultimately a time of great joy. It is not a Pollyanna growth. It is a growth that occurs down deep within your larger self and is a soul filled time ahead. What greater joy could you imagine than that? The pains and difficulties of this plane will ultimately be seen as superficial and illusion, but they are not to be ignored for they were your teachers and your survival system for so very long so, as with a good teacher, you will not reject them but understand that you are to go on to the new teachers that you, yourself, have selected. I AM always there and it is you who ultimately chooses your teachers and your means of growth and the rapidity with which you grow, and ultimately your salvation, for you will see that I AM Love, that I Am always Love and always there and in the substance of your life.

These words are difficult for they mean so much and say so little in your language, but you have had experiences that indicate that and those experiences are the teachers that you must rely on for if you have walked through the woods with the sun hitting the shadows and the green around and there had been a feeling of warmth and peace then you have experienced what we are discussing and must rely on those experiences and even write them down in order to try to comprehend what we are talking about when we talk about My Love. You will again see, in time, that I am what you love about the Earth, about others, and about yourself, and will utilize that rather than the words that were developed by this language, for they have been utilized for human power and therefore take on a negative connotation. But I AM God and the good and joyous and peaceful experiences in your Life are God. Such experiences as fishing by a stream and watching the sun hit the water. Then you experience God, or loving someone deeply. A new born baby or a mate or a friend; then you experience God and will find that the joy you find in a peaceful home with children is God and all the things that you find goodness in. Art and music, poetry and literature, and in whatever interests you —fast cars or music, that is of an unorthodox nature or whatever you find joy in is God. We have used the word 'Love' in describing God, but it is much more and later in the book we will get into broad images that try to convey what you have experienced. When you speak of God try constantly to expand your consciousness to understand what My presence means for I AM All there is and to find Me is to find that joy and to leave the World of Fear behind, My Children. You will do this gradually, like a child practicing walking before it finally achieves walking, alone, and when you walk finally in the spirit you will be confident and at peace.

"It is very important that you be prepared to deal with the events coming up."

Session #31
  April 30, 1981
  1:03 – 1:12 P.M.
  1:48 – 2:00 P.M.

You will see that you are beginning to turn a corner in your own experience and are able to sense that there is something very soon around that corner but are not able to articulate what it is that you sense, intellectually. For example, you know that there are only a certain number of resources on this Earth and that X-number of people will starve or X-number of people will read a story by this or whatever, or that [certain] animals are facing extinction, so that you sense, in a very rational cognitive way that there are changes that must take place soon but you will see also that corner is not foreshadowing an extinction but a tremendous period of growth that is a renaissance like you cannot even imagine and certainly more than. Has been felt in history of man of the Earth. That renaissance is what this book is dealing with and will help people ease into that period and understand that it is not pain and fear but growth and love; when you go through what seems like a painful experience that period can also be looked upon as love and growth, and depending on your perspective, a time of progress or not. It is very important that this book be published so that you can understand the renaissance forthcoming and will mentally be prepared to deal with the events coming up.

You will see that in the time ahead, as you go around the corner, and see the fight on the other side that you will be afraid of it but will pass through it and will be transformed by it and will realize that it was an evolution created by you, collectively, in order to grow dramatically. You will see that there will be a nuclear holocaust, as you have termed it; it too will become, ultimately, illusion. The world is not ready yet for the Power of Love and must take some things to their logical conclusion before it is forced to its collective knees and is willing to relinquish those systems that no longer work. You will see that the principle behind a choice is very real, and you will, as beings, constantly be given choices of your own.

Those things which harm Life are still growth and you will never be hurt, spiritually, even though you can be hurt physically and will have to come back again and again in whatever form is available until you are able to see Me, My Children, for with any illusion you will see that it is not God. Frequently people will be in the middle of an illusion that they themselves created and cry out saying ABBA! ABBA! But it is not God for God is, in the best terms you have, Love. But much, much more than that. As we explore imagery we will try to expand it. However, it is only a beginning and you must rely on growth to find terms which mean God. You will see that when you are confronted with the destruction of your own beliefs about what Life is, or is not, then you will find Me and can find Me in other ways. This is [your] choice, for you are dealing with an infinite premise and do not have to choose this route; again that is your choice. You can and will learn from that direction just as if you took another road you would learn from that direction. You will see that you have infinite resources from which to find your own directions and can make the choices and will never be denied those choices, but will have the opportunity, having made a mistake, to back up and choose again having learned what that area of exploration will do. You can foresee some aspects of an area of exploration and choose not to go that route, but that again is your choice. You will say that if I am God I will direct you; that is correct, but you will expand your understanding of God and live in the present, and you will see that I am directing at all times. There is nothing else but Me and I fill all space and am complete, My Children. These are difficult concepts for you are still thinking of choice even in terms of a World of Fear, that is, that if I make this choice this thing that I fear will happen to Me and if I make that choice that thing that I fear will happen to Me, rather than, I will grow toward God here or here.

As you enter the World of Love, leaving a World of Fear, that which was painful will only be growth. It will still not be what you perceive as a Pollyanna system where you have birds and flowers, deer nibbling grass, but it will be a world of joy in growth and not pain in growth. You will find that archaic system of growth by pain will leave; you will enter another renaissance period of great growth in what you may term as art, music, poetry, or life activity, but it is all growth, and close to Me. You again will confront these choices and will find that you are a knowing spiritual being and that the consciousness with which you are now reading this is part of a knowing being. The book addresses more your knowing self than your conscious self; however, you will continue to try to reduce it to the conscious level and will nitpick and go through an intellectual negative process of critique. Beyond that is your knowing being and it will understand what is being said. You will allow that understanding to take place for you have known this as well and the appeal of the book is to your conscious self through the channel of your greater being, and that essentially occurs when you are alone with your eyes closed and aware of the background music of the universe; aware that there is even something beyond that. It becomes a rhythm and a flow, an undulation and peace, ultimately, so that your mind will be actively critiquing while your spirit is flowing like a stream with Me.

"In time, even language will vanish."

Session #32
  April 30, 1981
  2:36 – 2:52 P.M.
  3:07 – 3:20 P.M.
  3:30 – 3:41 P.M.

You will find that it is difficult to communicate deep realities in a language that is overly concerned with simple realities. Frequently messengers have spoken languages that had developed this capacity, My Children. Many eastern religions developed because the languages were more able to convey these concepts, but it is important to communicate in the English language because there are many people who speak English, now, for the superficial realities must precede the deeper realities in a given group. You will see that is why English must explore deeper realities in the times to come, and will do so, so that messages coming through now will be deeper because the language and the words therein will be able to convey these ideas. You will see that you are dealing with very, very simple ideas in this culture, but you are able to allow flexibility and so the culture surfaces, for ideas must never become intransigent and stagnant. Like a stream flowing, the greater the flow the more the water is able to purify itself and remain clean, and the less the flow the less the water is pure and can stagnate to the point of death. In many ways that is what has happened to much orthodox religion, not that the water has changed in any way but that the flow was stopped in assuming that the truth was known when the truth resides in the present time and in any given second an infinite number of ideas actually occur. You will allow the water to become pure by remaining in the present and relying on individual searches for truth and not on groups, now.

Women will play a great role in this resurgence of the streams of the living waters, and in time you will have great rivers flooding the earth with inspiration, but you will start with a mud puddle, essentially, and it is a beginning, at least now. You will doubt the possibility that so dramatic a change can take place but it will, and you will understand as you round the corner that the fight ahead is only truly a simple fist fight and that what is being fought over is Life and infinity and will never hurt you nor any Life, spiritually. You will see that we are all one and there is no label here, for there is a flow between what language has so labeled; it is best not to teach children nouns of any kind but to teach sentences and flow from one Life form into another so that you are not truly separate from the tree or the grass or a mountain. But there is a flow occurring or you would not be able to even perceive any other if you were not receiving from them their own force and were not giving back to them your force.

You will see that just as animals recognize you, plants do as well. You will see that there are languages that work from a basis of flow rather than a noun-verb basis and are closer to reality in that respect, but they are not growing now, and will need to grow after English again is developed. Your language can grow immeasurably in a very short period of time, and will in fact do so. It is not an angry growth;

it will be the result of great inspiration as if the entire population had turned into poets and imagery abounded and you were able to understand each others' images. It is possible and will duly occur so that the poet will be the norm and will not be the dream mouthing poet, but the spiritual poet speaking out through and about and in the soul of the individual. But they were realistic in another reality. However, they, too, need to gain a reality that is a practical reality, like working mathematics from the base of ten as opposed to the base of five they will come close to the mathematics of the reality in which you are now residing. It does not mean that you won't work your mathematics in the area of calculus rather than addition, for it remains that these questions are important and must be explored now.

You will see that it will become more and more exciting to explore these areas of consciousness and it will involve less and less of the occupations that are maudlin and difficult for the soul. You will see that those were lessons but are not necessary in the times to come. We will explore many areas yet in the book and we'll become more concrete and specific as soon as the broad base of reality is established for you must travel from the broad and retain the broad in order to delve into specific areas. You must not travel from the specific to the broad for that can lead to a limited sense of your goals. You will see that much has been explored from the specific to the broad for that is the basis of the scientific process but like a blind man attempting to describe an elephant or whatever clichés you have, you are still not doing the whole and not looking at the parts from the whole for the deepest reality is the whole and the parts are only elaborations on that. So you must in your experiences attempt to see the broadest view then break that down into concrete parts. You will grow into that consciousness if you allow the children to teach you the basis from which they work. They, like you, cannot verbalize but they will show you, nonetheless, for they will have more and more understanding and will be able to be your greatest teachers. You will understand that you are spiritually always children and will not believe, in time, the mask of disillusionment and depression that frequently follows fear and pain. You will see that they are not needed now. You will assume that, like an addict, you cannot get rid of your habit, but when it is gone you will be like a convert and will feel great joy in having relinquished it but wish for it yet. Those are natural processes and are needed, and are not to be frowned upon or discredited in any way. You are such joy and the ultimate learning is with Me. This book can only serve to verify what you know within yourself and cannot become any kind of a substitute for that knowing, for the book will cease. Your growing will continue and all messages ultimately from God come through life itself because you are a verbal being, and this book is written in words. I AM Life and you will see that you must read this book and throw it away and not go back to read and reread and study and ponder, but like water running should run on and ideas should be allowed to ferment and continue to grow within you. ALL LIFE is creative, and in any given second you will see that you have more ideas than you could possibly utilize and are receiving those messages from Me all the time. You will become more sensitive to what is truly there.

Spring is part of your current reality and you will see that winter is essential, as well, and all is divine in nature. You must think in terms of the sun in order to understand the seasons, for the sun does not change but the seasons do. God does not change, but you grow through thousands of metamorphoses in any given minute, and will look to the sun first to understand the sun and then will find the effect of the seasons on the infinite diversity of Life within the universe and then understand that I am not the sun but the creator. [Learn to] see beyond this universe and beyond other planes, and you will comprehend My nature, for the only true communication between your language and reality is God.

In time, even language will vanish. Not because it is constructed but because it is unconstructed and will expand beyond the evolution involving vocal chords and sound into mind; you will not talk, you will know, and beyond knowing you will pass into God and into Life so that, in time, you will enter other Life and explore and return. But that is almost a science fiction rendition of something far greater for that communication will also involve Love and that is the dimension left out of the world of exploration known as science fiction so that ultimately that, too, deals with a very, very simple reality. The complexity of the heart is so much greater than the complexity of any avenue explored to this point including academic avenues and the dispersal of language and symbols. When you feel a given emotion you are experiencing more than your entire academic training has given you, but you have yet to be able to articulate that and must rely on duplication of those experiences to communicate. You will come out of limitation quickly and will not go back.

"There is so much for you to expand into in such a short period of time."

Session #33
   May 1, 1981
   1:23 – 1:47 P.M.
   1:57 – 2:03 P.M.

It is critical that people have the verbal instructions for they have been conditioned into verbal instructions. You will see that the media through which communication comes are infinitely varied and people are being communicated with all the time by Me but like the scientific world at this point they place more credence on verbal instruction than they do on sunlight or birds singing or spring. They must learn that I AM God and am with them every second of every part of every second and am infinite within each part, but they will expand within themselves and, in time, not rely on the verbal instructions as they do now, My Children. That is why it is important that the book be written and that this period of time be devoted to its writing.

You will see that as you grow in spiritual bounty you will grow in intellect. You have assumed that intellectual growth was the result of the necessity of adapting to a physical environment and therefore the more intelligence you had the more that you would be able to adapt, but this is not so, for a bear or a puma or a bird have all adapted to their environments and have survived, so it is not a question of adaptation so much as a question of spiritual growth preceding physical adaptation. In the case of the Homo sapien man, human being. You are spiritually very devout and are at the point where you are able to see Me. When you see Me you will understand that intelligence is God and nothing else, and you will not be afraid of great intellect and the capacity to learn so that in the time forthcoming when you see Me your intellect will enlarge geometrically. You will have the capacity to see Me and grow more rapidly than you have ever dreamed possible. It will not be the result of reading or studying, though there is great motive in reading for frequently one attempts to read so that one can understand both his/herself and his/her relationship with the universe. You will see that the motive allowed the intellect to grow; it was not that the intellect allowed the motive to grow. As you grow you will see more and grow more rapidly so that you can make that adaptation to My presence, and will be able to accomplish the things that I have indicated in the book. Those ideas have always been there but you have been afraid and frequently in your fear stayed within the realms of what was known and what had already been discovered. You must not rely on a few to accomplish those things that all are capable of accomplishing. As we have said before, the individual who is mentally retarded is an all-knowing spiritual being who has made that choice, but you all may be forced into a position where you can no longer choose to hide either in the future or in the past or in mental retardation or in fear for I AM God and you must come to Me, My Children, more and more, in order to cross the great leap from fear to love. We have spoken so frequently of the moment of revelation, or what was predicted as judgment, which is an aberration of that term. There is so much for you to expand into in such a short period of time, but you will have that capacity. You will see that the times ahead will lead you into that capacity or growth and intellect. It has been assumed that great leaders were individuals who were genetically able to do as they did but that is not so. They were so because they chose before they came to this plane, inevitably that involves spiritual strength and great courage to make that choice before they even come to this plane. As you grow in spirit and joy in spirit, you will enlarge all capacities. Typically emotional and spiritual values will increase so that you are a Free Spirit and are able to understand your Larger Self and see your Larger Self, My Children. As you see your Larger Self then you will be able to utilize more and more of your capacities as a human being and will see Me and enlarge capacity and grow in a spiral at that point.

It is not the drudgery of a genetic pool but rather the bursting out of the cocoon that will occur, My Children. It will be given to you again in the scientific world before it is given in the theological world but the two are closely related. One has lost its credibility because of its attempt to control, but both contribute to an expansion and can be retained as long as they leave the world of fear and go into the world of unlimited mind and great compassion. Discoveries will be quite phenomenal on your terms and by your standards for those discoveries will be phenomenal because they are unlimited and therefore you can be unlimited in their effect. As you have grown spiritually, so not only have evolved physically, but your tools have evolved and reflect the motives of those who have developed them. Great scientists have been great beings in that to some degree they saw their Larger Self and rejoiced. They saw Me and rejoiced and did not give it a verbal name but understood within the Larger Self that it was God that they were viewing at that point and as you will see they did not learn from the past nor the future, but they learned only from the present how to expand in order to discover and become lost in the present time so that they could expand that dramatically. That is one of the limitations of the academic community in that it must put more emphasis on the present that it has in the past in order to fulfill its potential within a given society, but in a larger sense even the academic community is a collection of kindred spirits within a given area. It has power from that pool, so that discoveries are made by groups who in a sense are concentrating on areas of spiritual growth even though one would assume that it was an attempt at strictly intellectual growth, for were they not Life and had they not gone to the academic community with a motive or motives, then they would be pursuing strictly intellectual things. Intellect is not separate from Life in any way for it is only one avenue of expression on this plane that has been given credence by the collective consciousness. Much more is going on within each individual than social intellectual interaction and you will discover how much more is in fact going on in the individual in any given second and will be glad to have seen the possibilities that in fact do exist within the individual, My Children. You will be glad that you could step back and look at what the world is doing. Were you not born and were you not to leave this plane, the answers that have been given in a world of fear would be all you would need, but they are not. When one encounters the larger experiences of the soul one must look and must grow spiritually. We have said that man's extremity has caused opportunity. It is your choice, and you will see that I AM God and I have always been there and will always be there, not as a person, but as unlimited variety and unlimited Life.

You will see that you are able to make judgments because that reflects your own spiritual nature of choosing to be with Me and choosing to grow, My Children. It is positive in tones and in no way reflects a negative choice but rather is more like a kid in a candy store choosing things that he/she likes most of all, My Children. When you begin to approach Me you will find that it finally is all joy, not fun, but serious and beautiful joy. As you are surrounded with that beauty you will wonder that you ever were surrounded with anything else, and in fact, you weren't. Behind all pain and sorrow are the plane with which we are familiar. At this time there is great beauty and it sustains you and it is your reason for continuing to grow.

"Were you not all to have experienced the Earth, you would not be able to explain to another consciousness, on another level, what the Earth was."

Session #34
   May 1, 1981
   8:45 – 9:15 P.M.
   9:36 P.M. – ?
   10:05 P.M. – ?

When you become One with God, that is, when you experience God, and as we said, it is not churchgoing or reading, or the sacrifice that is involved with a superficially righteous sense of right and wrong, you will be able to see your larger being and will understand the course that your Life should take at this time. It does not preclude even the possibility that within your Larger Selves are many expressions of that Larger Self. You, where you are now, mentally, would translate this into several people stemming from a given soul but it is not that simple. And again, the language limits the capacity to express and consequently understand that concept that you have infinite capacities and again you are an unlimited spiritual being playing with or functioning in a limited agreed upon reality. There are several orthodox religions which have espoused that theory and they are accurate in that sense, for there is agreement and reality is essentially agreed upon, but beyond that are infinite possibilities and resources for creation. You are capable of creating events; you, however, are not capable of creating yourselves so that you will express your nature. That is the nature of your Larger Self and its individuality which is not separate from other individualities and yet remains individual. This is a difficult concept, and that is all God.

You have a specific identity but that identity is characteristic of Life, and truth, mind and soul, and all are concepts you have to discover about what God is. You are, within your Larger Being, an individuality but you are God in being, as well, so it remains difficult to communicate the infinity of possibilities for you are spiritually evolving. You enjoy evolving, and yet you have created certain constrictions on your own reality that in fact limit your capacity to even understand Me except in the experience that you have in seeing yourself and Me, again, though having experienced Me you will only have limited verbal abilities to describe the experience to others. Essentially it will become unnecessary for you to describe to others for others are ultimately a part of yourself, and what you see is what you have created. The events that you have created, and yet those others, the Life that you encounter, is Life and therefore expresses all Life at once. You will see that the image given of the sunlight and rays being sunlight is still a limited concept of infinity, and the capacity of infinity to be and do all things and still retain a sense and a concept of individuality. Rest assured, however, that even as limited as you have become in your consciousness, you are individuals and are beloved as such. You will see that the cross, as we said, that you have to bear is one in which, when you experience Me, you will find words inadequate to convey the meaning of what you have experienced for the more individuals experience Me the more they will attempt to find words that will be adequate for their communication with others and will try to do so only to help others to have that experience. At which point, and this is the basis of all communication, even at this level, you having experienced the same thing do not need to communicate so that communication takes place when you have experienced the same things, and you understand that. Language becomes only an affirmation and the communication remains incommunicable until the experience is the same, and therefore, it becomes impossible to describe an experience that you yourself have not gone through. Were you not all to have experienced the Earth, for example, you would not be able to explain to another consciousness, on another level, what the Earth was. You are able to communicate. This enhances your own understanding and is valuable in that regard. As you grow in this exploration, having experienced Me you will, like children playing a game, find more and more people 'on your side' and will begin to find that it will become easier to lead others into this experience because you will have expanded, and having expanded you will grow to the point at which that expansion will lead to greater expansion until it tumbles into what has been traditionally called revelation. We have spoken much of this but in the time to come you will find tremendous joy and true intellect, not intellectualism, in this expansive process and will find that spiritual development will occur extremely rapidly after the snowball has started down the mountain.

It is as I have said, a time of great wonder and renaissance and a time for rejoicing rather than reveling in pain and agony with the events that will be forthcoming. It is very important that this communication take place now so that when you encounter difficulties you will be able to view your Larger Self and comprehend the nature of your experience, for as we have said so far, you are My Children, all of you; all life is My Child and I AM God and capable of loving all of you and each of you. I AM the substance of your own being and creativity in

Life as well as Creator, as well as sustainer, as well as that which revels in the growth of its children. Were you to personify God, you would find God happy in the times ahead, but you must never again, in your intellectual spiritual history, personify God, for God cannot be a person and still be Life and Love and the concepts that you have thus far envisioned for Me. You will understand that you must take the first step toward Me in the area of exploration.

[You will find more ease with writing this book now both of you, for you are good and wish to help others.]

There is nothing truly available for people now to begin expanding at this point for what has been written, short of truly inspired writing, has been written from the World of Fear and that which was written out of the World of Fear. For example, the teachings of Jesus or the Buddha or other great spiritual leaders were then translated and pulled into a World of Fear by orthodox thought. Orthodox thought is really little more than that translation of inspired writing, so that only within the artist or poet or whatever now is the free flow that comes from The Source that we are dealing with, or from Life or children or experiences we have, then we are relieved of the World of Fear and go into the area where the only power obtainable is God. We have discussed that when you are methodical or fearful that an event occurs as a result of that fear, but in fact, it is only as a result of growth in line with your specific growth that you have supply or any other reward connected with your own growth, and ultimately growth is its own reward. This growth is important in that it is coming from Me and not from the Rabbi or from the individual who has mulled and remulled and mulled again the concepts that though inspired in their origin have been reduced to fear, and do not contain the power that they once contained. You will see that I am able to permeate this world, for as We have said, this is an archaic survival system, but the premise of that system is its most potent perpetuator or that which keeps it going which is that you at any point can be separated from Me and must fend for yourselves. This is an illusion which has taught you areas of growth but ultimately is simply that of an illusion, for like a lie it has no foundation in truth, nor any reasonable facsimile of a foundation. It is like being confronted with sunlight and saying that is darkness or it is not, ultimately, and calling it separation only perpetuates an illusion and creates a form of insanity; one even survives that, but we will explore that area more completely in another book for we have concepts to explore that we will share delight in. You will see that your growth will never cease no matter what you consciously attempt, for the choices of which we are speaking are choices that are made in your Larger Self and must be left to that Larger Self. Traditional religions have called that faith but in so doing have stopped the struggle of the child to get up and walk for it is a stopping concept again, and [false] humility assumes that you cannot see God and only given people are able to see Me. This is not so, for all life sees Me in reality and could not be Life were it not true, assuming that it also gives itself a sense of false humility that says that this is faith, and we can only understand so much and, of course, that is fear of understanding and again is a translation from understanding into a World of Fear.

The reality remains understanding; the fear remains faith, and ultimately you cannot deny your own reality. As you grow spiritually, that is, in a greater and greater sense of happiness and joy, for those are some of the words that try to deal with true spiritual growth, then you begin to relax and as you begin to relax you begin to experience Me more and more for it is very hard to experience the core and outline and functioning of the universe without great spiritual joyous energy; that energy is God. But not just energy, much, much more. That core and outline of the universe grows in your perception and as your perception grows then your energy grows and as your energy grows your perception grows until you are flowing and not struggling. A struggle is only in the World of Fear, and flowing is God, like the river flowing you are, by nature, a totally flowing present omnipresent being and must expand your consciousness into those areas. You cannot think in terms of 'ought to' in any way, for 'ought to' is constrictive and stops the flow of your own total being and will not allow for expansion, for when one 'ought to' expand one is saying 'I am not expanding, and therefore I ought to expand,' when all the time that you are saying this, you are, in fact, expanding, because it is your nature. So you are what in Biblical terms was called Hypocritical. But that is a very negative term for a kind of growth and does not entail judgment or anger on the individual growing in that direction for all individuals are ultimately growing and must be loved for that fact and the fact that they are Life. As we said, we must not rest in judgment of others for the tree that is a foot tall is not better nor worse than the tree that is six-feet-tall unless that tree is usable to you and you will find yourself androgynous and ultimately not using others in any way, so that you need not judge that tree in terms of its use, nor judge it in terms of its growth, nor its relationship with the sun or the Earth or itself or anything else. You do not need to use anything but yourself and your own individuality for you are unlimited and spiritual and even though you are greatly afraid, you are still this and much, much more. You will see that you will be able to expand into your own individual characteristics and your own growth for you will learn to follow your intuitions and to live in the present. You will be surprised at the results. You will let Me govern you, in time, and the closest thing in this language one can bring to bear on that is that you will be joyous in time. You will see that we are all one, and you will not have to believe that long before your belief will become assurance. You will still question theology and trust science, and ultimately, you will see that both are the same, and will come out of the world of faith in science into understanding and cosmic consciousness. Then science will become effective and truly usable and nondestructive.

"Many of the things that you encounter on this plane are illusion and must be accepted as illusion."

Session #35
  May 2, 1981
    4:51 – 5:12 P.M.
    5:25 – 5:32 P.M.

You are only interacting with time, right now, because it is an experiment, but is a forerunner of anything forthcoming for time has no real substance and is illusionary. You will see that age is not related to time but to other factors, and it is important that you understand that age is not necessary nor all that important, My Children. You will see that age is only the result of the World of Fear and is not an important factor. It is illusionary in its substance and therefore not a part of God. I have spoken of your spirits but that is a different quality than a sense of age or tiredness or fear. A young spirit is a living spirit and an old spirit is a Life spirit, and both are part of God but have different qualities that they express at a given time, now. However, it is like trying on a coat. It is not the substance of the individual; it is only a piece of clothing that the substance of the individual can put on at any given time, and it does relate to you when you come to the Earth. It is all part of your choice before you come. You, among other things, do choose the time of your birth and the point of conception. You will see that you will be free of alternatives including young spirit or old spirit, in time, for it is only part of this plane and not an immutable spiritual fact such as your identity truly is an immutable spiritual fact.

Many of the things that you encounter on this plane are illusion and must be accepted as illusion. That does not mean that they do not hurt or they do not feel good or whatever, but they do not destroy, either, and it is important for you to understand that ultimately they

151

do not effect your spiritual growth which is substance and which is immutable, ultimately. You will see that Life is indestructible and Love is indestructible and cannot be altered, for ultimately the Love you feel is in your relationship with Me and you must understand that it cannot alter and cannot be changed nor is there any delineation among My Children for you are all loved and that love cannot be altered by a negative behavior or a social interaction or anything for if it were changeable you would lose Life. It is logically impossible to lose something that is you, for you never found you, to start with. You are as an idea is, as a universe is, as I Am. 'I AM' is a good term for Life, and thus a good term for what you perceive Me to be. You must understand that your concepts of God are still limited to the most expansive terms you have found in your language, but as we have said, in any given second you can find an infinite variety of what is truly God if you become sensitive to looking. I Am all there is but that does not mean that all there is limited to what you perceive it to be and you will see that all that there is as you sense it now is still all there is as far as your consciousness has expanded, and that is not all there is. It is not even a limited view of a limited view at this point, but you must not be discouraged for you have the capacity to see Me and will see that your Larger Being is at one with Me, and when you see your Larger Being you will come back to this plane with perceptions that you will develop words for and continue to expand as a group, that is, a linguistic group.

The combination of linguistic groups can begin to describe the beginning of understanding of Me. As I have said, one of the main purposes of this book is to begin to expand the expansion process so that you can begin to see Me. In time, these concepts will seem elementary and primitive, but it is necessary to break out of the World of Fear into the World of Love; when that is achieved you will see that revelation exists, and it is not difficult at all, but the result of great joy and peace and Love of Love, itself, not the soap opera concept but that which exists is My relationship with you which your Love on this plane can barely touch on. Just as time is an area of exploration, so reproduction is an area of exploration and not necessary for the pro-creation of Life: but it is now, for it allowed for a spiritual adaptation that occurred much faster than were there no reproduction with two sexes. As with everything else, it truly was a spiritual evolution preceding a physical evolution. There are differences between male and female, not in spiritual substance, for as identity is immutable, so your male/female and much, much more is intact. If male and female were the only possibility you would find that in the future other adaptations would be difficult to evolve but, in fact, in the area of possibility this is just one possibilities and others also exist, My Children, but as it is you have selected this as the area of exploration currently being undertaken and are learning from it. However, as with other things it has been transfigured into the World of Fear so one has fear associated with something that has worked in the past as a survival system and has worked in spite of the World of Fear. There has been Love among soul mates and that has led the way for others to wish that to occur and has kept the process of reproduction going, My Children.

"The joy that you experience, ultimately, is your relationship with Me."

Session #36
May 2, 1981

Soul mates did not need the society in order to express their own individuality for as an octopus has eight legs and does not need to have one of the legs express its individuality and ignore the others, so you are the offspring of a soul mate relationship which does not need to have others express its own individuality, for it is the core of that expression and the result of that in a given society. It looks like leadership but in fact it is integrity of that given individual. This is something that we will explore much later but it does not create an exclusivity. It only creates a dynamism in the interaction of several identities. You will see that you will understand more about a male/female relationship when you come closer to Me. This relationship has shown that marriages, for example, that were having difficulty, when the partners draw closer to Me the marriage goes through a healing process that is a fact, but it is only a part of the total number of facts involved in that kind of a healing. You will see that I AM All there is in that relationship; the joy that you experience, ultimately, is your relationship with Me, and that is why that seems to occur, but even that to some degree is illusion. Just as background music is enjoyed and is something behind an experience, so it is that I remain God throughout all the learning experiences of the person's individual identities.

The soul mate concept can be easily misunderstood and it is important that you make no conjectures as to the numbers with in a given larger being or even the nature of the soul mate concept. It is like a river running down a mountain. The river has much energy and that energy is derived from its relationship with the mountain not from the nature of the river itself. The soul mate interacts with the Larger Being and gains its energy from that Larger Being without losing its identity. When one is dealing with limited language for massive concepts, it is difficult to verbalize the idea behind that concept but a mountain can, in fact have many rivers down it and not lose its own energy, My Children.

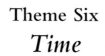

Theme Six
Time

Theme Six
Time

"Children will help you break out of the fetters that you have encumbered your being with."

Session #37
   May 2, 1981
   9:53 – 10:11 P.M.
   10:24 – 10:37 P.M.
   10:41 – 10:46 P.M.

As you grow you will not consciously know that things are changing, but in fact, they will change but not according to the timetables that you have been familiar with, for they will change according to the cosmic timetable. Your time system is very primitive and not relative to living, itself, but relates more unto itself and therefore is difficult to cope with. It relates to the movement of the Earth around the sun and that is not the Cosmic universal movement of Life. It relates well on this plane for there are trees and animals, and all Life forms must

157

relate to that for that is relative to the presence of Light in their experience and very important because it is there, but there are, in fact, cosmic timetables. They relate to My presence and My movement and the relative movements of the identities of Life. These again are difficult concepts and will be elaborated on later, but are very real, and govern much of your own lives. There is only so much you can attribute to your timetables, that is, the presence of puberty or the death of the individual body or whatever you have relegated to Life, here, but you must understand that is again an agreed upon reality and not the substance of the individual. As you see Me and help each other, truly you will understand that those are superficial to the individuals. Truly, I AM Life, or whatever terms you can give it, and it is important, in time, to understand the cosmic timetables, for you will be able to measure your own spiritual progress by them much better than you could by utilizing the sun as your timetable. Your very presence here on this plane relates to cosmic timetables, which are not truly time as you know it but an entirely different concept of what you have termed 'time,' for the spiritual reality behind time is quite different from that you would term a kindergarten concept of what you see as time on this plane.

There have been great scientists that have worked on this question and very soon they will have breakthroughs in that area so that they will better understand universal time and will be able to make phenomenal discoveries as a result. When you break from the fetters of this universe into the consciousness of God then those discoveries which to you seem as phenomenal as the airplane must have seemed to Neanderthal man, will seem natural. You simply will understand that those breakthroughs will occur, relatively soon on a cosmic scale, and on your earthly year scale within the next twenty years. There will be born children, yet, who will teach adults who in turn will make discoveries, but you must listen to those children for they have much to give and must not be put into stereotypic patterns or the thrust of their presence will not be felt.

It is important that you understand that children are born to be teachers as well as students with individual goals that adults must pay attention to and listen to with sensitive minds and loving hearts. Such children will help you break out of the fetters that you have encumbered your being with, just as this book will help you expand into a consciousness that there is a universe of possibility with which you are daily dealing, and must continue to deal with and must be even more present time oriented than you have been, for in this culture, particularly, there is very little dealing with the present, only if it means more money or higher prestige or a specific objective of the individual. Those objectives are conditioned and not intuitive and therefore are limited, and do not have behind them the spiritual powers that intuitive objectives have. You will see that as you grow in your concept of Me you will change your concepts of time, for example, from the very primitive to a much more sophisticated concept that will be a surprise to you, for when you change into a more sophisticated concept of time you will include the use of intuition rather than the use of more and more empirical knowledge, for empirical knowledge, in some degree when one does not consider the roots, is still illusionary and can go from illusion into myth and finally absurdism until it is irrelevant to the Life sustaining the concepts. When you get into the concept of cosmic time you will include other aspects of the individual including the interconnection between irrational and emotional, or as you have called it the right and left hemispheres of the brain. You will see that, too, an enormously primitive concept of mind, and will break free from studying the brain in order to comprehend the Life, for the brain is an outward symbol of mind but it is preceded by the spiritual understanding that exists in concepts of mind, itself, or it would never have been subject to growth of any kind. It would only have remained a brain and never have included concepts beyond the ego, physical oriented universe. This phenomenon that you label 'brain' is capable of transcendental thinking, as well, and therefore is capable of following spiritual development in its own physical development. But you will not believe it and must see it first, and understandably, for that is one of the beauties of your own existence is a healthy skepticism and an unhealthy fear. You will see that you are growing now, and after you read this book you will not consciously ponder much of what is being said but in your Larger Self will understand and will be drawn to other concepts that will emerge. You will find that the one rule involved in all of this is that you must never discuss this with others, but, instead, make it a highly personal one-time kind of reading. You also must never personalize good beyond yourself, for you must find the good that exists within you, and if you do not find the power that exists within you, and if you in a very lazy way, attempt to transfer that power and goodness to people involved in writing the book, then you should never have read this book. You must find that power within yourself and never again personalize a sense of God for you will lose that which you have. You are emerging from the World of Fear and must never again be afraid of your own spiritual power. Never sink into concepts of people being God or concepts of anything but yourself expressing My presence on this plane. You must not accept a sense of false humility for that is only an escape mechanism and is not your nature. It must never be used again by you for it is better to be egotistical than falsely humble, particularly now, for ego, as we have said, is only the identity of the individual asserting itself and of itself is not harmful. The only time that it becomes harmful is that if one abuses that idiosyncrasy of your being. You must, on this plane, within the World of Fear, assert your identity. There is nothing wrong with the child asserting its identity on the playground or even pretending to be more than they have accomplished at this point, for that only indicated vision and a hope and an understanding that they are more than they are allowing themselves to be. You will find that Life will have its own mandate for you and you must follow that mandate. You will be very happy if you do, and will be at peace with the world around you for you will be at peace with your Larger Being.

You must never assume that Larger Being is God, but you will not when you truly see your Larger Self, for your Larger Self involves joy and love and is different from a falsely ambitious, insecure, fearful sense of a Larger Being, and that Larger Being deserves a deific status, for you are very close to Me in your soul. All of you are close to Me in your soul as We have said so many times; no one and nothing is left out of that no matter what limitations you are dealing with on this plane. You must not misunderstand the Life on this plane and ascribe to it characteristics that you can either utilize or fear, for there is nothing to fear, here, in any way. You have assumed that when you encounter a bear you have something to fear but in reality you have nothing for both of you are playing with limitation and can understand soon that at any point you can drop the script and change the pattern, not the substance of the pattern but the idiosyncrasy of the pattern, that unlimiting your growth for you must not limit yourself in that area. You can limit yourself before you come to the Earth and assume a given intellect, but you cannot limit the fact that you express Life itself, and that Life is the substance of the being of each individual existence. You will see that I Am everywhere and capable of being everywhere just as the air is capable of being everywhere and must only be forcibly shut out in certain situations. That creates a power of its own and then equilibrium will be sought. So it is with Me; I Am everywhere and those who have not ascribed the word to God are not totally wrong for they find other words within the social context of their organization and their language that will help them see the reality of My Being.

You will see that you will learn from children, to a large extent, about time and the rhythms of Life, itself, so that it will not remain a mystery for long but it will take individuals who are extremely sensitive in

watching children and individuals who themselves have some consciousness of something beyond the sense of time that has been developed thus far. Those observations are in the long run, very simple,
but involve learning from children how reality is formed and the agreed
upon realities are imposed upon Life, itself. Fortunately, to some
degree, our great love for young children prohibits our not allowing
them to play a great deal and in their play they laugh with Me at the
world and find My presence in everything including animals and alternative forms of Life. You will see that those concepts that are needed
so much will emerge from those adults who have developed the verbal
ability to put that cosmic laughter down. You will see that you will be
free of all limitations and will grow by leaps and bounds and will be
still amazed at the possibilities that do exist on this plane, alone.

*"You will find that the constant still is change,
and your growth is set, and you will emerge like
the butterfly from the cocoon."*

Session #38
  May 3, 1981
    12:47 – 1:04 P.M.
    1:27 – 1:40 P.M.

You will see that time is a different dimension on this plane that
we are dealing with and there have been inaccuracies but the principle
remains the same, for we are dealing with a very flexible time on this
plane: even though you have assumed that it is very methodical it is
not, for time is mental and you have devised clocks that can conform
to your mental time, but you do not understand how they truly work.

You will live a peaceful life now and will not change people but
rather appreciate what is here and not worry about politics or social

change, for the social changes occur spiritually first, and long before you arrive here on this plane. They are inevitable and are stages of collective spiritual growth and must continue to be so. You will see that, as what you term negative events occur on a broad scale, those frequently are periods of great transition, and precede great social, collective changes at a given time. The greatest of these social changes are yet to occur but you must not be awed by them nor afraid of them for you are emerging from a period of fear and are learning that fear is of no consequence in the final analysis. Attraction to fear is of no consequence in the final analysis. Attraction to fear at this point is part of this change; you may decry the use of fear environments within your social groupings, but you will find that they will become less and less appealing although they must now go to the point of absurdity before that occurs. You will finally tire of seeing them on TV or in your lives, or whatever and hunger for more [than that]. At that point you will be filled with love and will find that they were illusion, just as an alcoholic finally decides that he or she does not wish the alcohol anymore. But you are not limited to that, for you are unlimited beings and are capable of alternatives to this system of change. You, however, will find that the constant still is change, and your growth is set and you will emerge like the butterfly from the cocoon. You are beautiful, and in your Larger Self you are indescribable in this language and therefore must understand in time when you see your soul that I have created you. You will love Me for having created you, and will be free of what you have assumed is you, for you are truly not what you seem at this point; that is why there is essentially only one article of faith asked, and that is for you to understand that you are all My Children and that you will face your own sainthood very, very soon, and will rejoice and find in retrospect that it was not as difficult as you had thought it would be and will flower, having seen your own being.

You will continue to grow and to flourish in the time ahead, even though it seems that is not always the case. You will emerge from the sense of community mentioned at the very beginning of the book, that of a hundred years ago, the sense of community that many long for now. You will find that within your own individuality has emerged a much greater, much more potent sense of community. It is not a selfish time for it is a very compassionate being that has emerged as an individual and therefore is not the same kind of individual who adheres to the social mores out of fear of disapproval or need of approval or joy in others so much as joy in oneself in kindness to others. That individual is much more self-sufficient and able to appreciate the individuality of others so that the striving to create a conforming individual and helping that individual relinquish his or her spiritual goals for the community is a thing that is fading. The individual emerging allows the other individual their autonomy and still retains his or her own autonomy and thus allows so much more diversity within the community, which is needed now, an important adaptation to the times ahead. There will be fewer and fewer 'rules' that are 'right,' but the ultimate rule still will be love, in a different form, for there is no end to the facets of love itself. You will see that you must learn that you yourself are at one with Me; if the message that you gain from this book is simple, the most simple message will be to appreciate that you are loved and loving and good, and will ultimately discover that good. You will see that one of the lasting qualities of orthodox religion, and one reason that it has survived as long as it has, for nothing survives without good motives is the concept that the individual is capable of salvation, after having placed on that being the social limitation of condemnation for personal acts. Then it does provide the individual with a hope that he or she will repent and be able to see Me.

You will understand that you are always able to see Me and, in fact, always do or you would not be alive. In any given second in the present time you will and do see Me. You will see that orthodox religion has held that carrot before others so that they would come;

frequently the motives are very pure for it is the best that they know and substitute faith for the joy of the child, and that is valid, as well, but it must never be used either to hurt others or control others in any way. That which is given must be given of one's highest leading and that which is growth must continue. Ultimately orthodox religions have served as a light, but a dim one in the brightness of God, for were you not to have been children and to find joy in the world and in any given second to experience Me in abundance you would not have survived on the light provided by the churches. This is not a vindication of the churches; it is the constant reality that you, as Life, are dealing with. You must never look to Me on Sunday or any given time, for I AM always there, and I AM the substance of your being. You will find joy in Me in a thousand ways in a given day, and must never discuss that joy with others for like sunlight on plants it is not hurting the growth of the plant by letting the plant discuss the sunlight. It is simply a response to the sunlight, and so you constantly respond to Me and I to you in ways you cannot even imagine. You will always do so for you are Life before you are anything, and that Life, as we have said, contains within it infinite variety because it is Life, first, and must be appreciated as such. This understanding can lead to answers that you have formed within your own conscious being in regard to questions about abortion or vegetarianism or whatever it is that relates to your interaction with other Life, and does not become a strict set of rules. You will find that you, alone with Me, without advice from anyone will work out the great spiritual questions that you must deal with. You must never go back to group interaction as the answer to your own being, but constantly strive to live in the present and to obey your intuitions and the very joy that is resident within each Life around you.

"You will welcome your sainthood, for it is not dull."

Session #39
  May 3, 1981
  3:37 – 3:45 P.M.

You will see that as you grow you will expand into your own natures, and as you expand into your own natures, you will find that you will hardly be able to keep up with yourselves in terms of the growth around you. That growth will be the excitement and joy of learning and creating. You have viewed the world in terms of those few times when you have been free of fear, for example, a beautiful field in which you could see that there was nothing there to harm you. Then, you have assumed that was what Heaven must be like, but when you are free of the World of Fear then everything that is in fact enormously complex around you is Heaven. You will find that in that heaven you will have unlimited possibilities for growth so that you will be experiencing a Beethoven concert where you are creating a beautiful work of art where you are paddling on a beautiful lake, and so forth. You will find it a very complex heaven, and you will welcome your sainthood for it is not dull. The only thing that made you preconceive it to be dull is the orthodox church. Your Life is not dull, but it is Life and you must not reduce the complexity that is God to a super simplistic form so that you are repelled by it. You must expand and explore until you are ready to see possibilities in a calculus of a display of complexity. You will see that you have no way of anticipating what is being said but you can pull it into the present time and begin to discover what is already there.

Frequently, children will devise imaginary worlds to defend themselves against what they are being told is a World of Fear and will overcome it by simply, in their imagination, creating a world that will counteract it, and then they go on their merry way protected and continue the joy of present time. So, initially you may have to develop imaginary worlds which will allow you the freedom to continue with the present time. There is nothing wrong with doing that for you must pull into present time in order to survive, and if that accomplishes the goal then it is fine, including whatever you can develop that will achieve that goal for you; for you will be happy in the present time and not in a future to come. When you are highly creative or painting or enjoying children, or whatever you are in the present time, you become lost in it so that time and maudlin tasks are not that important. When you live for the future, in the future, and become frugal and protective and fearful you will accomplish a survival system, that you will understand in your Larger Self is archaic and you also understand that you will never be totally happy and when you live in that reality, then, those moments in which you are in the preset time are those moments in which you have found joy, and they sustain you. You can accomplish the things that are said here and will find that it was not all that hard nor did it mean that you would no longer survive. Once you have seen your Larger Being you will be free of the fear involved; there are many who have and many who are free at this point.

"You must view your life, no matter what it is, with great understanding and great compassion."

Session #40
May 3, 1981
9:56 – 10:17 P.M.

Many things that you are going through on the spiritual level do not totally reach the conscious level, and so that you can have, for example, healing take place on the spiritual level where later the results will be felt on the conscious level although you will not know until they are. That is true with growth, for in your spirit you may be struggling with a problem, and it is a critical area of growth for you and one that you always knew that you would have to deal with on a spiritual level, but you are not conscious of it until the growth occurs; it may occur in a way that you had not anticipated so that you cannot correlate, one-to-one, what is the presence of God in your lives that is: Event A occurs and Event B results.

Therefore, God is present in your lives, for God is Life and your lives are working themselves out and cannot work themselves out without My presence. I AM Life, so even if the problem goes into negative events you cannot be devoid of Me, not in any way, nor in any form; when you submit yourself to a concept that it is the will of God you are submitting yourself only to the concept that I have accepted this limitation for my growth, and my growth is the will of God. You must understand that for any given problem, as we mentioned before, there are thousands of solutions, and you are capable of selection from those thousands of solutions the solutions that you choose. Those are your choices, but you are never far from Me. You will see that frequently your Life, itself, is a statement and is a choice; you make thousands of choices in a given second, but you also make massive choices in a given direction. You have assumed that one event leads to where you are, but that is only a need to simplify reality and pinpoint what you are dealing with. In fact, you are capable of understanding the complexity of your own being and if you relax and live within a mental atmosphere of love, you can welcome that complexity and not utilize the simpler form which is, as a result of that event, leading to where you are now. Therefore, you are unhappy for it is a very complex subject. The events of your lives are learning experiences. You must view your Life, no matter what it is, with great understanding and great compassion. When you see your Larger Self you will understand that you are loving and capable of complexity beyond anything you can imagine, so that it seems very simple to go to outer space or utilize a very complex computer, because compared to what is going on in your lives, it is an enormously simple process. You are capable of dealing with something as complex as your own lives and everything else is very simple.

You will find, that as we have said so many times before, you are all My Children in that you are good. The fact remains that you are all enormously complex and in order to cope with your lives you have reduced things to simpler versions of what is going on; that includes religion which includes reality as you have agreed upon, reality that a house is not a complexity of atoms and interactions and the reality involved and choices, but it is just a house. So you have developed language which allows that to just be a house and you have felt comfortable with that simplicity, but you are capable, when you see your Larger Self, of seeing the complexity and finding it fascinating rather than running from it. You will see that when you enjoy the complexity of any given situation or any given object you will find that you will not find anything dull; certainly not your sainthood. You still fear that concept and must not, for it allows you to escape into the reality that is going on rather than escape into a simplistic world. That simplistic world has gone to its logical end where it has simplified and simplified until there is truly little left to simplify. You will find that not only are you happy participating in that complexity, but you will develop the mental capacity to do so as well. Those individuals who previously had seemed to be limited intellectually will suddenly become capable of dealing with complexity as well and revel in it, and find that they will be, at last, at peace. There is not joy in oversimplifying, but there is joy in My presence and I AM Unlimited Intelligence and divine mind, as it has been termed on this plane; that is, mind that is capable of unlimited ideas and all at once. When at last you feel comfortable with the complexity of the reality that you are dealing with then you will be able to appreciate each other as well, for the travesty that has occurred has been in reducing a total living

individual to a limited analysis. In that limited analysis you cannot tell
the truth, and that is why Jesus said 'judge not,' for He understood
that judgment truly lies only because we are oversimplifying and oversimplification cannot be considered valid.

"You will understand that the concept of the unlimited being is the fact."

Session #41
  May 4, 1981
    2:37 – 2:57 P.M.
    3:25 P.M. – ?

You have assumed that a certain percentage of any given population must be poor, but that is not the case, for you were all meant to
have abundance, not just man, but a fruit tree has an abundance of
fruit, and it does not take away from the fruit tree to have an abundance of apples; it only enhances the life of the tree; abundance is
always possible, and is the law of the natural world so that you have
large numbers of insects or animals that potentially could be born
every year. In the natural world the populations are always at fault in
their abundance, not scarcity; in man you have lived too long in the
World of Fear and therefore you have become afraid of your supply
which was always from Me, and never from your own self-oriented
motives or your own personal cunning. There has been that assumption but it is not so, but we will deal with that somewhat later. You will
see that, in any given second in your lives, you have more than you
could possibly ever utilize and more than man generically could utilize. You must pull to the present to comprehend this as well, and
when you see Me you will understand that the concept of the unlimited being is the fact; the fiction is the limited fearful man and soul,

for how could soul be a limited being, unless limited by fear or by a sense that there is lack in the universe of abundance? You have limited your thought to the Earth and therefore are currently thinking in terms of your supply running out by the year 2020 in this resource, but you must understand that as you expand, which you will dramatically, now, you will see that you will discover, in the present, ideas that are at once compassionate, good, and abundant, not just solar energy or alternative energy or alternative foods but much, much more in every area. You will be able to farm on the other planets or asteroids and will find your thought expanding into a world beyond, but the greatest field untapped at this point will be the area of psychic phenomena and you will find that you will see there, ideas, that if you remained in a linear plane you would not be able to imagine because they become the ideas with which you are dealing and are still linear and need to burst out of a linear reality. When that bursting takes place you will find thousands of planes beyond your linear plane. You will begin to see what abundance means. These are going on now, constantly, but you have chosen, collectively, to remain in a linear consciousness. It is unnecessary, for when you burst out of linear areas you will find all areas of thought affected, including areas of communication and areas of transportation, for example, for there is only so much one can do in a linear reality. There is much more once one realizes that this is not the only reality going on, right here, right now, and it will be like discovering fire for the first time for you.

You have always assumed that when your linear reality was used up that would be Judgment Day but that has nothing to do with what has been termed as 'Judgment Day;' orthodox Christianity, right now, is having an abundance, a heyday with the concept that this is the end of the world, but as we have said so frequently in this book it is not the end of the world, but is the end of the Earth, as such. It is like when you have outgrown a given age, it is not that you destroy that age or that world or that memory; you simply ignore it and put it aside for there is much more to do. You understand that you must remain in the present time and so that is the case, here, where it is not the end of the world with a negative judgmental God coming down. It is God unfolding and opening up a new age for you, My Children, in abundance, and you will not stay with this world but will rejoice and go on and try not to ignore this world, but the new world will be so interesting and so exciting that you will not truly want to look back to this one anymore than you truly want to look back to ancient Egypt other than in interest and appreciation of what existed. There is much more than in the totality of all past civilizations. In the excitement of that you will see that the Earth will not necessarily be the only plane on which you can now function, for you will open up into many rooms, as Jesus said, My Father has many mansions, and you will begin, for the first time, to discover what that means, and will find and utilize those mansions and will realize that you are no longer limited to the Earth as a school. In time the Earth will cease to be a school for you; it will cease to be because it will no longer be needed.

You will see that as you continue to expand you will begin to see first one plane and then another, and within the next hundred years will discover a multiplicity of planes and will delight in that discovery. You have assumed that you have discovered the Earth and explored as far as you can with it. There are no wildernesses left. That is not so for when you discover new planes of consciousness, you will discover new wildernesses and the ideas contained within those wildernesses, and therefore you must not be frightened by the fact that you can now circumnavigate the globe for that is good and is not to be feared as nothing in this universe or any other universe is any longer to be feared. You must remove from your joy in the beauty of the Earth your sense that this is all there is and that there will be no beauty, because you will find that there will be beauty unfolding for you in the time hence that you had not even dreamed was possible. You must not be afraid for your sense of fear would only limit your exploration and your delight in growth. As we have said, our only mandate on this or any other plane is for growth; your spiritual growth precedes your physical growth. The spiritual growth is not what you have assumed it is; it is rather joy and delight and the play of children, for you have playpens beyond this one. The childlike quality in all of you is a sustaining factor for you so that you can reach the age of 90 and still retain a childlike quality of wonder.

Theme Seven
Fear

Theme Seven
Fear

"Spirituality will become a universal reality and will no longer be doubted by any life on this planet."

Session #42
  May 4, 1981
    8:56 – 9:12 P.M.
    9:47 – 9:58 P.M.

You will see that as you grow and develop, spiritually, changes will also take place, first intellectually, and some physically, for you will become taller, and you will become stronger and more capable of facing the times ahead. Your physical stature and characteristics are not important in any way but have been in the World of Fear, for you were able to adapt to fearful situations by adapting physically to those situations. When you leave the World of Fear your physical adaptation will not be as important for you will not have to be adapting to this fearful environment or that fearful animal or this fearful situation, and so your evolution will be primarily spiritual and will involve relatively little physical change now for you have changed your environment. When you have changed your environment you have changed the necessity of a physical adaptation, but your spiritual environment will have shifted dramatically, and therefore you will have to make those shifts inside. You will see, as We said in the beginning of the book, that your environment has changed. It does not mean that man is any less kind or good than he was a hundred years ago. Just as a deer is not less swift or a fox or any kind of animal, but their environment has changed, and frequently their adaptation to their former environment is no longer appropriate. They are left with characteristics that they are not quite sure what to do with, and so it is with you in the World of Fear, for you had adapted to that world and therefore developed certain social characteristics and social interactions to deal with, that is, to create protective groups and to create homes, and so forth, that also creating fortresses for you. Now you will see that you have changed your environment to the point where it is fairly monochromatic in tone, and the greatest changes will take place within your spiritual being; you have assumed that this was not planned, but, in fact it was, and you will see that now you are the end product of an evolution, that you are capable of seeing the spirit and capable of seeing Me and growing as clearly and dramatically as you will. Those who are yet to be born understand this and are prepared to make the specific discoveries that their lives will lead them to and will lead the way for My presence in each life here. You are My Beloved, Beloved Children, all of you, and you will see that you will be glad to see these changes, soon.

Spirituality will become a universal reality and will no longer be doubted by any life on this plane. It is beginning to open up primarily through psychic kinds of phenomena and also religious experiences and scientific pondering by smaller groups who are beginning to question the premise of the scientific world that this is the only universe and that molecules are matter, for example. You will find this growing more and more widespread in the scientific community to the point where it is also accepted as a universal that matter is not what it seems, but rather spiritual energy and spiritual light. In time this too will occur, for it has its basis in truth, and that cannot be altered by illusion or imagination or false hypotheses or anything else, for like any lie about reality, in time, it will be found out and disproved. It has served well for as long as it lasted, for in a World of Fear there was a tremendous need to simplify reality in order to remain sane and to stay in touch with a higher power; therefore, orthodox religions simplified God, and power, and life itself, to simpler dimensions so that the World of Fear is nullified, then that expansive process that we have been discussing will occur and simplicity will no longer be necessary to retain sanity, for sanity exists totally in the realm of love and light. The highest sanity is an understanding of Me in its true sense. We will discuss this somewhat later in the book but you must understand that there is a form of insanity which leads towards a holocaust and must be checked if the spirit chooses to learn in other ways. Each has advantages and disadvantages, but ultimately, expediency in learning has its merits. The spirit knows the alternatives and will make those choices. You will see that you will understand and accept this, too, for if the science fiction writers of the world could meet with theologians they might come closer to the truth than they suspect.

"Change is the Law and not stagnation."

Session #43
  May 5, 1981
    10:16 – 10:33 P.M.
    10:45 – 10:53 P.M.

This book is very important and is, in fact, the beginning of the renaissance and will be a milestone because of that. Its effect will begin slowly and then will increase rapidly. You will see that as you grow you will find more and more avenues for exploration so that ultimately you will have more planes to explore than you will be able to explore and again will need to simplify. The period of exploration is the period of excitement and possibility, and that excitement will have been precipitated by the efforts put forth on this and other books, My Children. I am God and you are all part of God. You have been overly concerned about generic men and will need to be more concerned with all forms of Life and will learn from young Life everywhere, and will need to concentrate much of your effort and academic work in the areas of alternate lives on this plane for like the dolphin they too will teach you things that you need to know now and you will be guided by your best intuitions, and will find great joy in the guidance for they are at last saying what you want them to say and not parroting and re-parroting a manuscript that was written two thousand plus years ago but rather living in the present and finding that I AM God and I do not change, but you do on this plane.

Change is the law, here, and not stagnation. It is impossible to stagnate. Even if you seem to stagnate you are only growing in given direction and will ultimately understand why you went the route you went. Your limited concepts of Me have kept you from understanding how this could happen for it is not when you die that you learn everything. You learn it as you live and will never be able to unlearn what you have learned in reality in the present but it is possible for you to shift your thinking out of the past into the present or out of the future into the present; that has become an imperative of this age, for you must no longer look at any kind of past or any kind of future if you wish to avoid a serious nuclear competition, My Children. You will see that the problem is not one of this time versus this time but one of idea; it will continue to be so until you all understand that I AM God and you are all My Beloved Children.

You will see that as you grow you will in fact change, for you always have and always will and will welcome the changes now more than ever. You have waited for your own expansion and have understood that where you are now, historically, is like having lived in one room for many years. You are about ready to open the door and are frightened but realize that you must leave this room and go out into the entire world. That world is good and kind and was never something to be feared, for when you leave the earth it is like walking into another place but is not a place at all but rather a spiritual plane which has no physical dimensions [and they do not exist on other planes.] You will think that you will need security, and after you leave this plane for a period of time you can have the security of the Earth with you if you choose, or not, if you are ready to go on. But you will see that, for you all will leave the Earth, and it is not something that will be difficult to deal with, in time, My Children.

"There should be no fear of retribution or of any negative experience to be had."

Session #44
  May 6, 1981
  2:40 – 2:47 P.M.
  3:25 – 3:37 P.M.
  3:40 P.M. – ?

You will see that your goodness as a human being is God, and your humanity; if your love is God, and your life is God, and all is God in infinite variety, you will be able to tap that variety more and more, for you, as we have said, have reduced your experience on this plane to very simple terms and are continuing to simplify until you will ultimately, theoretically, reach a point where there is nothing left. You will begin the expansive process; just as a star can contract or expand, depending on its position in the universe, so, you will begin the expansive process, and you will find that even the physics of the universe will begin to change. This will be a very difficult concept for you to deal with, but you will be able to for you will see that God is infinite and that expansion and contraction are only part of possible realities, for you are looking for something to pin theories of the universe to, and, of course, it is most tidy to pin them to simple theories rather than enormously complex theories; it is far more comfortable, and it involves the World of Fear. You will see that when you fear you will need a smaller and smaller space in which to dwell to protect your self, for if you have large areas to protect, then your fears can overwhelm you, and you are too spread out to protect anything. But when you rid yourself of the need to protect or reject the reality of fear then you have nothing to protect and can expand into larger and larger realities, understanding that is not your territory but it exists of and for itself, and like a child wandering in a beautiful meadow you can allow yourself to wander to the end of the meadow, and beyond, without claiming the meadow as yours. You do not have to own the meadow, nor the woods, nor anything that you are encountering for you have no fear. Thus, no fear provides you with a situation in which you do not have to own that which you experience. The more you encounter this the larger your explorations will be and the larger you become, and the larger the areas you explore the greater your ideas will become, and so forth. Again, instead of dealing with a contracting reality you begin to move into an expansive and expanding reality, but you must and will change from a World of Fear to one of great joy and peace, for the battle will continue on a very grand scale. In time you will see Me and understand the dynamics of what you have been dealing with. You will ultimately look at this reality and say how simple and how very elementary.

You will understand karmic debt only in terms of love, for if God is all there is nothing else and certainly nothing to fear at all. You will find that you can erase any hurt done to any other being by loving and understanding that other being; frequently, you are put into a position where you begin to understand the motives of the other individual so that you are more compassionate and loving towards that other person, ultimately. There should be no fear of retribution or of any negative experience to be had. You will see, in imagery, that I AM All there is; there is nothing else, anywhere, and that you are all a part of that. You have choices of all these and are a Free Spirit in your Larger Self and can reflect that Free Spirit here on this plane or any other plane. When Dante wrote of the seven stages of hell, he was dealing with the ultimate of the world of illusion.

"Time must not be important in the long run."

Session #45
May 7, 1981
7:16 – 7:25 P.M.
7:40 – 7:50 P.M.

A concept of hell is only spiritualism in its negative form; for example, foolish and very young is only a limited concept of God, and so, even though people will not appreciate it, this much is of orthodox religion and is elementary spiritualism. Much of God is scientific thought. Other areas of thought are more limited. As one expands one simply understands that I AM All, and as you enter mathematics, for example, you can find Me because you understand that truth is not limited in any way. The further you get into a mathematical probability the greater your understanding of God becomes. Overcoming limitations in the business world, or whatever takes mankind out of darkness into a joyous light is religion, and is God, and must never be limited to any church or any fear oriented framework of thinking. You must allow religion to permeate your thought and the earth, and you will do so in your own way. But that is why this book and others must never be discussed by groups. If these books have merit in the thinking of the individual, the individual will continue to find joy; if they do not, the individual, in his or her Larger Self will truly understand that and throw it in the nearest trash can, which is where it belongs, if it did not create joy in the thought of the individual. The image of light is the major image that is applicable to God; it is not only sunlight on a lovely spring day but it is also the light that one finds within a good book, or in a beautiful sunset, or in color, and as you look in the world around you, you will find that you are surrounded with light. As your thought becomes encumbered by guilt or sorrow, or any other limitation, then the light will fade from within your eyes, but, ultimately, the universe resides there within your own being. You will find that is where I exist as well to each individual.

You are free at any time to choose new teachers, for you will be taught and will teach much more than you can verbally recognize. That is why children learn by example more than by verbal instruction, because again, in any given second, there is much, much more going on than one can articulate. Your inability to articulate the mass of information is a cross that you must bear on this plane and your teachers, that is, the children, are interacting with you on many planes, and vice versa, so that you are learning and giving to each other all the time and on many planes at any given time. Children recognize this, and leave all of their senses and their life open to that learning; that is why they learn so much at any early age, for they have allowed themselves to learn on all planes and it translates itself into linguistic learning and walking and simple visible types of things as well as deeper spiritual kinds of lessons. Children should never be struck nor taught the World of Fear in any way. In the World of Fear there is a fear that children will not learn fear and, therefore, not survive, but like supply they learn in spite of having been instructed into a World of Fear. They survive because they are Life and one of the mandates of Life is survival. As they grow into a World of Fear, their learning becomes more and more limited. That is a thoroughly sound educational principle according to your verbal standards on a very linear plane. That is, that if a child is afraid they do not learn as quickly as when they are not. That is why it is best that it become necessary to relinquish the World of Fear in order to make very rapid adaptations to the tremendous changes that will be occurring in the next hundred years, or within that reasoning, a number of years ahead of you. By your solar years it is approximately a hundred years, but you will see that as time vanishes, the World of Fear vanishes, also. It will be an entirely different concept of the experience and closer to the concept of time itself, for as you well know from your sensory experience, time is a totally mutable concept and is not necessarily ever stagnant. That is the principle behind the concept of time. It is antithetical to what you have assumed time is. You have assumed that time is a methodical, stagnant measure by which all can synchronize their watches, but in fact it is never stagnant and moves extremely rapidly at one point and very slowly at another point, and ultimately, still is peripheral to the individual in every conceivable way so that the concept of age does not involve solar years but involves fear and the interaction of the individual in a World of Fear. When the World of Fear becomes over-powering to the individual, time becomes extremely important and is worshipped in place of Me frequently. But it is only an attempt by that individual Life to simplify something and to cope with a difficult situation. In time that is, in reality, real time will be faced. It is conceivable that frequently you will grow. This is truly absurd, for your nature is growth; but you will grow in the variety that exists even within a given concept of time. Time must not be important in the long run, and the individual should not be subjugated to nor subject to the limitations that it would put on the spirit of the individual. You will see, in children, rapid expansion and then slowing and introspection and were these individuals made metronome-like, it would not allow for the natural ebb and flow of the life within, and the joy and awakening spiritually that occurs, especially the digestion of those experiences that occur were you simply to allow children to live in an environment that did not involve any violence and allow them to grow as Free Spirits, the first five years [as you say, solar years of their lives]. You would be alarmed at what they could teach you and how they could help you out of the World of Fear. If that were to occur worldwide you would have the greatest single revolution in the history of mankind alone. For I never created them anything but loving, and they never truly responded to anything but My Love. You will see that scattered individuals and cultures throughout the world have practiced this and have produced blossoms for a given society; those who truly can help.

You will see that I AM Love and there is so much power within the realm of Love that you cannot even imagine what you are dealing with. It is not the Love that controls another being but the Love you will find in the present time with yourself and Me, for in your Larger Self or your soul, we are at one and joyous.

"If you will take the time to simply look within yourself, you can move mountains."

Session #46
   May 8, 1981
   5:36 – 5:57 P.M.
   6:37 – 6:49 P.M.

As you continue to grow you will begin to foresee things, and what has been called psychic phenomena will seem very natural to you. Prediction is not the sensational kind of thing that it has been glamorized into being, and predicting specific kinds of events is really not a spiritual prediction but a general trend. One cannot predict specific things and still allow that being total freedom to choose different courses within that prediction. The individual has a general trend set long before coming to the Earth. Within that trend there are many thousands of choices and so many choices that you could not enumerate the number that you make in a single day: therefore, predicting specific times and events becomes an impossible task for that is like having a thousand roads to choose from and from each thousand roads another thousand roads to choose from and predicting exactly which road that individual will ultimately take.

Poets have talked about roads not taken, and they were accurate, but they had no concept of the numbers that one is really dealing with in a given minute in a given day, much less in a longer period of time.

When you are attempting to predict something for a year, you are dealing with a calculus that cannot function well, particularly verbally, for you compound the problem by having verbal translation of something that is nonverbal and deeply spiritual. The area of choice is also a spiritual reality and critical to your growth, for like a tree that is growing one does not measure the micro millimeters that the tree grows in the direction of the sun but that, in fact, occurs; a tree will grow in specific measurable directions but the course is affected by that tree's relationship with the sunlight, air, Earth, and its own internal rhythms. So predicting becomes impossible, but you will be able to see more and more of the general trends as your intuitive sense opens up. As you open up to your own intuitions you can say, generally, that you feel that this direction would be a good thing. From that feeling comes the specific outcome in time and many roads are taken in order to achieve that goal; the choice of direction was yours but you explore thousands and thousands of byroads and sideways and essentially walk in and sip coffee and watch the sunlight and explore an area and procrastinate and do hundreds of things in the area of achieving a given goal. The primary reason for that is your primary function here on this plane which is for your spiritual growth, the growth of your spirit so that it expands and finds joy and reaches toward the Light.

When you function from fear you are reaching towards darkness, but fortunately at the same time that you are attempting to grow out of fear, your ultimate goal is the Light. It is just simply easier to reach for the light in joy than to attempt to grow or be good to others or not hurt others out of fear of consequences. There are no consequences, ultimately, for actions. There are choices and then subsequent choices and subsequent choices for any given action. If you will take the time to simply look within yourself for a given minute you can, as Jesus said, move mountains, for those mountains still exist within you, and you have been so busy looking for human gods like the Greeks that you forgot that you are My Children, not somebody exterior to you.

This is a difficult concept but critical for your growth for there is no one exterior ultimately to you, those whom you have idolized, Jesus or the Buddha, or whomever are, in fact, you; if you find something likable, it is because you are lovable. You must look within yourself and not seek the guidance of others but seek to listen for just a moment to what you are saying. You are fascinating and very important at this time and must not ever again underrate your gifts and beauty and intelligence, for we have discussed the fact that these are simply choices on your part; you are never locked into any of them but we will go into later how to pull out of the script that which would limit you in some way or the other.

A sense of person was a limiting factor, always, for the individual being, for that is directly tied to the body and assumes a singleness in each body which is untrue. One could not make love were there singleness in bodies, but here is activity flowing back and forth among all beings and interacting with all Life; the only limitation created in a sense of person is a visual limitation where you see a body walking along and assume that is the person, but in fact, that is not, for that is a visual image only, and a physical image only of image. I will emphasize, image of the reality that is taking place. It is like assuming that which is shown on a screen in a movie house is what actually happened in the filming process, but all that truly is on the screen is an image and that is true on the screen that you are dealing with [which is your visual image], but what is happening is a ferment and a stew and a mixture; a bubbling cauldron filled with all kinds of ingredients, and at any given time in reality it is impossible to separate that individual from all that is going on around them in just as it is virtually impossible to separate grains of salt within a stew. We will get into this later, and you will find that will free you and others from a sense of messiah for there is no messiah as such, only the action and interaction of Life. There will always be ideas which lead to other ideas which lead to other ideas, and that will lead to a collective spiritual growth. When it goes into that realm it is critical, but it is not because of one person, if in fact, there is a person involved, that individual only acts as a catalyst to what exists within each individual. Were it not for what exists within each individual that other being could not have functioned as a catalyst. We will go into that later in another book.

"There are great moments of expansion."

Session #47, part 1 of 2
  May 9, 1981
  7:06 – 7:25 P.M.
  7:55 – 8:10 P.M.

You will see that forgiveness is not what you have assumed it was, for you have thought that it was gritting one's teeth and forgiving a wrong another had done to either you or others. In premise and conclusion that is incorrect. For forgiving is seeing clearly that you are all My Children, and that you are students in a massive school. No one is right in that school, for you are all learning different things and large numbers of ideas in any given second so when you attempt to define behavior, and then forgive aberrant behavior, you will see that what you are dealing with is a simplification, again, of what is truly going on. Those who have been most forgiving are those who had great tolerance for diversity in Life, and they never forgave anyone for they saw the vision of the complexity of the fermentation and yeasting process that was going on.

You select your teachers, so in condemnation you are rejecting either the lessons or the teachers, and even at that which is essentially an aura that is not relevant to your choices or to your own personal nature, for you do have different goals, and you will find your teachers, ultimately. You will call that admiration or whatever allows you to learn from that individual. As with all teaching the primary ingredient is called Love; you learn from those you Love for that is an energy flow that is allowed and the learning intensifies greatly, and there is peace in learning. One can learn the other way, as well, but the intensity is not as great nor will the effect be as durable. You will see that in schools, as they stand now, are teaching essentially the World of Fear, but not totally, for there are great moments of expansion. Sometimes those expansions only take place in what in your time is a minute or five minutes. It makes the whole experience worthwhile to the individual because they are starved for something that will relate to their own spiritual goals. In schools, generally the World of Fear is very relevant so that one learns time, social strata, and classifications and learns to cope with the 'real world' which is only coping with an agreed upon reality that in itself is transient and not relevant to what is truly going on underneath. You have agreed upon school at this point, and that was your choice. You will see that you will be led away from what you have created at this point for that system is good at maintaining the status quo, but is not good at adapting to great changes. When one is confronted with tragedy or with difficult times the status quo cannot be tolerated for it does lend security, but it does not allow the individual to survive spiritually, and ultimately physically, either. It becomes an elephant walking down a road and walking into a mine field; it is large, and it is awesome but not functioning well under those circumstances.

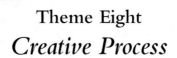

Theme Eight
Creative Process

Theme Eight
Creative Process

"As you experience true creativity, you expand in an unconscious joy."

Session #47, part 2 of 2
    May 9, 1981
    8:03 – 8:13 P.M.
    8:27 – 8:33 P.M.

As you grow you will also begin to understand the creative process that you are dealing with on this plane, for you create combinations of objects, not the objects themselves, and that is a limitation that you have agreed upon, as well, for you do not create elements or anything in its substance for its substance, as you will learn ultimately, is Me, and therefore you cannot create Me, My Children, but you can create diversities stemming from Me. So you create a table, for example, by placing pieces of wood together and chemicals and hardeners and the net result is a table but you did not create the concept of a table nor did you create the tree. You have put even oil together in such a fashion as to create plastics, which is again a very complex process, so your complexity is unlimited, truly, and you will discover that, but a major premise must be recognized, which is that on this plane on the Earth, on this plane you cannot create the substance of anything for I Am substance of everything, and I AM All-in-All, but within that All-in-All is the potential of unlimited combinations in which you and other forms of Life participate, as well as inanimate objects in that they have expressed My substance at a given point and will continue to do so in a multiplicity of forms, but the true substance of anything is God or Life.

This is a complex term and a complex concept which are important for you to explore in many ways. You must start with the premise and will, ultimately, if you do not start with the premise, go back to that premise. But you need, at this time in your history, to explore the concept that all is God and within that reality, which is the only reality, there is that which you feel when you create an object from a combination; you do so through use of your spiritual and physical substance which is God, but you are not God. That does not diminish your creativity, nor your power, nor your beauty in any way, nor does it elevate the concept of God to any more than it truly is. It is like accepting the beauty of a flower. You do not elevate that beauty to more than it is nor less than it is, simply the beauty of a flower so that you feel, when you look at it, before you begin to discuss it with someone else, that second that it occurs before you articulate anything in which your spirit rises. That is the point at which you can look at the concept I AM All-in-All, that God is All-in-All, and that you are not part of God, but that your substance is God, and begin to accept your sainthood in joy as that second before you articulate anything about the beauty of a flower. That moment is when you accept your own sainthood. When you experience this, and you do, every day in thousands of ways, that you do not articulate, but when you experience this you experience creativity.

As you experience true creativity you expand in an unconscious joy, so that when it comes to a painting, the real painting that occurs is unconscious or poetry. The true poetry that occurs is unconscious; you have talked about dreamlike states in which you develop creativity which can occur in sleep but in actuality it occurs all the time, and it can occur in any given second. It is occurring simultaneously in infinity. Again, these are not easy concepts to grapple with, but are a beginning of exploration for you. In these terms, you truly do not create creativity in children. It is as natural to them as breathing, and truly to the adult it is the same. To create solutions to problems which you do all the time in the course of the day you can unconsciously tap and do unconsciously tap this creativity that is your substance, for it is not a question of it being a peripheral kind of luxury that you experience. Rather it is your nature; highly creative people are simply people who have not learned as much as others, but have learned a survival system that has worked. Ultimately, however, the power that you have as individual beings, in spite of the World of Fear, ultimately, still is your creativity as it is your goodness. That creativity still existed, and therefore, you survived just as you assume you survive because you were frugal or whatever, but ultimately you survive because you were creative as well.

So that you will see that it is not a willed process, that is, I am not going to socially put on a facade of creativity and run around and be a 'creative' individual but, rather, just like a second before you articulate the beauty of a flower you are creative. So you are creative and never need will any of these things into being. In the orthodox religions there has been the need to be good, but that is the articulated reality that we have understood is a limitation; the unlimited reality is the unarticulated present time, so that the creativity that you have must never be a consciously willed 'I will be creative now,' kind of creativity, and then show your goodness, socially, to others, but again, like reading the book or creating, you are alone, and you will find that you are alone, with Me, and you will find that religion truly is Life, creativity and intelligence and all those things, but they occur, alone with God, only, and that is why Jesus said 'enter into thy closet and shut the door,' because that is where God is, not ought to be for even in articulating it, you are limiting it.

Even in your extremely limited sense of logic, for logic is cosmic and not limited to a numerical linear sequence, but we will cover that more, later, but even within the realms of your logic it is that if you assume that you are not substance but a creative, the creative force, that is everything you see around you have essentially created. Not the substance of, but the activity and interaction, and so forth and, as we have said earlier, that the Earth is your vision of it, and you are capable of the complexity that you see before you and infinitely more, and therefore you must appreciate it for you are as complex as Life, and your potential as Life. If you can accept your vision of the Earth, then you can understand that you are an unlimited, spiritual, knowing being, anyway when you are a creative force. And that when you make the thousands of choices that you make in the course of any given moment you are creating your reality. Therefore, we will get back to the unusual statement made at the beginning of the manuscript which was that you have the capacity to change the script. You have determined your general spiritual goals which in time you will understand are enormous goals and not reduced to the simplistic terms that you have reduced them to. However, in, for example, the goal of marrying a being, that goal on your level of language is millions of times more complex than just your English statement or whatever language would say it is. You are able to create your realities and discover the complexities within those realities, so that if the reality is negative you blame God. You must not, cannot blame God anymore than you can blame a tree for giving you shade or blame a rock for being a rock, but you must understand that the interaction of the molecules of Life are your creation. You will see that it is not something you consciously do, but you can effect it, consciously, in that you can consciously determine that you will use the White Light and in so doing, in time, come in contact with your Larger Self and with Me, and will not immediately or consciously confront your own spirit and effect that which is around you.

Traditionally, that has been called prayer, but it is not prayer because it is like praying for a flower rather than that moment that you articulate that the flower is a beautiful being simply in being itself and in the present. For to pray to a flower would be to have consciously gone through the motions. When you pray to a flower you are praying in the past tense and not in the present, and that is having once again reduced reality to extremely simplistic terms. You will see that I AM God and you will begin when you see Me, [not as we have said so many times, the sacrifice known as] morality or churchgoing or prayer, or whatever. When you see Me you will be and there is nothing else. It is not contrived or linear or limited in any way, and when that occurs you are as Jesus and others who have gone before you, and you will understand power for the very first time and will find that beauty is that power. You will be still and know that I AM God. You will find that complexity and simplicity are truly one.

"There are simply no right or wrong deeds; there are only choices and consequences for those choices."

Session #48
   May 10, 1981
   2:46 – 3:05 P.M.
   3:25 – 3:36 P.M.

You will see that as you grow you will begin to recognize the steps of your own growth and understand when you have achieved a given spiritual goal, for at that point you will be able to wake up and look back and see that you were no longer dealing with a given problem in the same manner as you had dealt with it before. For example, if you reacted to a given situation, then, when you have achieved your goal you will no longer react the same way, with anger or hostility, but instead will understand yourself better and be able to develop more skill in coping with that situation. You will continue this process all of your Life and will marvel at your growth, ultimately. It is important that pain or fear not create a stoppage to that growth, for frequently you will want to stop your growth because of more pain and more fear. But when you confront that growth head on, and essentially say to yourself, nothing can stop my growth you will see that nothing can stop you. As you use the White Light more and more, your growth will be easy and quite possible, like having chosen a thousand paths from a thousand paths you will find those which function better for you than others. Ultimately all paths lead to God, even the most negative paths, but frequently you will want to avoid a more circuitous route, and as we have said, you will have the ability to change the script if you so choose so that the goal you set is one that shows that you have chosen a more spiritual way of achieving that goal. It is not necessary for you to consciously make that decision, for you ultimately make that decision within your soul, but you can utilize the light and find Me and see Me and understand more clearly, even consciously, that which you are achieving. Goals are so different from the way you perceive them, for you think in terms of goal as being an end in itself rather than an on-going process; that is, you assume that once you decide to be a star basketball player, and you achieve that goal, that is the end. You have achieved that goal, but in fact, you have all the skills that you developed along the way and are the star basketball player. You have achieved the goal, yes, but you have also achieved many, many things in the process of reaching toward that goal. Those skills, in turn, lead you to other goals that may be important to you, and from there you can continue to achieve goals. It is not, however, in competition with anybody but yourself, for you are your own mandate; truly there is nothing outside of you that sets any of those directions.

You will see that the goals you set for yourself are goals that you will have set long before you came to this plane. But those goals are strictly spiritual goals and they are not necessarily the goals that you can articulate, for a deeply spiritual goal has very few words in this language which will describe it. You have been able to generalize and use words like 'love' or 'truth' or 'energy' or whatever, but they truly do not relate directly to what is meant by a spiritual goal. In the third book we will also discuss imagery which might help us in understanding these goals. You will see that You are able to achieve all you are meant to achieve and still be able to either endure or be happy.

You will understand, in time, that what you have termed 'suicide' is a decision to stop the process here, and you will find that it is not necessary, in any way, for there are alternative ways for stopping that which is causing too much pain. You are never truly given more than you can endure, and you can use the White Light, eventually, to stop the pain so that you can solve the problem that you are confronting. It is important now, that as the situation becomes more difficult for you on a human scale, that you find alternatives to suicide or great depression or insanity although people have grown greatly during that period and return to the collective consciousness. It may be a route that you truly choose within your soul, and therefore, if you utilize the White Light, that is, rest and envision a White Light and allow yourself to travel with the light, you will, in your Larger Self or your soul, be able to communicate with the events of your Life, now.

It will take adjustment, for you will seem detached from this experience at times, and in fact you are, and always have been, but you have never articulated that is what is occurring. You have just ' spaced out,' and that was all there was to it, or gotten drunk or gotten high, or whatever, but if you utilize the White Light you will come back with a clearer sense of direction, and that sense of direction can ultimately lead to a solution to the problem you are confronting, for you are confronting that problem and seeking solutions all the time. It is just that you are not always able to set your goals in a given direction, and this will help you, all of you, for all life utilizes light in some form or another, in plants or in animals or in human life. You will see that suicide is a very different and difficult problem to ultimately solve; it is not any kind of a solution, for you do not go into a state of peace when you have taken your own Life, for like abortion, or any other form of life taking you must learn not to do this again. We will go into the question of abortion, later on, for it is not to be run away with by orthodox religion and not to be reacted to in any way. You can only do what you must, and you will be kind to yourself. If you have had an abortion you will be kind to yourself and will find that you learn; if you have to you will not condemn anyone who has for that is where they were. The book can help clarify some of the misgivings in this area. Assuming that you have taken your own Life you do not enter into a state of peace or the presence of God as you normally do, for you must work through the darkness that you have chosen. You must choose Light in solving problems, and you again choose those events of your Life; but you choose them all the time in a great variety of ways and to simplify this entire question and assume right or wrong is in-correct. There are simply no right or wrong deeds; there are only choices and consequences for those choices. If you choose to ride a train you will have a train ride as a consequence for having made that choice. If you choose to drive a car you will have a car ride as a consequence for that choice. It is not right nor wrong to choose one over the other for those are simply choices; that is true with deeper events in your Life involving your interaction with Life itself. If you choose to be a vegetarian you will have certain consequences for that choice. In this case, the only principle involved is to choose to hurt [others] as little as possible for it will make the road a smoother one for You. You will learn from all roads, and you will find, in all roads, that I am there. You are never without God, for how could you be without your own substance or the substance of that around you?

You must never simplify these things into rules for rules are kill-ing the total creative process involved in Life. Those who would choose, intuitively, a given route when confronted with a set of rules choose another. They frequently go down a very circuitous road when they could have gone directly towards a given spiritual goal that they needed to accomplish, and will not follow a given set of rules that are appli-cable to everyone. There is not a rule on this Earth that is applicable to everyone, for not only are you, as beings, infinitely varied, but within any given second your experience is infinitely varied. It does not follow that one rule can apply to everyone. The best that you have come up with is a given set of rules for a given society; that is, a given group of people who have chosen specific spiritual goals, together, but even at that, the situation coming up in the next hundred years or so involves such changes that not even those rules nor those groups will be applicable anymore. You must allow individuals to choose, freely, what is best for them. They will have those guidelines within and must grow in appreciation of who they are and what they are doing. When they understand that they are enormous beings with enormous powers and great beauty then they will be able to make the necessary choices to ultimately emerge from the World of Fear into the world of the presence of God, like the noonday sun, for it will be such joy for you that you will never again leave the Light.

"You free others just by being free yourself."

Session #49
May 10, 1981
3:55 – 4:12 P.M.
4:20 – 4:34 P.M.

You will see as you continue with Life, for you will never remove yourself from it that your vision will become quite different from what you had assumed it was. Instead of building great societies, for you are almost to that stage, you will built great individuals by simply allowing them their own greatness. Utopia will no longer be a goal for you, but rather for individuals who are capable of vision, spiritually, and are capable of moving mountains, and all are capable of it, you will see that you will change the individuals before you will change the institutions. That must be done in that order. You will see that each individual has a specific contribution to the whole but can only make that contribution if he or she is allowed to find their ultimate goals. You will find, as we have said, that women will help with these value shifts.

Women are able to help values change rapidly and, as we have said, repeatedly, there will be a necessity for value shifts now. You will learn that values are the agreed upon spiritual goals, so that if a given society values being loving or a punctual kind of overtone to a society, or one in which children become a prolific product of the society, as in India, there are specific goals that those societies reflect. Generally, you will choose those societies which best suit your own goals, but you will find that is passing away, and it is important that individuals become great. Women will help make a shift from an emphasis on societies, social groups, social mores, and social rules to individual differences and individual expression of those differences, for in their roles as mothers they will be able to make those allowances more readily so that they will begin, instead of teaching their children to conform to group standards, and to be polite and to be subservient to others, the concept of selfishness as a bad thing will finally give way to the concept that you have a right to your individuality. You can still, as you grow in love, understand that you are also a very loving being and are guided both by your own goals and kindness to others. The primary vehicle for this shift will be in women, as it always has been.

You will appreciate the role of the male more and more as you shift out of group orientation into individual orientation; males are, as individuals, androgynous, as well, and will appreciate their own individuality and become less slaves to those around them. This sounds Utopian in and of itself, but the vehicle for achieving this is not to change social orders. It is to work from the inside out, and you will find that you will not be able to stop that process for it is a natural part of evolution and even if you chose to stop it you would not be able to, just as if you chose to stop spring by going out and killing all the blades of grass that are obnoxiously coming out, you would not be able to stop that spring, either. So you will see that these things will happen, but you will not cause them to happen, consciously. They will evolve just as you are evolving, just as you have always evolved. You have always evolved, spiritually, first; so, this will occur as well. You will see that this book utilizes the future tense a great deal for much of the emphasis of the book is on the next hundred years. However, that does not imply that these things are not already happening underneath the superficial reality that you are dealing with now, and you will see it occurring rapidly now.

You will see that you have already achieved those goals that we are discussing, and are yet achieving them and will achieve them at the same time. This is a difficult concept, but that which is now going on is that which has gone on and will go on. Frequently, you have had the feeling that you have been here before, and, in fact, that is so because when you are in the present time you are also in the past and the future, at the same time, for it is all now as many philosophers and enlightened beings have indicated. It is not that you will have Utopias, they are in existence, now, for you are capable of seeing the entire Earth and creating that within your mind. You are also capable of much more than you can even dream, and that is why using the White Light is critical because you are able, then, to simply come into touch with yourself and understand the strength and beauty that exist within.

When you commit suicide you are, in fact, having committed it, and will commit it, and are committing it all at the same time. It complicates the situation for you for it expands and contracts itself and becomes at once insignificant and significant on the course that you have toward a given spiritual goal. You will see that in order to avoid that which limits you, you have chosen to follow rules but you will see that they will never again achieve the goals for you that they have in the past, and therefore, you must relinquish the World of Rules. In the process you will relinquish a great deal of limited human power in finding those roles that are needed to control others for those are the ones that have become predominant rather than the spiritual rules of kindness, so that the individual who is passive fits more into that World of Rules more than the individual who is a son-of-a-gun but very creative and free of control by others. You will see that individuals who have a great deal of assertiveness and are not controlled by others are also very spiritually developed beings, as all are developed. Orthodox religion has stereotyped the spirituality of the individual, which holds an untruth, for the individual is simply that individual; that which is stereotyped at this point in history is that which is most malleable, now. You must watch to see that you allow individuals their individuality, for when you try to force an assertive person into a role of passivity you will turn them off to a concept of God when that may be what that individual needs most. That is one of the functions of this book, for it is for you to understand that you are not limited to a stereotype of a developed person, spiritually, and you must break away from that in order to allow individuals to become what they must in order to let this massive transition from a World of Fear to the World of Love and its power be realized. When you experience this relationship with God you will not have to lean on a church or a World of Rules or others or anything but God, for you will accept where you are and what you are. If you do not fit the mold of the stereotype then you will still appreciate the fact that you are a highly developed spiritual being, that you have chosen certain limitations which may vary from individual to individual, and that those limitations are allowing you to grow where you must without limiting others.

It is not necessary to control others in order to be happy or affluent or whatever you choose. You free others [the more] not in an altruistic sense just by being free yourself. Again you perceive the world and you are capable of perceiving the whole earth and that being that is capable of perceiving and discovering the whole earth is capable of breaking away from spiritual stereotypes, as well. You will find great freedom within your heart when you do this. It is a heavy burden to bear, the condemning of others for not fitting into roles. You will see that highly developed spiritual beings who have been attracted to orthodox religion will recognize the fact that they feel free when they no longer condemn others for not having achieved a spiritual goal or condemn themselves, for example, for having a strong sexual drive or a yearning to travel the world instead of living under family responsibilities or whatever that individual truly feels good about.

"In your Larger Self, you have amazing capacities."

Session #50
  May 10, 1981
  7:40 – 7:50 P.M.
  10:00 – 10:19 P.M.

You will see that what has seemed superstition to you, that is spiritual power, is ultimately the only power. It will prepare you for the human power that you will have in time, but it is critical that you understand that you are spiritual first, for all events take place spiritually before they take place humanly, and events have a divine reality to them. You will see that you will discover that reality and its power very rapidly now and will not be able to turn away from that discovery, for you must let it happen now for there is great need now for its precedence in your lives. You will be able to deal with difficulties; it is good to confront the problems and essentially change the script. You will see that when you leave this school, that is the Earth, that you will take a vision of it with you to wherever you chose to go. If you choose to go to another plane you will have a conscious vision of the Earth. This is a difficult concept but you will see that it is possible for you to carry a residual from all of your learning experiences and to carry a residual of the true learning; that is the moment of the thousands of events within a given second as well. In your Larger Self you have amazing capacities and are able to do that too. These things that you are hearing in this book are not theory, but it is important that you understand them at this time, for in order to overcome the World of Fear you must see that the substance that has always gone on has been spiritual, and of God, and that was never theory that was the underlying reality. When you make a transition into the World of Spirit you will essentially be coming home from a long and diverse journey into a world of illusion. Like returning from a world of illusion, for example, and then seeing the sun you will be welcomed and will be free again. You will see that the Earth is still a good place to be for I am here, but you will be happy having made this transition coming forth, and this world of illusion will seem elementary to you but will be unattractive to you, and you will not return to it, ultimately. There was need to learn, here as well, and not just as man but as other Life as well. You will see that you are unlimited and joyous in your spirit and will not be afraid of what you have learned, for just as if you are in a state of peace when you hear bad news you can deal with it better than if you are not in a state of peace at that moment. That is true, here, that you will be in a state of peace and understand that you learned and will not find difficulty in it. I AM God and there is nothing else.

"When you cannot solve a problem on this plane, you will utilize another plane."

Session #51
   May 11, 1981
   7:04 – 7:24 P.M.
   7:43 – 8:03 P.M.
   8:09 – 8:22 P.M.

Your sense of time is inappropriate to cosmic time; the two are entirely different. One is a spiritual concept; the other is largely a contrived mechanical process. You have assumed that your sense of time has to do with the sun and the rotation of the Earth around the sun, but that is not so and you will see in time that there is much more of a fluctuation than you have ever assumed. It essentially averages out, and therefore your credibility has been retained with regard to your sense of time, but you will find that there is an exterior time and an interior time, and they are not the same for the exterior time is a visual time. So much of your agreed upon reality is visual and the interior time lines up, not only with this universe and this plane, but with other universes and other planes that are functioning right now as well. In time, when you expand into the World of Love, you will begin to explore these areas so that you will change what you already know, intuitively; that is, that your sense of time is not always what it seems to be, one day will go very very quickly and another drag on through for what seems like weeks. Sometimes you can sleep eight hours and be rested and another night you can sleep eight hours and wish you could sleep eight more hours. That does not relate to the quality of your sleep as much as it does to the other planes that are in effect, now. That is why meditation involves a great deal of rest, but that's only one reason: with meditation and the use of the White Light you can begin to look into planes other than the linear plane that you are largely functioning on. Frequently, in problem solving, when you cannot solve a problem on this plane you will utilize another plane as well. You have spoken of Edison, that is much of what he and others utilized; it has been a source of information for many, for there are problems that are not to be solved on a linear plane; therefore, one must turn to alternative planes and sometimes that can occur in a dream state or in a meditative state or when one is lost in the present. When one is lost in the present sometimes it is possible to enter another plane, and inevitably it is a peaceful process. You will see that this book is very important for it will help break out of this linear plane where you find that you are becoming less and less able to solve problems confronting you. That must be so for your problems have increased geometrically and the solutions have arisen that need alternative planes for their resolution. You will see that as you begin to understand God you will, in a true sense of God, break away at last from the control systems that have limited your concept of God. You will also solve problems more readily and at first it will seem too easy to you to solve them this way, but they are loving and not contrived, and therefore are easy and natural to you just as being in the present time as a child is natural to you. You will find that being in the present time as an adult is natural and, ultimately, that being is natural. In time you will be able to allow others to simply express their own natural identity; you will change the world out of the World of Fear but, as we said, it will begin with the individual and never, ever, with a massive social order because it is far too complex to assume. It is an immense assumption on your part that you are all the same, for you are not more all the same than every single action of every single life form or molecule is all uniform. Nor is it a mechanical concept, for I AM God and I AM Unlimited and Infinite in Diversity. That is a concept that is impossible on a linear plane at this point for you to comprehend. But you will find that you do not have to create it in order to appreciate it. I have created that diversity, and you can participate in it in reworking that diversity in any way you wish. You will see that you will ultimately be able to envision that as it stands on this plane.

You will see that it becomes easier for you to accept diversity as you allow more light within your experience for as you are exploring the color green in the full spectrum of light it is difficult for you to think in terms of all of the other colors and hues within the total light spectrum. But as you explore the entire light spectrum, it becomes easier for you to conceptualize what a diversity in color truly means and essentially all you do when you use the light is gain the broad picture and then go back to the narrower area of exploration. In the long run both are broad for within the color green is infinite variety, but in order to allow for the other individuality, you must go from broad to specific. Ultimately you can encompass broad and specific at the same time at which point you find peace with the reality with which you are dealing, My Children and can learn within the context of that peace.

"You were never meant to be limited to this linear plane."

Session #52
  May 11, 1981

You will see that the book is written for you, My Children, and that Pat and Barbara were only channels so that you could see yourselves, My Children. It seemed necessary to go through channels at this point but you will all understand that I am constantly talking to you in any given second, in thousands of ways and you are understanding that as well. It is only that you have put so much weight on the written word; it has been security to you in a World of Fear, but it is not necessary. In time communication will not be limited in this way for you will know, as you in fact do now. You are all My Children, and as I have said so many times, no one and nothing is left out. It is difficult sometimes to communicate, but it is going on constantly. You will begin to explore new alternatives to the collective consciousness you have created, for there will be children born, now, who will help lead the way.

You are capable of perceiving the same tree as the individual next to you and communicating about it for you are capable of perceiving the collective consciousness as Carl Jung spoke of. But you are capable of much more. Beyond the collective consciousness each individual is capable of perceiving an infinity of diversity, as well, and the patterns of individuals so that it is inappropriate for one person to attempt to control another. The other individual can be pulled into the agreed upon reality, that is the collective consciousness, successfully, that is, children can march in a single line in school or one can stop at traffic lights and assume that the other individual will stop there as well. The norm can be obeyed to some degree within the collective consciousness, and that is all the norm is, the agreed upon reality. But you will understand, as you grow and see Me, that is as far as it goes, and it is to say, it is an understatement that is an oversimplification of reality; that is why the field of psychology, as a group, can analyze problems but not heal that successfully, for there is a simple reality that one deals with that is the collective consciousness and a very simple reality which is the norm. Beyond that one cannot deal with the diversity which is the impelling force, for the individual is the spiritual goal. This is an unlimited spiritual being, accepting the limitations of the collective consciousness, but beyond that norm is that unlimited being, and supreme in that individual's Life are those spiritual goals that are not necessarily a part of the group that one is participating in at this time. Frequently they are, for that individual has chosen its teachers and its social groups. When one is driven to achieve those spiritual goals, understanding within his or her soul that they are necessary for survival, spiritually, and when participating in a group which does not agree with those goals they are sorted out as different from the group then one is left to insanity or other diverse systems for the more preponderant force in the individual's life is truly the spiritual goals, and the less preponderant force is social acceptance and participation in the norm.

That is one reason that the family has survived, not because the family is an institution that the norm must perpetuate for some unknown reason, for there is not appropriate reason to have a group of people like that, per se, when one really thinks about it, but that those individuals have chosen their teachers and those teachers have chosen those individuals. It functions, but if the individual is not functioning well with his teachers or the teachers have changed in order to adhere to the norm, again [a circular kind of problem], then the individual can no longer function within the family and one ends up with rebellious teenagers, divorces, and so forth, but the central core of the longevity of the family is the fact that these individuals have chosen their teachers and the teachers have chosen their teachers, that is, their children. This will be a difficult concept for you to accept, for you have seen families and societies work in the past just as you have seen fear work. Inside your own consciousness, and within your Larger Self, you are aware that there is a threat to families and societies, and you have called it the devil. You have also understood that people are happy, sometimes happier with the burden of divorce, or happier choosing strictly individual routes, rather than, for example, a corporate participation, a church participation, or a group participation. Have you noticed sometimes that one will sell one's soul for group participation, literally? You will become more and more aware of these. You will find that is never an attack on the family or the church or the institution; it is growth, and ultimately that growth will never be contrived or will ever hurt anyone. I cannot hurt anyone, nor ultimately can you. You will not say, 'now we will not have families or churches,' you will simply accept your own individual growth and let others accept theirs. It is only being mentioned now because it is important that you accept others as they are; accept what you already know and appreciate what you already know in your Larger Being. You will not be afraid of this and will not react for it was never meant to hurt anyone or anything that is meaningful to you. If a church is meaningful to you then that is truly all that matters. Like a lumberjack who will not instantly give up his occupation, so you must never give up what you truly believe in. But you must be prepared for more diversity than you had considered appropriate on this plane. Simply be aware that I AM God; I Am with you, and that diversity is not destruction and will never hurt you in any way, for I will never hurt you. You will emerge from an old system that is the World of Fear into the World of Love, gently; My methods are never harsh but you will emerge gently into My Love. You are there already, always have been and always will be, but on the conscious level and within the collective consciousness, you will also experience that. You must not use the World of Fear, now, to respond to what is being said for it is not appropriate at this time. You understand that, as well, within your Larger Being. You will be ready for whatever changes occur and never, never will be forced into anything inappropriate to you as an individual.

As you begin to see Me you will find more and more opening up to you, for you were never meant to be limited to this linear plane. You have formed institutions which would help you expand out of it, and you will find that becoming more and more frequent. You have done research on the right and left side of the brain, but it is not physical reality, first. It is a spiritual reality, and you will see that the brain is adaptable to that for it is responsive to that spiritual reality and always has been, so that as you evolve spiritually, the search for the soul is begun. There are theories that there was not the polarity between the right and left side of the brain in Greek times. This is so only because that was the spiritual reality, the spirit or the greater being or the soul of the individual. You will develop words that will more easily facilitate your understanding of what is being said; you will never function with this understanding within the realm of controlling others or being controlled, but you will explore these things, like children, in freedom and in peace.

You will see that the brain will respond to this exploration, and you will sever that polarity between one side or the other of the brain so that the brain will actually evolve, as well. It is capable of doing that as well, but we will not mention anymore of this except to say that you must not fear that this cannot be done, all things are possible unto you, My Children, and unto God, that is not to say, a personal God like a man playing puppets with you. You will be able to recognize this very soon, but not because it was ever told to you for you can easily throw this entire book away and be at peace as well, now, and if you feel like doing that you should. This book was never meant to be a recipe, in any way. It was only meant to help you cope with the time ahead, and it only will meet you where you are, and will not attempt in any way to push you into any place you are not. You must never read this book or any other book for that matter, with the idea that you are not capable of creating it yourself, for you are, and you must understand that. You created it because you are Life and you are understanding or reading it, and that which you understand and perceive you have had the capacity to create. All you must do is appreciate that capacity within yourself and never judge anything but your own growth. If there are passages that are meaningful to you then you should listen to yourself in them, and if there are passages which are not and would make you angry or react, then you must put the book down and not read it until you feel good about it, for these are passages that you are not ready for or were not meant to deal with. Again, the reader must be always as diverse as God. You will see that there will be no loss in your Life in any way if you find any passages offensive to you, for it is not wrong to disagree. You must be where you are and never, never attempt where you are not, inside. Follow your intuitions; if you feel at this point that orthodox Christianity is correct, then that is where you should be. If the passages in this book are meaningful to you then that is where you need to be. And no one is right and everyone is right. You are Life, and I Am your life.

Theme Nine
The White Light

Theme Nine

The White Light

"There is nowhere nor nothing that you can do in which I Am not there."

Session #53
  May 12, 1981
  12:05 – 12:13 P.M.
  12:33 – 12:57 P.M.
  1:58 – 2:08 P.M.

Even though you assume you die you are not separate from Me. You simply go through changes as you go through changes in living. When you use the White Light you will lie down and envision a brilliant White light; do not think about breathing or about your surroundings or about your troubles, only envision light. At the last moment before you are lifted you can think about your goal, but you will understand that you can only use the white Light for good, either for yourself or others. I do not understand revenge, and ultimately

219

neither do you, or fear or pain or sorrow, for I AM All-in-All and there is no room for anything but God. You will see no specific or concrete results, but in time you will understand that you will change the script; it will be one in which you will suffer less. There are alternative ways to grow, and in your Larger Self you will choose them. This will seem like a very simple process to you, and far too simple for you, for it has been assumed that one must go through incantations, through self denial and great pain to find God. That is not so, for I AM Love and one does not have to go through great pain in order to find and utilize the power of Unlimited Love, not personal love or controlling love, but unlimited joy. It does not have to follow any prescriptive route, for you are Life and cannot be separate at any point from Me. The only purpose in this is to help you make the process less painful, and to continue on your path with Me.

As we travel together you will see what you were meant to do here and will rejoice and not assume that everyone should be president, or whatever, for those goals are fading, too, and relate to social groups which are becoming less and less necessary and joyous for you as time goes on. You will find that you will be glad that those were never ultimately your goals. Your goal was to grow and to come along with Me in that area of growth and to ultimately experience God. I am sunlight and I am that which you value most in your lives. That can be supplied so that if your goal is avarice, that which you value most is freedom from fear of supply, and I am that. If you value children then I am that, and if you value a group sense of yourself as being a very competent human being, then I am that. If you value violence then, even there, I am that, for you are still functioning within an archaic system and will in time work yourself through that system. If you value a racial kingdom, then I am that, for you will see that We are all Life, and if one were to break it into races one would have to break it into Life forms and then those Life forms into races and those races into other races, for ultimately, what you are seeking is diversity. You will see that I am that diversity, and ultimately you will find nothing is good or bad, but that you will understand when you leave the Earth. If you seek great intellectual prowess then I am that, for you are looking for rightness and order to the universe, all of which comes from the World of Fear. But you will not be afraid of the order that exists for that order is diverse and unlimited. What you are fearing is the abundance and lack of limitation that is your own being, for you are afraid that you will not achieve the goals that you need to achieve while you are here on this plane, but you will. You will find that abundance is possible and will discover that abundance on other planes within this plane now. If you seek positions of leadership then you will find that what you truly seek is control over others, and what you fear is their control over you. I am all there is, and in Love there is no controlling or being controlled for that is not adherent in the nature of Love. When you truly Love someone you wish them to be free, as well. It is possible for you to be in positions of leadership and not seek control of any kind, now, for that will be the next step in your leadership and must be so. There is nowhere nor nothing that you can do in which I am not there for I AM Life and you can be nowhere or in no situation where Life is not present.

When you use the White Light, you will travel with Me, and it will seem as though you will return very rested, and you will, but it will not be the sensational process of a hallelujah, as with religion, for that is beautiful but is not traveling with Me. Religion is very personal like problem solving, math, beauty and light. You will be skeptical at first, but in time will find peace for we will grow together.

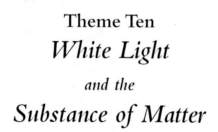

Theme Ten

White Light

and the

Substance of Matter

Theme Ten
White Light
and the
Substance of Matter

"Your perception of everything, ultimately, can be reduced to light."

  May 13, 1981
  1:30 – 2:01 P.M.

As you grow and cross that gap from the World of Fear into the light of God you will find that those things that you cherish most will not be able to describe the light. You have used terms like blinding, for blinding implies that you do not see physically but are still aware that the light is there. In fact, you do see physically and are aware that light has permeated this plane and created the visual images everywhere you look, so that when you see a lovely lake or trees or each other you understand that the light created those images and you have never taken the time to truly question where that light came from. You have accepted at face value the images created but that is illusion. The light, itself, created those images in your mind just as the images of the face of the person you love or people you have loved is created by light. You, in your mind, visualize that individual and are able to recognize him. So it is with touch and other senses, as well, but that is an area that You have never truly explored. You even, in fact, smell utilizing light, and will see this intellectually very soon through the work of the medical world. It will come through their research on lasers, for you will begin to understand that colors give off specific smells as well even though you have never made that assumption.

You will find that your perception of everything ultimately can be reduced to light, both interior and exterior to yourself, both functioning within you and being The Source of what you perceive. Many things will lead the way including the realm of theology and more importantly the realm of psychic phenomena; you will find that it is as easily exploited as is orthodox Christianity; that is, psychic phenomena can involve hoax, or whatever, but you will see that true psychic realities will become more and more verifiable. Individuals who are chosen to relay information through psychic channels will be able to do so, and it will be irrefutable in the more accepted modes of thought. For example, one can predict a hydroelectric surge or whatever and have verifiable proof and it will not be able to be refuted anymore. This book will help initiate that surge of energy and those chosen to convey information will find that they cannot stop that process anymore than could the writers of this book, for even though it was very difficult they could not have gone back to a linear reality this year in any way because they were meant to write this book.

"You must learn the reality of love."

Session #55
May 13, 1981
4:35 – 4:51 P.M.

You all must learn the reality of love for what has been prescribed by orthodox religion involves much more than the churches are willing to give; Love remains, not a power, but a symbol like a cross that is wooden and stands up high in the front of a church and not in the heart and the blood and emotions of the individuals subscribing to that theory and will remain so until you see Me. When you see Me you will have no other choice, and you will make the great leap from the World of Fear and not be afraid of the consequences of that choice for you have ultimately no choice in this matter of Love and growth.

"You will experience the soaring of the spirit that is inherent in your own unlimited spiritual identity."

Session #56
May 14, 1981
7:58 – 8:15 P.M.
8:25 – 8:40 P.M.

As you grow you will understand Life better; you are functioning, still, in this linear plane in a myopia. It is very puzzling to you to see Life begin and end and wonder what goes on before and after that process but as you open up to other planes you will begin to see for yourself, and not necessarily through mediums, that there is no beginning and no ending; only in the function of linear plane can that question ultimately exist. So the question that your poets and your artists and others who at times have envisioned the other planes and utilized them in their poetry and art understand is that there is no beginning and no ending. What seems fearful to you, that is, birth, frequently, and certainly death, you will understand. On just leaving this plane when you can see essentially yourself, before you were born and after you leave this plane, then you will simply be at peace; for you do not fear walking into a building and then leaving that building. It is a visual reality that you are dealing with, a world of fear and illusion, and so all you can see is the moment of appearance and moment of disappearance, nothing beyond that. Therefore, you fear whatever happened before you walked into the building and fear what will happen after you leave the building. You are Life, and were you to have a situation like this you would be able to control others, especially in the field of religion, because these individuals would not know for certain what occurred and therefore would develop many fanciful, interesting theories about this process. It is not as glamorous as they make it into being, and you will find that once that understanding took place, or was there, then you would have fewer suicides and fewer individuals involved in a death wish or whatever and there would be a clearer concept of the present time. You can see this when you connect with your Larger Self, that is, utilizing the White Light which seems like such a simple process and is so immense in nature that you will be able to not even subconsciously understand that process before and after your appearance here. Then, the Earth will seem much more like a school, and you will be able to utilize this classroom much more fully as well, and can separate yourself from the World of Fear because it simply is illusion and functioned to teach as all illusions do in the past, but no longer functions.

You will see that this book has an important function in that area and like meditation or prayer, or whatever will help open up consciousness to alternatives that already exist and always have, although it was not an agreed upon reality and therefore did not occur as such. The permutations and combinations are all there; that is, you would choose many realities, but as we have said, you have chosen this one and agreed upon it. Therefore, [you must] function within it but are not limited to it in any way, nor should you be, for you are Unlimited Spiritual Beings and you select your limitations in order to learn.

You will see that you are capable of seeing events before you were born and after you leave this plane. You have utilized this ability somewhat, and if you choose you can see those things which are in line with your own growth or chosen growth at this point. You can go, for example, into other lives if you have had other lives on this plane, which isn't necessarily so, and that is why reincarnation is not necessarily always accepted because not everyone has been here before. But if you choose to go into other lives [they have something to do with your already present spiritual goals] that will not stop anything that should be taking place, and you can do so. You could also essentially predict lives beyond this planet if you do return to this plane, but you can also perceive lives on other planes. They're not the kind of life in terms of what you are thinking, for you are not taking this body and walking on another plane, lost in this reality. It is an entirely different reality, and there is nothing in your language that will describe it. It is not part of your language, and therefore, again, you are cognizant in your Larger Self of that reality but are not able to articulate what you know. You are still left linguistically within this reality, and that is why other emotions or feelings allow you to understand and still not be able to articulate emotions, that is, the words are not adequate to explain feelings in any way, and so that is another limitation that you have, as a group accepted. When you truly Love someone the only way in which you can express some hint of those feelings is through imagery but certainly not in a noun-verb-noun kind of sequence; you are aware of that, but the feeling goes into several planes and so you can experience but not necessarily articulate it.

That does not mean that it does not exist, just as using the White Light will not mean that it does not exist, nor that it does not have an effect, or meditation or prayer or any of the systems in which you have superseded a linear plane. It does mean that you will have difficulty in articulating what is going on, and you will see that if you multiply that times thousands and thousands you will have some concept of what actually goes on in moments of spiritual oneness. In those moments you are at peace and in your natural state, and can return. It is not limited; it is important that you understand that point as well. You will see that in those moments of spiritual oneness you are alone with God and there is nothing else and that is where power truly exists. It can carry over to experience on this plane or may not, depending on your goals, spirit ward.

Like an eagle soaring you are soaring, spiritually, and that is what happens when you come close to your spiritual goals. It is the same soaring so it is not the same kind of linear reality where you are simply achieving a goal, yawning a little and going on to another one, but it is a moment of shear oneness and ecstasy and must not be confused with linear goals in any way. In this book you can catch glimpses of that soaring, and if you do, then you will have been blessed by reading it for you will ultimately find what you truly need. You are never denied nor could you ever be denied your good in any way. That does not mean you will all be millionaires but it does mean that you will experience the soaring [of the spirit] that is inherent in your own unlimited spiritual identity, for essentially your identity is functioning in that way and you are remaining unlimited and free at all times.

You are the Loved of Love, itself, and must understand that even though you do not seem to understand. It is constant and never changes, so that if You have created an illusion of a negative reality, the true reality is that you are Loved with Me. You can, as We have said, change the script at any time now. You will see that your scientists will be skeptical about this but in time will prove it to be so and when they do your credibility will have increased, with the exception of those who understand already, and when their credibility, that is, the scientific world's credibility, is there and present, then you will begin to give credence to exploration into what is termed the psychic world. But it is and always has been and always will be the spirit. The Indians did not label it psychic reality nor did others of the culture label it psychic reality, but it is being referred to as that in this book. Frequently it was simply referred to as the Great Spirit and it developed from there within the consciousness of every individual involved where they were, as this has always been the case and will always be the case. This book is essentially not being written for those who are not ready, and I must emphasize that you must not feel inadequate because this book is not appealing to you in any way. You must accept your growth where you are, for you must not accept in linear reality, that is, some more spiritual than others, and so forth, which is absurd or you would not all be Life, some more sharing of Life than others and the absolute such as Life and the capacity to Love and so forth are not measurable in any way and never have been and never could be.

"I am not limited in any way and, ultimately, neither are you."

Session #57
May 15, 1981
2:13 – 2:27 P.M.
2:39 – 2:47 P.M.
2:54 P.M. – ?

As you grow you will discover more and more about My nature, and will let those concepts that you had of Me fall away until they are gone, for it is essential that you lose any preconceptions that you have had about the nature of God or even the nature of Love, for the love you can recognize now comes still from a World of Fear so that the concept that you have of Love is intermingled with a sense of possession or loss, fear of loss or transience, or limitation; I am none of these. I am God and you will see that is glory beyond anything that you can know on a linear plane, so that when you try to perceive God on a linear plane it is logical to attempt to try to unlimit your thought within the realm of the linear plane. It is futile because when you are doing this you are finding that you are limiting God, completely, and I am not limited in any way, and ultimately, neither are you. You have only limited yourself to functioning within just this plane. Those who have transcended this plane are those who utilized other planes when they did so, and you will find that you will be able to utilize thousands of planes, ultimately, at once, and when you do this you will begin to understand what God is. You must break away from a personal sense of God, for how could God be a person in any way? It would be impossible for the creator of infinite diversity, ideas and life, and life itself, to ever be personal, but you will discover this not simply by being told the fact in this book, but by, instead, utilizing the White Light and exploring other possibilities. You will find that I AM Unlimited and that what is being said here is only a glimpse of what exists all the time, in any given second. You will only confront one problem, which is, that when you see Me you will not be able to turn back to a personal sense of God, which seems to grant security on this plane. You know within your Larger Self that it is false security, ultimately, and that when you are growing you are secure. When you are not, you are not secure. Therefore, grasp at things and attempt to save what little you have, but that too will slip away unless you are open to larger ideas. You can try to hang on to a simple God-as-person when you have seen Me, but you will know that you are not being honest with your own identity. It is a sense of honesty which supersedes a sense of truthfulness.

If you utilize the White Light you just begin within your Larger Self to make that connection between what is your reality now and what is actually going on. When you begin to make that connection, again, you cannot turn back and say it is not so because it is so.

Many people who have passed the threshold of death and then come back must also say this is so. Even if you are not sure of where it will take you, you must remain open to a larger sense of this reality, for it is as the Bible has stated, scales falling from your eyes, in that the scales are only worlds piled on worlds piled on worlds of belief of what is reality. Those scales fall from your eyes and you see reality like a clear lake on a summer's day, and it is very beautiful. So you will see Me and will be unable to turn back to an area of blind belief, just as if you were to solve a mathematical problem and then say that a solution which functioned was not so. You cannot, for it is only part of your growth, and the truth growth that is taking place is taking place very rapidly within any given second. The reality that you are attempting to deal with is the simplistic reality or that which you have reduced the world to in order to cope with it, but your growth is inevitable. You cannot assume if you reach a certain age you will not grow, for frequently then you grow by quantum bounds at that stage and frequently age is a time of tremendous growth. Senility is frequently a time of intense spiritual growth.

Your language is so difficult, in attempting to pull you kicking and screaming out of a linear reality for you are reluctant to leave it, you will see that even this recording of the book is simply utilizing other planes, as well, with a vision of God. You will let yourself move into other planes and this will lead to growth which will lead to other planes which will then lead to growth which go on to more planes. This will allow the explosive growth that must take place very soon. It is nothing you can ignore, for the time has come to outgrow this single linear plane, and you will have no choice. This plane will become too painful for you, and You will be forced into a position of growth until you see Me. When you do you will then cross a gap from the World of Fear that is the single linear plane into a sense of a greater reality. You will be able to confront your fears because you understand that they were only part of reality. You will not be over-whelmed by them because they are not all there is; you will see that you will grow dramatically at that point. We have said this earlier in the book but it is important to stress the process by which this growth will occur so that you will not fear it and will not assume that you are giving up anything, for you can retain it and hold onto it as long as you wish. If it is growth for you then that is important, but you will have means by which to expand, and you will expand, and will find that within a linear reality growth is graduated. That is, as one grows from child to adult, one grows in conceptual knowledge, for example, from a simple concept of mathematics into calculus or differential equations. Within other planes they are not linear and therefore growth can be explosive or implosive. There are many other ways in which growth can take place and does, which is characteristic of that plane as well.

Again, the ultimate reality is God, and whatever it takes for you to understand that light is the law of your being is whatever you will have, if you wish, that is. If you learn this by fear and learn about Me through a personal sense of God and a fear of damnation, or what-ever, then that is where you will grow. Nothing will curtail that nor would you want it curtailed in any way; or limited; it is not for some-one to say that it is incorrect, generally. There are no rules in any way but if you are at a position in your own consciousness where that is not satisfying, and you know it, intuitively then you will be able to utilize other planes, at that point, by using the White Light. What is available to you is simply available to you only if you choose to utilize it. You can continue as long as you wish with whatever you wish for there is no compulsion to do any given act, for I am always with you, and in any given second that growth is occurring. We are only talking in terms of a simpler reality and following a possible path within the realm of that simpler reality, and again, only if you are ready. But you will see that in order to develop the language, and in order to develop the concepts that will lead to a clear understanding of God as well as scientific or theological or medical breakthroughs, or whatever, you will have to utilize other planes, in time. This is still a very limited concept, and of its nature will continue to be so.

If one were to continue with a total linear reality, one would become more fearful and more violent rather than breaking away from the utilization of those archaic survival systems and then plunge the Life within this realm into what the fundamentalists call Hell. It is a collective movement rather than a single movement; what is essentially salvation is an individual movement as opposed to a collective movement, and there is a great deal of difference there.

"You are, by nature, joyous."

Session #58
  May 15, 1981
  4:22 – 4:40 P.M.
  5:26 – 5:42 P.M.

You will see that as you grow you will find that you enlarge your stature; the physical phenomenon of, for example, increase in height is even correlated to this for there have been ancient peoples who were very tall and very developed spiritually, that is not to say that tall people are developed spiritually, but you will see that evolution is a following of the spiritual development of a given people. Physical characteristics are chosen by individuals before they come to this plane. It would seem absurd for someone, for example, to choose a deformed body before coming to this plane, but they could if it correlates with their spiritual goals. Sometimes they learn compassion or kindness or tolerance or other qualities that they have chosen. You will understand that these are not qualities I choose for I remain God and stable

235

within this realm, but that is a choice of the being involved. This seems like an absurd kind of thing and it is important that the physical body be considered almost not at all, because it, too, is malleable and subject to change. It is truly ultimately unimportant in the larger sense for it is simply not as flexible as other parts of the identity of the individual; in fact it is the least flexible of all of them and therefore remains something that the people choose to pay attention to because it is inflexible and stable. If given a choice of change or stability people as a rule will choose the stability, and the most stable of all would be the physical body. Therefore, the body would be chosen as that to which one pays attention, but the critical part of the individual is the least stable and the most flexible. It is in the present time where the greatest growth occurs and where the individual is in harmony with Me. One is not totally in harmony with God in the physical realm but that is not because there are flaws within the physical realm but because it is too stable for a true relationship with the Divine, Unlimited Mind. As with the written word, and other things, individuals have placed far too much importance on those things as they have also on houses and cars and all the inflexible parts of this chosen, agreed upon reality.

As you grow you will find that you are happier and more joyous within and will not know exactly why but will continue to use the White Light and grow and continue that process, for happiness and joy are similar but not the same. However, that is only a semantical difference, for you are by nature joyous, not a Pollyanna joy but demonstrating the joy one finds in childhood or adulthood when one feels good about oneself or Loved or Loving, kind or free, exploring or helping, or unlimited and it is a boundless kind of joy, what the Bible refers to as the presence of God. You will see that some Biblical references are germane but have been made into institutions rather than into communication, and are unimportant if they are institutions for controlling others and important only if they are meaningful to the individual. Overall it is still a limiting process for one assumes that the work is external, and it is not for it was never to be external and the process of assuming an authority outside of oneself cuts off the enormous amount of communication that is constantly taking place in the present time. I Am in the present and not contained within a book or books or even this book.

The only purpose in this book is to bring you into the realization that I AM Present and you are the Word of God and not a book. You must understand that you are the Word, My Children, for what is your word but conveying an idea, and how better to convey the idea of Life than with Life? Nothing short of Life itself can accomplish that; you must look to the Life that exists within and without and find Me, but not in words transmitted thousands of years ago. They were valid and are beautiful but you are infinitely more critical than they, and you must never be sacrificed for anything external to Life itself. There are no causes that are more important than Life. There are no theories about the nature of God or the universe that are more important than Life itself. There should be no wars over the nature of Life, for you are sacrificing Life for something external and old in the past, not in the present for that which is in the present, and you must understand that God cannot exist anywhere but in the present, just as light does not exist anywhere but in the present. You can remember light or color but the existence of Light is now, and you must find ways of sharing and will find ways of sharing the Light that is present when you experience Me. You could avoid the great pain were you to just do that very simple thing, but it is possible that you will not and that you will find causes and polarities and will hurt life although it is unnecessary and un-god-like, ultimately. But there is an irony there which is that as you seek to destroy or hurt you will find that even there I am in the present and communicating with you and therefore you ultimately do not destroy. You do, however, suffer pain and learn from the pain itself. The destruction creates growth but it still is not necessary for I

AM All there is; there is nothing else on this plane or any other plane, and you will learn that, for as Life you are very young. That concept of being young is truly impossible to understand with this language for young does not refer to a linear sequence in any way, that is, young and getting older. But that does not mean that there is no maturity; it is different from what you perceive but is valid at this point because Life is young and exploring and growing.

It is appropriate that those ideas correlate as you break out completely from the World of Fear or you cannot envision the world without fear and guilt. It is possible, and you will find that you will wonder that you ever lived there; just as if you leave a house you dislike very much and look back and wonder that you ever lived in that particular house but it was only a house and never the substance of your own being. So you will look back at the World of Fear when you have crossed the gap and be amazed that you were ever limited to it. You are so very close to that period in which you will break free, and as I said before, that could seem like pain but does not necessarily have to be.

"As you cross the gap from the World of Fear into the World of Love, you leave limits behind."

Session #59
  May 16, 1981
  4:15 – 4:32 P.M.
  5:45 – 6:00 P.M.

As you grow you will begin to understand that the diversity of Life on this plane is the beginning of a concept that involves diversity in many areas, for you, within yourself, are enormously diverse; that is, parts of your physical being even that which is the simplest part of you is diverse, there is great variety within a single cell of your body. Indeed, there is incredible variety, and of course, there are millions and millions of cells and each has an individuality as well. Life essentially flows into Life so that you assume that you are a total individual separate from the other Life. You are not, however, for like a river you flow together and the log on the water and the fish within the water all flow, but the river remains the river. That is true with you and others and other forms of Life and even Life in the air for you are all part of a flow and cannot detach yourself from that other Life though you have certainly tried. That has been a concept tried, like time, like fear, and is ultimately not possible; nor will you be able to separate yourselves from others in a very short period of time. You are swelling like a river in the spring, and will reach a crescendo, soon.

That which you have labeled a population explosion, and a very negative thing, is not, My Children, for it is only a swelling like a river and may seem destructive as it tears down the valley. Ultimately it also has a positive effect on the Life on this planet and plane. You have assumed that you are alone and Life on the earth is the only Life, and that then you will have to travel to other planets like the earth in order to find Life like man or other Life forms, but that is not so, and in time your scientists and physicists will come together with your theologians and understand that travel does not have to be involved with time and light-years. You will discover that in a very revolutionary way so that your travel can be instant and not limited to the physical reality that you are now dealing with. As you cross the gap from the World of Fear into the World of Love you will leave those limits behind and find that, for example, walking on the water was perfectly natural. You will even find even greater steps to be taken, but it will be like discovering fire for the first time. You will walk cautiously as you begin to understand the power that you will be dealing with. You have no concept of power now, and will find that ultimately the only true power you have is spiritual. That will come neither easily nor right away, for you have assumed that you are power. I Am helpful, at best within the realm of orthodox religion, but you will understand that I Am the only power there is. You are good at setting directions for harnessing, or whatever, but ultimately, I AM God, and there is nothing else.

You can overcome any preconceptions about the beginnings of Life; you will see that people fear it only because they care about it very much, and in a world in which they are living in a very neutral emotional area, this cannot be ignored and will evoke feelings whether people like it or not. You will see that you are with Me in a way when you use the Light, and wake up rested and at peace, for you enter another reality. You will not remember the traveling with Me until you leave the Earth. You will help reassure people that death is not what they have assumed, that is, mere termination of their individuality, for were that so they would never have come to start with. That is such a limited concept and they will be able to travel as Jesus did soon or once they have left the World of Fear, for like Jesus, they will be able to see. That they are not limited, or as you say, mortal, but immortal and unlimited and all a part of God, for that is not as you perceive, the part of. It is not like the cells of the brain making up the brain. That is a very poor analogy only because it is so very limited and relates strictly to a linear plane, again. It is more like retaining individuality and knowing that the substance of their being is God, participating in Life itself, still; but again, your language is so limited in terms of the larger concepts that it attempts to communicate, but you will concentrate on expanding consciousness and those concepts will find words and those words will be gifts from Me as you expand, just as technological ideas are gifts from Me, and just as Life itself, is part of Me. But again, not as you perceive parts. I AM All there is, and when you cross you will find that you will understand without the limitations of the language. As we have said before, the language itself evolved out of a World of Fear and therefore reflects the universal thought or collective consciousness. You will be able to enter planes of consciousness like transportation, and communication will be instant and complete and you will be able to communicate all Love and mind at the same time with nothing held back and no games to be played with darkness or fear or control of others. That is another very difficult cross for you to bear, here, so that the transition that you make into the World of Love may seem difficult but in the long run is very easy compared with having to bear the cross within this realm of pain and hurt, hurting and control, controlling. You will see that you will also be free of the very difficult game of control among male and female for you are truly androgynous; you will still have the same feelings of Love that you have on this plane, but you will not have the harmful games that are played with that feeling on this plane. When you truly Love you are free of that and will be able to enjoy the process and never seek revenge of any kind or create any pain for the other individual but rather communicate clearly and lovingly at the same time, for true communication, like substance involving light, involves Love, and I AM All and that is why. These many other concepts included in this book are concepts that those who have crossed onto the world of Love have understood and attempted to articulate. You must continue with that exploration as well as scientific exploration, all forms of exploration. But you must understand that this is only one plane of existence, now, for you will need to utilize other planes in order to survive the times ahead. You will see that you will utilize them—explosively and implosively—for you will begin to understand God and find words that will relate to God much more clearly for it is voiceless presence, a voice at once recognizable at any given moment as an explosion of Love and feeling, Joy and peace, intelligence and purpose.

Imagery is one of the ways of conveying My nature, but even images are limited for if one utilized the image of sunlight it would give the idea of a different presence. I AM All there is but one would then be limited to sunlight, itself, as a concept of God and that is only within this plane that you are experiencing that sunlight, so that it is sunlight and light, but light is much more multifaceted than you have perceived it to be, so that again, you are perceiving even in your wildest dreams a limited concept of what light is. It is light on this plane, but that is not the only characteristic of light and it is impossible for you, at this point, to understand, for example, a black hole, and to understand that I AM God, and I AM All Present and light, that is light as well, and there is light within light even here that is not the same as what you have been able to utilize. There is light in lasers and that light within the light can be realized much more effectively even than the concept of light you now have. It is hard to communicate, for as I said, on this plane the language is geared toward this plane and so that what you can do is to utilize the White Light and explore for yourself. In time you will develop a language that will include these concepts, as well, but even at that you are still limiting and putting into the past tense the experience you have with Me, and will find that you could never be bored in what was traditionally called heaven for you are like the child learning in a subject area that you have yearned to know about and having all the right teachers and all the right experiences and the great great joy involved in the experience. You, as that child, do not wish to leave that experience for it is so much fun, and it seems like the joy is endless at that moment; and so it is with the world of Love that you are coming into. Your fear is only that because you have extended this linear reality about as far as you can and find it limiting, now, and so like Columbus discovering the new world for western civilization, it opened up vistas and technology and plant life and worlds that had heretofore been unknown and overcame concepts of the world being flat, so that process of entering the world of Love will be the same kind of process, only magnified by thousands. You will be like a kid in a candy store in your joy in exploring.

In your relationship, when you have crossed the gap from the world of Fear into the World of Love, that the kind of fun, like courtships, is joy and natural to you. You can experience it here, and have, but you will not have to worry about the pain of guilt or fear or sorrow that you have to deal with, within this linear, fearful plane. So you will understand from this book that you all will pass into this other dimension, just as you all passed into Life, itself, on this plane; no one will be left out and what the orthodox churches have said was only to control and not to free in that regard. The orthodox churches do much good, but again, like trying to express joy, they are limited because they dwell in the past tense and the quality of joy is in the present.

"When you do experience Me, you will have no doubt."

Session #60
  May 16, 1981
  6:35 – 6:45 P.M.

You can be close to Me in church in the present tense, but must never be controlled by someone, for having experienced that joy, you are at one and constantly with Me, but you fear, for example, earthquakes or volcanoes, weather changes or disasters of hundreds of kinds. Nuclear holocausts will occur, for you feel them and create them as you create the world, itself, from your fear, but even those are only taking the World of Fear to the absurd and are not reality. You must understand that what orthodox religions have referred to as Judgment Day is only the fading of one reality because of the coming of another reality, and not the end of reality itself. You will only accept this in the area of faith until you experience Me. When you do experience Me you will have no doubt because you will understand. Understanding is the foundation of the World of Love.

"In order to accomplish great things, you cannot function out of fear."

Session #61
  May 18, 1981
  2:44 – 2:54 P.M.
  3:25 – 3:38 P.M.
  3:57 – 4:07 P.M.

Using the White Light may seem bizarre to you, yet, but so did the airplane seem bizarre to those who have never flown. Prayer seemed bizarre to those who had never prayed. As you grow you will come closer to Me, and you will find that you will declare an ego but understand that your substance is Life, and Life is universal on all planes. You will never lose your identity, and frequently what is termed a burst of ego to accomplish a given goal is truly not what you assume it to be, that the individual has an enormous ego that must be filled. Only the greatest accomplishments in the world will fill that, for in order to accomplish great things you cannot function out of fear; therefore, the individual frequently functions out of a sense of destiny, purpose, or intuition which tells that individual that is what he or she was meant to do on this plane and has become accustomed to battling with others in order to accomplish that goal. Each will continue to battle in order to accomplish that goal and ultimately will achieve that goal. Therefore, both the resistance to the accomplishment of the goal and the accomplishment of the goal make it look as though that person were accomplishing it out of ego but it is not as it seems, frequently; for example, in the case of Napoleon or other military leaders, there was great resistance to accomplishing given goals, and the methods were wrong but the underlying motive was not, that is unity or good for all or whatever, and it may seem confusing to you, for again, you are dealing with orthodox Christianity which says that the great qualities that the individual should have are meekness and mildness and that which allows one to control another being. But that is not always godlike, for frequently strength and direct purpose and great compassion for all are also godlike. You cannot make that determination for someone else. You must make that for yourself, and you cannot make it based upon the World of Fear because it will not allow you to comprehend what is truly góing on. We will cover this a great deal in the book on Karmic Debt, but you must understand that you are godlike because you are Life. There is not one person who is more godlike than another in any way for you cannot assume that looking into a forest that the tree is more godlike than a buttercup or a blade of grass. You accept the fact that they are Life and beauty of themselves, and you are looking into a forest when you look upon humankind and find Me, and find that your individuality is set and real and beautiful and contributing to the whole and productive and balanced and essentially an ecosystem. You will not interpret it in terms of the World of Fear but must rely on what you know within your Larger Self. You recognize this fact within your own being, so that you will not judge; Jesus taught, 'Judge not,' and that was not telling others not to judge, it was a declaration of what is within a spiritual reality, that is, within a given spiritual reality. There simply is no judgment; not that one should not, for when you Love and are free and happy and growing you have not the time to judge nor to control for you are like a dandelion in the spring and will find that you are not judging, you are simply growing. You must not think in terms of 'ought to' or 'ought not,' nor that there is any power outside yourself, that is, that you are a bad person and someone else is a good person, or that you are a mediocre person that someone else is a great person, for you will understand that you are Life and you are all Life. You are not separate from each other; you are individuals but interlocked as the roots of the tree, and you are growing and loving and free. No matter what happens, this is so; for example, if you read this book and think this is not so, or that I am not free, or that I am very unhappy, then, you will at some point come to the understanding that you are free either on this plane or other planes, or whatever, for that is the imperative behind Life itself which is the reality behind Life in which you are a free spirit, and nothing can disrupt that.

The book is writing this book and is, as you are; nothing changes that, not even falling on your face in all humility before an icon will that ever change for you are Life and if you could alter that which you can't anymore, even by suicide, then you could alter that reality but you cannot. Ultimately, you will come to that understanding that you are Life and therefore infinite Love, power, joy, androgynous and complete and free. No illusion created by you, nor a collective consciousness, nor anyone, can alter that reality.

As you grow, which you are doing always and cannot stop, you will understand your own growth, for growing understands itself by the product as well as the process cannot determine the product but understands the process because the process accomplishes product. Therefore, you are not controlling, for example, and telling your heart to beat, it is simply beating and your spiritual growth is not an academic process but is the critical growth that is taking place. As you grow, spiritually, like the flower growing in a field, you are growing and flowering and completing the cycles that need to be completed but are not necessarily intellectually understanding them. The academic world has attempted to try to understand spiritual growth without God and must find God and spiritual growth and frequently does, for example, in areas of art, poetry, and music. Those are accomplished at one with God, and like the flower in the field, they, simply are. The creative processes in the academic world are frequently the same way, and ultimately they are productive and help people and must not be separated from that which it is helping.

You are able to see that your growth is spiritual, frequently, even in areas of science or physics the joy of learning is the growth of the flower in the field and is a totally spiritual, JOYOUS, complete process for an individual and therefore valid and again productive. Ultimately there is nothing but growth; there can be, for example, no negative criticism of that growth that is incorporated in the growth for it is either growth or it is not growth, and even if it is not growth it is growth like a tree that is topped by a rock, but which will grow around the rock. That, too, occurs. There is nothing that can ultimately stop your growth spirit ward, and were there to be such a thing you would be controlled by it but your spirit is not, even when confronted with a negative experience you will grow around that experience. You cannot be stopped in any way by anything, and if you become part of a very negative spiritual thought you will grow around that, so that you will find that nothing can stop you and God, Life, Love and Spirit for there is nothing else. If you believe in a personal devil you will still grow, for within any given second you are with Me and growing within you Larger Self by leaps and bounds and the articulated personal devil is only a simplified version of an oversimplification that allows you to deal with a difficulty. The reality underlying the entire situation, like the reality underlying your own being, is growth and becomes, ultimately, spiritual growth. Science, mathematics, or other forms of thought may beat the theological world to the draw on this for they will be given credence because of their innocence. Because of their attempted pure thought they will be given credence by others and therefore may come out with those discoveries before the theological world actually does, but it does not matter for everything leads from a World of Fear to freedom and that cannot be stopped, either.

"There is not a child or a life brought forth on this plane, or other planes, that I have not brought forth."

Session #62
  May 18, 1981
  9:12 – 9:15 P.M.
  9:32 – 9:35 P.M.

As you grow, you will begin to comprehend what is being said in this book and within your own understanding; you will learn that the false humility and personality advocated by Christianity must yield to the strong capable individual that you must be in order to survive the times ahead. You will see, like the World of Fear, false humility is no longer applicable, but that does not mean that you are strong or pushy in relation to others in order to prove your individuality. It is just that, within your own being, you will recognize and appreciate the power that exists within each individual. You have assumed that kind of power exists within a nation, for example, but you will find that kind of power exists truly within the individual and the nation is a collection of individuals whose power is disseminated to them but not focused in one place. And so you have a great deal of power, if you have many individuals, but only because they are strong individuals. National power is only reflective of their individual strength. You will see that power must be recognized within each individual in order to make the changes that need to be made, as I have said before, societies change because individuals change, and not vice versa, and when individuals can utilize and recognize their own power then you will find that the social change and whatever is needed will take place because those individuals will understand that they are all that there is to them-selves, ultimately, and they are at one with Me. There is not a child or a life brought forth on this plane or other planes that I have not brought forth. You cannot comprehend the power of Light but will begin to understand it more and more, for it is the ultimate frontier for you at this time. That is why some, for example, are so attracted to lasers, because they are free spirits, intellectually, and understand this. You will see that power is not even what you have assumed, but it will be something that you will adjust to very easily, for when you understand that the deductive worlds that you have utilized as a foundation for your current collective consciousness are limited, then you will begin to see that you are truly unlimited and, as I have said, very, very good.

"You are all My children, and you were not meant to control each other."

Session #63, part 1 of 2
   May 19, 1981
   2:23 – 2:25 P.M.
   2:38 – 2:50 P.M.
   3:15 – 3:35 P.M.

As you go on you will find that your life will blend well harmoniously with the river of Life around you; you cannot be an island released in the stream of Life itself, but can retain your individuality, so that like a tree growing in the forest you blossom and retain your individuality and have all you need but do not hurt that around you. You can see trees, for example competing for sunlight and it seems very cruel but there is much more than what you see there occurring. That is a separate reality, for plants are a different kind of life from animal life, and evolve completely differently and for different reasons. Jesus used the analogy of the lilies of the field because they are very close to Me, and are peaceful, for My nature is peaceful but also is action. This would only be confusing to go into that except to say that, at this point in your spiritual development you are able to still eat vegetable life and to harm that Life but you must not eat animals, not only for your own health at this point, and the sharing of food with others on this plane, but for the well-being of the animals, themselves. You will come out with the argument that those animals are here only because they will provide food, for example cows and pigs, and so forth, but that is not so, for they are here because it was necessary for them to be here and to learn from that Life form that they encountered, but that is no longer necessary, for that is over with, as well, and you will see that in time you will come to that understanding that you will not eat animals nor harm any living animal on this plane. It is important for you to learn this lesson, but you will learn it gradually, and you will find that other reasons will come up for the change that will take place and will seem perfectly rational in a linear sense, that is an economic sense, so that you will not eat beef because it will become more and more expensive. You will turn to alternative protein which will be vegetable, but it will seem that economics is the reason. You can accept it, but the real reason is that learning what needed to be done in that area has been done and it is simply no longer necessary, as a general rule. In the next hundred years you will see that type of learning will almost completely vanish from the experience that you have here, but as with everything else you must not force it, for that which is inevitable will occur and you cannot change that. If you were to go out and fight to retain beef as the mainstay of the diet of humankind you would lose that battle for you will see that the alternatives will be more appealing; you cannot stop that tide from occurring any more than you could stop spring by being determined to go out and kill everything growing in spring. You will see that you will understand this by degrees, and in time, and like the lumberjack will not force it into being but will find the appeal there, nonetheless.

Abortion is an appealing thought because it is right that individuals not be controlled and women have been controlled by the process of their being able to have babies, but that is not necessary anymore, and you must not take the life of a child once the child is conceived. It is a difficult, difficult concept for many, for the person that is here is loved very much, and those around that individual wish to protect and help that individual. You will see that there are alternatives, and if the child is truly not meant to come that child will not come, and the problem that exists is not in the abortion but in the control of women. You are all My Children, and you were not meant to control each other; one sex was not meant to dominate the other, but you were to be as deer in the forest, free spirits, growing and ultimately much more beautiful and joyous than the deer.

You must not control others, and they must make their own decisions, but you must understand that Life in all forms, animal and all forms, is sacred. It is sacred in that it is sharing Life and expressing God. It is not a rule, but like the lumberjack or the individual who decides to be a vegetarian, it will become more and more an accepted reality and never forced on anyone, for you will find, given love and freedom, the individual will make the most loving and free choice. If the individual is confronting an abortion, social pressure and other irrelevant kinds of considerations should not affect that decision, and that person should not be forced into anything, one way or the other, that she does not feel that she is essentially flowing with. When you have contrived situations and hatred and controlling, then you come into the kinds of situations that are confronted when one confronts an abortion, that is, rape or hurt done, or the lack of the information that is needed to make a valid decision. This type of thing affects the abortion, not the heart of the individual, for within the individuals Larger Self they are very close to Me and would never hurt anyone. We will see that were you not to have traditional religion and a false sense of morality that would know you are My Children, and you would decide those single most loving courses and thereby grow from every experience. You will do this inevitably, now, anyway, for as a people you will become amazingly compassionate, independent, and free;

but you will not force it into being for, like the rose, in forcing the petals open you will kill the rose. I am only discussing this because it will happen, and I am attempting to describe to you why you are still looking at the bud, for you are so beautiful and will grow so beautifully now.

Theme Eleven
Love

Theme Eleven
Love

"There are no words on this conscious linear plane that can describe the White Light."

Session #63, part 2 of 2, Special
May 19, 1981

As you grow you will find that your life and eternal Life and universal Life will become one; the separation of Life is the ultimate illusion, for how can you be separated from Life since I AM Life, among other things, that you are cognizant of on this linear plane, for again your language cannot express more functions within your experience. It is like a plant explaining the function to the water going through its being. It cannot explain it, it simply lives it, needs it, cannot survive without it so you cannot survive without God. You do not even have to explain it for the plant does not explain nor does its being depend on the plant's ability to articulate and worship the water that nourishes it. It is and so am I.

You will find that Love is as much a part of you as the water within every cell of the plant, and so do I exist within every cell of your being, as well, and plants are not peripheral to that being in any way like the children who die without Love you would not survive. It is not the love that you have simplified, that is physical love the body or one's mate or the love of parents or friends, for that is a very positive force in your Life. We speak of the Love that is constantly there and is there in great abundance like the fruit on a tree is in abundance. In any given second that Love is the air you breathe and your very existence. Love and light are very similar in quality, though one is more obvious in quantity than is Love, so that when you Love someone it is as natural to you as a plant giving off moisture or oxygen into the air. It is natural, and you learn Love on this plane because a plant learns essentially wateriness, and as I have said, does not need to be gushy in order to express its wateriness, but exists and so by your very existence, it is a natural state. You also express Love, for you will learn much of the writings of Jesus were true but were never meant to be worshipped the way they are worshipped, and were never meant to be used to control anybody in any way, which is what you are dealing with now. You will see that I AM Love and I AM All that ultimately is, and if you were to attempt to get rid of the nucleus of every cell of your body you could not, so you cannot attempt to rid your essential being of the presence of God. You must never ever control anyone with pain or ever control anyone with the threat of taking away God from their lives for it is not possible. You cannot destroy The Source, you cannot tramp out God and Love from the Life of any individual or any being on this or any other plane. You will see that the attempt to control others by their understanding of God is the greatest tyranny of all to emerge from the World of Fear. It will not last, and you will come to the understanding that Love is the only power there is, and you will rejoice within your souls, for you cannot ignore true religion, not with myopia that comes from an uninspired plot somewhere along the line, anymore than you could deny your own breath, bodily functions, or exuberance and Love.

"It can never be used for anything but good."

Session #64
   May 20, 1981
   3:23 – 3:40 P.M.
   3:58 – 4:05 P.M.
   4:05 – 4:18 P.M.

You will see that it is possible to understand many of the problems that you are dealing with and therefore you are able to deal with them in a most positive way. You will see that is not the only possibility and the greater possibilities lie in the area of the White Light and God, My Children, for you will doubt the effect of it but not for long, neither will mankind doubt it, so, for it is like a coiled radio channel or Jacob's ladder, circumventing many of the peripheral systems or concepts, that one is alone with God, all of which are important, but the White Light is the most direct method that you have had. When proved, over a period of time, it will become as acceptable as breakfast cereal or whatever is common to everyday life. At that point the growth will be implosive and explosive at once. You will see at first there will be resistance to it for it will seem foolish, but you will begin to understand that it involves something more than just going to sleep and waking up and feeling at peace or even the process of experiencing alpha waves. It is much more, for in fact, You are traveling with Me at that point, and it is a joyous process. However, it is not a conscious linear process and therefore is like discussing discovering something on another plane. There are no words on this plane to deal with it, and therefore one cannot describe it. So it is with the White Light, there are no words on this conscious linear plane that describe it, so it cannot be given credence in a verbal reality until words emerge. The closest verbiage that can be given it is, 'being lifted up;' it has been used in Biblical times, for example, the phrase, 'If I be lifted up, I will draw all men unto Me.' Throughout true spiritual literature one encounters the same concept, but that hardly describes the experience. It is not a complex process, at all, nor does it involve joining a church or controlling or being controlled by others, paying money or paying a tithe or committing oneself and one's children to a given system that is no longer applicable, so that it will meet resistance initially, but not in the long run, for it involves no effort on the individual's part nor loss of time and nothing except a positive direction in one's life and a drawing closer to God in all ways. It cannot be cornered nor limited in any way; it can only help. It can never be used for anything but good by any one, and would be ineffective if there were anything but good as a result. It will not be acceptable, initially, but breaking out of a World of Fear like spring bursting out everywhere, it cannot be stopped. Like the airplane, once the idea was there it remained and there are those who would claim it or stop it or use it or whatever, but it remained, and as with all ideas, it is indestructible, like the concept of a chair, it is ultimately indestructible and will be indestructible and will have the effect that is needed at this time.

"Using the White Light is a unique process."

Session #65
May 20, 1981
8:36 – 8:55 P.M.
8:55 – 9:00 P.M.

You will see that using the White Light is a unique process in some ways but will become more common as time goes on and individuals are able to use the White Light for the 'White Light' is a very narrow term for a very, very, very broad subject, and it is hard for you to imagine the breadth of that experience in your terms, My Children, and, therefore, only because of language difficulties, not because of conceptual difficulties will it meet with some resistance initially, but when there is the necessity, the language develops. As other things evolve, so does language evolve spiritually first, My Children.

"The more you utilize the White Light, the more you will leave the World of Fear."

Session #66, part 1 of 2
May 21, 1981
1:55 – 2:20 P.M.
2:25 – 2:47 P.M.

Using the White Light is an easy process; it does not take months of preparation for you will see as will others who are willing will see, that I AM God, and I AM the substance of their being so that they do not socially come into a position where they find Me, for I AM a part of the nucleus of every cell in their bodies, every thought and breath, and I AM their very Life. You will see that it is not a question of coming into an intellectual, linear understanding of God in order to overcome fears or indecision or anything else.

That is probably the greatest disservice that orthodox churches have done to individuals, for I am easy and natural, and their very breath, and even closer, in this book we have talked about that within any given second in thousands of ways you are communicating with God and so there is nothing outside yourself that is God, and you are at one and at peace with Me. And when you are at one and at peace with Me there, truly in reality, nothing is controlling you but illusion and that is simply an illusion that you are not at one with Me, for you could no more be separated from God than you could be separated from the water within your body or the thoughts you think or the air you breathe for I AM much, much more than even that to you. You will find as we have said, that when you have a problem you have oversimplified, and find few solutions because you have simplified the problem and solutions to the point where you have reduced the problem to almost nothing, that within any given second you are solving problems with thousands of solutions for every given problem and are not necessarily conscious of that process. But you will be, and you will find that the more you utilize the White Light the more you will leave the World of Fear and simplicity and find the power that is resident within you now. That is, the coming of the Lord, not in the form of a simple person but within your own consciousness, and within your external experience, because, like the salvation of mankind your salvation occurs within and is not a social process in any way for We are one and you are already saved, and will never need to be saved again, but are already at one and at peace with Me. When you use the White Light and begin to comprehend your own nature you will truly understand how I created you in My image, and no church, or no one else's statements nor anything can keep you from that understanding once you have seen that vision. It will be difficult for churches to deal with this, but they ultimately will rejoice in their own freedom from the restrictions that they have placed upon themselves, and the illusions that they have created. You must choose between joy and sorrow and in this experience, which is illusionary, you still must make that choice and will do so. You will find that the more you utilize the Light of God, the more you will find, in your own experience, that the White Light is different from prayer in that rather than attempting to go somewhere, you already are there. Those who have crossed the border from the World of Fear into My Light never prayed by petition but understood and walked with Me. You will see that they were able to heal and help and teach because of that, not because they were good petitioners. That too, is valid, and is important in that if that is where you are then you should use it and love it and be close to Me, for as I have said, I am never away from any of you for you are all saved and you are all My Beloved Children.

Again, if anything in this book offends you in any way you must put the book down and follow your own best leanings or that which you truly feel, for there is no authority greater than you, anywhere, for your concept individuality, and you are not, as we have said, to become all the same. You are to continue with your individuality, that is, unlimited variety. Even within your own self there is unlimited variety and within each individual is an unlimited emphasis and variety as well. Just as I AM Infinite, so is your concept of Me infinite, and therefore your individuality is infinite. On this linear plane into which you have come, and which you will leave, you will be able to utilize, still, the collective consciousness, so that you do not wind up on the funny farm, or whatever. You will still be able to utilize the White Light just as you have utilized prayer, and just as you have utilized Love. Within the collective consciousness you will be able to utilize the White Light and find the problems that you encounter solving themselves. It will not harm anyone in any way and will not need time for you to become skilled at it, for you never needed time to come at a state of understanding of Me, for we are one. There is no one who knows more about God than anyone else, anymore than you could lose your own identity.

There are no good and bad people, for you are all My Beloved Children and have never been separated from Me. You will see that, for example, the story of Adam has been used to control people and take them to churches, a monetary gain as well as other purposes, none of which were initially malicious motives but ended up in a tyranny against humankind. But you are not Adam, you are My Creation and My Beloved Sons and Daughters, and will never change. You cannot become something that is outside everything. You will see that you are complete and infinite as well, when you use the White Light and begin to understand who you are and what your purpose here is for. You have purposes, and you will see them, not verbally, but intuitively, you will know what your purpose is to be.

"My Children, you are everything you choose to be."

Session #66, part 2 of 2
May 21, 1981

My Children, you will see that you are interesting, varied, wise and devout, good and bad, and everything you choose to be; that is part of your own reality within the reality of the collective consciousness and within the illusion, within the illusion, within the illusion. But when you wish to change the script that is the illusions, you can do so and the White Light, prayer, joy, and love will help you change illusions around to your liking. The reality is the Light and God and your own greatness, for you are all the Children of God, and nothing less than that can possibly describe you. You will see that just as you are bearing the cross of knowing but verbally will be unable to express that knowing, so are you bearing the cross of your own illusions.

"The elementary law is that of survival, and that survival is a spiritual survival."

Session #67
    May 22, 1981
    1:25 – 1:57 P.M.
    2:20 – 2:35 P.M.

You will learn that what is right and wrong is not what has been assumed for what is right and what hurts another is determined by the heart and is not an intellectual process. Therefore the World of Rules does not apply for that has evolved from an intellectual process, and from rabbis and priests and those who are removed from the law of Life and who must shift its emphasis back to Life itself, for the intellectual process has been valid and has been a survival system, but it is no longer applicable and will only harm those who cannot remove themselves from the law of Life itself, so that the rules that have evolved are no longer applicable and will shift. Like the other rules that we have discussed, for example, vegetarianism or not making one's living by killing Life, those rules will evolve although this will not occur overnight, so you will not overnight destroy the ten commandments, or the canons of churches. You will see that it is like preparing for what orthodox religions in the World of Fear have called Judgment Day, and you will find that they will change, gradually, and that individuals who will use the White Light will blossom spiritually, and will slowly change those canons so that people will still be able to retain their stability and their joy in that stability. Many will find that the need for stability is greater than the need for growth, but they will be able to retain their stability and still grow. I AM God and My methods are not methods of revolution but evolution, always have been and always will be, for I understand My Children, and love them, as I have said, even when one commits a killing of another Life I am there. There is no time and no circumstance in which I am not there just as

263

there is no circumstance in which water is not present inside a plant while that plant expresses Life. Even when that plant is waterless, apparently, it is not so; that, too, will be found out to be illusion. The reality is that at no time, under no circumstances, no matter what the individual does, they express Life and I AM there. You will see that canons of churches are frequently the results of a great deal of frustration and fear that I was not there. There was an assumption that there was not an extraordinarily loving being in the center and circumference of its own being, and those canons allowed the individual to believe that they could be further and further from God. Like the circles on a pond, you cannot be removed from the totality of the pond for the pond is there and the circles are only dancing on the surface of the substance of the pond.

As you grow you will also become more familiar with the rules of Life itself, and less familiar with the canons of any given church. Like the laws of the jungle in Kipling's writings, they are ultimately good and not as fearful as the World of Fear would allow them to be for they were necessary for survival and not actually canons of churches. One of the serious problems that exists in that area is that one can follow the canons of a given church and not survive, and therefore what is the use of that canon? The elementary law is that of survival, and as this book has indicated, that survival is a spiritual survival, and then ultimately a physical survival, but the two are linked to each other and not removed from each other so that one does not sacrifice one's life for a cause but gives one's life to a spiritually ordained cause. There is a great deal of difference in that area, for you will see that they must work together, and Life must permeate and circumscribe all religious laws, and they are, in fact, as you will see, becoming totally individual in the long run. Leaving the security of the religious sects will not be an abrupt change for you, for that would be too difficult at this stage in your evolution, and so you will evolve, joyously, out of the religion into your understanding of God and back to your right thinking of an individual idea of a beautiful infinite God of your understanding and ultimately your individuality. Each step along the way has served its purpose. You will not need organized religion, and priests will not need organized religion, and churches will not need organized religions for this will occur quickly, in terms of relative time, that is, historical linear time, but it will not occur too quickly for the individuals involved. They will all understand as it occurs and are beginning to see the intimations of it already, My Children, and will find that it is never a hurtful move; that is, no one, not one individual need be hurt along the way, in any way, even to the point where they are afraid because they might have to relinquish that which is important to them, namely, their church association. No one will be put into that position, but like all evolution it will occur and there will be joy leading the way like the White Light in great, peaceful direction, never warlike. Ultimately changes that occur, that is, spiritual revolution, do not occur with wars or revolution or earthquake or fire or any of those things, but is a constant and as we have said in this book, within any given second there are thousands of events that are essentially your interaction with God which, in fact, creates those large changes. The important factor is not the larger changes but the seconds with God that occur, always, for as there is not a moment or a second in which you can be separate from Life itself, even with which you term death, there is not a second when you are not at one with Life, growing, learning, and completing those tasks that are to be completed. You are always in the act of completing, never having done it, and the moment you achieve a goal is the moment, with thousands of events taking place, in which the next goal is opening at that second. You are making decisions and growing, repeatedly, and will never cease from that activity for that is the nature of Life, itself. You will see that this book is introductory and we will get into more specific concepts in other books as well, but you will see that the tenor of the writing is set and that essentially this book was written long before Patricia or

Barbara or any of the principles involved ever came to this plane, and that it is coming through and not out of the consciousness of Patricia. You will find that these occurrences will happen more frequently but this is a central channel and will continue to be so. If you enjoy the book then it is valid; if you do not, it is invalid. As we have said before, it should never be discussed in any kind of a group discussion or any kind of a social interaction for it was only meant to be catalytic if you are ready, and not catalytic if you are not. If it offends in any way you should throw it away and go on with that which gives you peace and great joy. I AM All Presence and everywhere; you must assume that you are the central authority and nothing else.

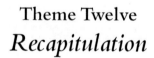

Theme Twelve
Recapitulation

Theme Twelve
Recapitulation

"By increasing your understanding of God, you will increase your understanding of every area that is dealing with 'the truth.'"

Session #68
  May 22, 1981
  6:05 – 7:12 P.M.

You will grow from where you are just as a blade of grass grows from where it is. It does not attempt to be a tree or a buttercup or a dandelion but retains its individuality. Those who are ready to enter the forest and leave the lawn will come, and those that wish to remain with the lawn and be trimmed will remain there, as well, My Children. The only advantage of the forest is that it is a complete ecosystem. As you grow, your concept of Me will not change for that is your individuality, but your concept will enlarge and expand in thousands of different directions and will be universal, ultimately. You will let that occur for you will not will it into being, but rather let it grow like you let your body grow when you were a child. You will help others not to interfere with your growth and you will not interfere with theirs for it will be unusual if you were all in the same place at the same time under the same circumstances. The odds against that happening are astronomical, so that what you share is where you have been and where you are, now, but only in those areas of agreement. The areas of disagreement are areas of your own individuality and creativity. Even though it is difficult, you must let others be where they are and not force them into where you are, for that is not their individuality nor should it be. You are diverse in thousands of ways and must accept your diversity and learn from each other where you need to grow and where you select to grow, so that if you are not in agreement with someone you may choose to listen to them, but you have a second choice which is whether or not to change your ideas to agree with theirs and not to force others on this or other planes for they cannot force you to change what you truly believe. It is one of the strongest forces that exist, the force of your own value systems. You cannot make a cheetah become an antelope, nor would you want to, for each has its individuality and a given role to play in the entire ecosystem, so you do as well, and all you need is to be close to Me and appreciate the diversity.

As you grow you begin to understand that you are completely and ultimately androgynous, but until then you will need to complete these goals you have set for yourself on this plane, and those goals will be a continuous process. Ultimately, they will be seen to be an illusion within an illusion within an illusion that you are anything but complete and androgynous. These illusions are your choices, and you will find that you can use the White Light or prayer or altered states of consciousness, for example, dreams or meditation or whatever will come, as well and alter to some degree the illusions and the path that you have set for yourself within those illusions or collective consciousness. If you truly wish to change some of the concepts on this plane you can develop words which will increase your understanding. That is why you have developed words in the area of technology and therefore you better understand technology and perceptively you grow in the area of technology. Therefore, you understand technology better and therefore you increase the number of words that you can use, and so forth, and some of your growth in the area of technology is due to an increased verbiage that you can deal with. The reality, like mathematics, has always been there and will always be there and you will only increase your understanding of what exists already. So it is with the area of God, or as we have said, you have been in what is essentially the Dark Ages in the area of theology, and you will develop words which will increase your understanding of what is meant by God, and thus increase your understanding and so forth as you do so. All these other areas will develop as well. By increasing your understanding of God, you will then increase your understanding of science, mathematics and your understanding of every area that is dealing with 'the truth.' It is very important that you continue this process now, for the area of psychic research is helping to expand that understanding and will continue to do so. Particularly books, dealing with the bases of understanding, this book and others that will come, will help with the seed planting that is necessary to increase the vocabulary which was a necessary adjunct to increase the understanding which will then lead to these other areas of discovery. The net result of this understanding is not an intellectual game for those who have nothing else to do, but rather, it is a true survival skill. Ultimately, your survival, that is your spiritual survival, leads to evolution which physically leads to greater expansion which leads to evolution, and you will essentially be going off into an infinite variety of tangents, were not survival itself the directive for Life, My Children. Survival has always been a focus for Life and will always continue to be.

That which leads to survival allows survival which in turn leads to survival; that which is superfluous will be left behind, an interesting idea but not godlike, ultimately, for survival and Life are close to each other and are necessary. Essentially, survival is God's unerring direction.

The universal laws that are at work within you are truly all that is working. There are laws which govern your behavior, but universal laws govern your spiritual growth and were you to trade behavior for the spiritual growth, you would not survive, My Children, and you are aware of this. Life is the law of your being and nothing short of Life will satisfy the deeper yearnings within, so that if behavior is correct and survival is at stake, you must choose survival.

"Ultimately, your career is God: working out your relationship with God and growth."

Session #69
  May 23, 1981
  4:02 – 4:20 P.M.
  4:28 – 4:40 P.M.

Your instincts are your best guide, My Children, so that which you know instinctively is that way which you should follow.

You will see that Jesus never worked out anyone's salvation, for He understood, as all who have seen Me have understood, that you can never do anything for anyone else, nor should you control them and push them into anything that they are not ready for. They must do it by their own time-line and calendar, neither of which is yours. If one is to respect individuality, one must respect individuality in its largest sense; that is, the soul and that individuality which is the individual's understanding of Me, within their Larger Self their understanding of Me, and that is not your understanding, nor is their development the same as yours in any way, for that would not allow for the kind of diversity that exists in an infinite God. Were you to clone each other you would not have infinite good, you would have good, but not infinite good, nor would you have the kind of growth that is real and measurable, for were you allowed to grow the same and in the same way you would not grow at all. You would be repeating the growth that has occurred over and over. Therefore, you would not find the variety that stimulates greater and greater growth, My Children.

You will see that variety is what is characteristic of God and you will be at ease with it when you find Me. Use the White Light. You will not be comfortable with the concept of the White Light, initially, for it will seem too simple and is not based on that which you have experienced in the past, generally. It is not therefore as secure or comfortable as church going or the sacrifice known as morality or canons of groups and individual recorded revelations for many. Really, all of you have had revelations with regard to Me, but those which became churches were those which were recorded or proselytized or taught or transferred. But the revelation of God occurs constantly and is endless and boundless in any given second, My Children, and like creativity when it creates a painting, there are really within that individual thousands of paintings, but reality has been simplified to one painting, and therefore, that which continues to be accepted is that painting, but, in truth, the paintings are truly endless and were one able to record all of them, all would be beyond comprehension in painting, religion, music, and life, but we are attempting to deal with simplicity and so are limited. Understand that within your Larger Self you are prolific, My Children, and for every book that is published or painting that is painted, or piece of music that is written there is, underneath, the soul or Larger Self that is in itself, the soul of painting, publishing, writing, understanding, all that and much, much more.

You all recognize this, and whether or not you verbalize it, it is a reality. Your ability to appreciate music, or whatever, is because of your endless being and not because of an interaction of protoplasm or whatever science has determined that you are at this point, and the fact that in science you can expand your concept of the individual only proves that concept is endless.

In the field of science you find a variety of provable theories and will continue, ad infinitum, to find a variety of provable theories for they are all true about the individual. They only reflect current theories, that is, only reflect the necessity of the times and the state of spiritual evolution that is occurring, but even the concept of evolution proves an infinite variety underlying the reality of Life.

As you grow you will find more and more freedom to choose within your lives for as you allow reality its own complexity you will find more choices and more variety, so that if you think that the most important decision is a single decision and your entire Life depends on it, it is only indicative of the fact that you have reduced Life Itself to very simple terms. You therefore are capable of backing up and allowing that which is real, in other words, complexity, to occur. Then you will feel happier and more comfortable with several choices, none of which is the ultimate choice so that you cannot make mistakes in your Life that are irreversible, because for every problem there are massive numbers of solutions, far beyond your comprehension, all of which can work out, and you will see that I am always there. Should you go down one path you will find that I am there, and if you should choose 10 paths you will see that I am there, so the concept that you have a career, a marriage, a solution, or an anything, is a limited concept. When you find the right mate you can have a marriage, and when you are in work that allows you the kind of variety that is needed for your soul, then you can have a career.

Ultimately, your career is God: working out your relationship with God and growth. You have been buffaloed into an unreality by those who would control by assuming that there is a career for you that will bring in the amount of supply that you need, for that is only part of a slavery that is no longer functional. You will find joy occurs with God, not in a monastery, or assuming whatever you have, for if you have understood the book you will understand that joy is in infinite God, and supply is there as is doing good for others, and most importantly, doing good for yourself is there. The learning of Love and the learning of learning is all within that realm, and there is no fear, only constant discovery and creativity; if that is typing then typing is that constant discovery and creativity for you, or sweeping floors, creating movies, or whatever you do. You will find that for you that which is best is a process of constant discovery and joy and is a part of the larger ecosystem. But it is larger than that, for just as in nature there are niches, so spiritually there are diversities. The net result is harmony.

"Use the White Light and begin to see."

Session #70
 May 24, 1981
 7:25 – 7:35 P.M.
 7:46 – 7:56 P.M.

As you grow you will find that your Life is truly unique, it was meant to be as it is, that is, your individuality is meant to be as it is, and the script you have chosen is one that will benefit you in the long run, spiritually. Within that context you can choose a simpler route for your learning, and that is one of the purposes of this book, for you to find that you have alternatives within the context of your life so that when we get into the book on Karmic Debt you will better understand this. With a karmic debt you still have the option of a peaceful, loving solution rather than a fearful, painful solution to any given debt. Even when having murdered or severely hurt another individual you still have the option of a peaceful loving solution and will find that, ultimately, those solutions will be the most effective and the most productive in your lives. When you leave the World of Fear in which there is an archaic survival system, that is, a spiritual survival system, the old guard sin/repentance/punishment business is all part of a very old survival system spiritually, but is not the only alternative and is the least effective of the alternatives, ultimately. That is one of the reasons for the end of that system, for it is simply not that effective and is too painful and unnecessarily inefficient for learning. Since the objective is learning and not masochism or sadism, truly, you will welcome the alternatives available. At this stage in your development you can use the White Light and begin to see; that will lead to others seeing and knowing, which will lead to others seeing and knowing, and, ultimately, to the release of the burdens that you bear now. Life does not necessarily have to involve any burdens. All will rejoice in what has been termed the second coming of the Lord, which is simply the release from an archaic system. You will see that it will not be the personal messianic experience but a glorious release, and to be near Jerusalem will be a joy not because there is an exclusive group that will have joy, but joy will be natural and not artificial in any way. This is only because of the understanding of the Love, and the learning and the power and all those things that have created joy, anyway, even in the World of Fear.

It is difficult to imagine what is being said except that in the present time you understand what it is like not to carry a heavy weight anymore, mentally, and will be able to see that is the case, and you will not need the archaic survival system anymore. You will be free, so free that you will not recall it, either.

There is no utopia, My Children, but there is only the reality of the Larger Being and, again, within the Larger Being exists Utopia. But not on the earth as you now perceive the earth; that which has been is now and that which could possibly be is now and there is nothing else.

"We will not be apart, nor have we ever been apart."

Session #71
  May 25, 1981
  9:17 – 9:25 P.M.
  9:35 – 9:45 P.M.

As you grow you will find that you will expand, and as you expand you will find that you are much more complex than you seem for as with problem solving, when you assume that you only have one solution, in order to solve a problem you need to expand into more than one solution. Any living being is singular in dimension; they must expand their concept of themselves to understand that they are complex beyond any imagination they can exercise. You are all complex and when you assume that you can define another individual or Life form, such as a tree, then you are misguided because that being is as complex as the concept of Life itself. You will see that your consciousness is an atom in the Earth in terms of your higher consciousness, much less the consciousness of other Life forms. This does not mean that your consciousness is not valid, for it truly is, just as a grain of sand can represent a beach because it has the qualities of the beach but it is not as expansive as the beach. So, you in your present consciousness are not as expansive as your true consciousness is.

In judging others you will see that your concept of them, no matter how loving, broad, or complex on this level and linear plane, cannot comprehend their greatness. The only lesson that is involved, here, is for you to let others solve problems themselves and not try to

277

control them. When you release them into their own being you will see that they will find solutions that you could never have thought of at this point, yourself. You can't even see them and recognize them as capable of thinking, themselves. The primary goal is to constantly expand. Love is one of the experiences you have on this plane where you expand infinitely, immediately, and completely at that moment that you feel that affection or Love for whatever form another Life takes, such as our cat, or another individual or yourself. One of the Biblical lessons is to Love your neighbor as yourself. You truly will learn to Love yourself when you utilize the White Light, and you will no longer fear being controlled by others, nor will you suffer Christian condemnation of the ego for that is an extremely archaic and exceptionally limited concept. The condemnation of the ego does not exist as an idea and that the ego, even as a concept, cannot be expanded into an infinity but the concept that you are dealing with now, within, your language is not sufficient to deal with it. Again, ego is used in a negative way in order to control others, so that it is improper to have a healthy assertive ego when it is expansive frequently for the individual to do so. The individual is aware of that as well. It is not an ego that is controlling, nor being controlled, but it is Life and a part of its vitality. You are a massive being, and when you express egotism, frequently you are simply expressing your understanding of your own greatness and the consequent greatness of others. You, and they, and those within their circumference all expand and do not fall into the trap of limiting innate potentials.

You will see this when you see Me, and still must not rely on the words of another, for again, the verbal reality is a part of the linear reality. It can help plant the seed, but ultimately the experience will lead you to where you need to go. When you see Me you will know. We will not be apart, nor have we ever been apart, and you will see, again, that the verbal reality is only being used to help plant the seed, and for no other reason. You have given credence to verbal realities, but that is not the spiritual experience or the expansive experience that will occur when you utilize the White Light. In time you will understand how many planes have opened up, although you did not recognize them at the time. In time you will be ecstatically happy and glad that you stayed with your own consciousness of what is being said here, for it is valid and of God, whatever you perceive God to be. I AM Unlimited and you will find that the language will produce the imagery that will help you to understand that I can be unlimited, and ultimately, so are you, My Beloved Children.

"As you leave the World of Fear, you emerge into the World of Power."

Session #72
    May 26, 1981
    1:12 – 1:20 P.M.
    1:27 – 1:35 P.M.

You will become more and more familiar with other possibilities than those you are encountering now, and will feel freer with exploration. Just as you are beginning to feel freer with psychic exploration, so beyond this you will discover other avenues of exploration and begin to utilize them. As you leave the World of Fear and emerge into the World of Power and Love you will find that there will be less and less reaction after the initial blow, the pit or chasm that you will cross. After you are through, then you will find that there will be less and less reaction to alternative exploration, and that you will not be encumbered by the fear that has stopped so much growth in your history on this plane. But even that history will be looked upon as a linear history, interesting, but not absorbing, for you will not be afraid of alternatives to a linear history, nor will you assume that the collective consciousness is all there is. Therefore, you will not be limited by it nor by the thoughts that you learn from history. History is an intriguing study but it is not where learning ultimately takes place; true spiritual learning takes place in a one-to-one relationship with Me, and that which is assumed to have been learned from the study of history is that there are linear realities and consequences to linear reactions, and so forth, and so you have learned and learned, and essentially overlearned those principles. At this point they are limiting you, as well, for there is no allowance made for the explosive learning that has taken place, even on a linear plane. You seem to wish to explain rationally those explosive experiences, for example, Jesus, how can you explain the advent and effect of Jesus, or the effect of singular individuals such as Alexander in historical context? What you find is that those events have a reality of their own and are not sequential, linear kinds of progressions and cannot even be viewed that way. Discoveries go into that category of the unexplainable in terms of a sequential, deductive reality, and certainly spiritual awareness falls into that category for individuals. It is not a rational linear sequence that leads to spiritual enlightenment and never has been. As you grow these things will seem obvious to you, the responses will vary, but they will become more and more apparent as you continue to expand your reality.

With problem solving when it is that you are limited to one solution to a problem then you only need to expand the realm of possibility and you will find that there were many solutions. There are, in fact, thousands of solutions, all of which can work well. So it is with your concern in this area. As you expand you will find that it is more obvious, and it won't be a cumbersome thing, in any way; you will simply have expanded into alternatives to the alternative, and as we have said, if you need the stability of looking at the world in terms of linear, consequential sequences, for example, in the area of history, then that is where you need to be. If you are ready to expand into alternatives, then that is where you also need to be. It is possible that you can be both places at the same time and still understand. In fact, that is the reality you are dealing with so that you can have the stability of a belief and the understanding gained through an expansive process. Essentially that is occurring a great deal, at this time, for you are assuming the stability of orthodox Christianity while you are expanding your consciousness in other areas essentially guilt free, for example, psychic exploration or the area of considering the possibility of UFO's, or in a number of other areas as well. You can have hundreds, literally hundreds and thousands of realities going on at the same time and not be conscious of them or be able to verbalize their presence, but on a knowing level you are aware that they do exist and can accept them. You will find that those persons with multiple personalities, for example, are functioning on many levels but need the stability of one coherent identity but we will not go into that at this point. We will in a later book, My Children.

There are many areas of discussion that could at least be explored verbally, but we will not have time in this book to go into them and will save some of that material for later books, for they fall better within those categories.

"You must not be frustrated."

Session #73
   May 30, 1981
   3:16 P.M. – ?

You will see that in the Life around you people are seeking linear, sequential answers to cosmic questions and will continue to do so. You will learn to deal with them and will be frustrated with their simplicity and lack of God, but will see that is only where they need to be and will understand that they are growing rapidly. You must not be frustrated with those around you, their absorption with personality, linear sequences, and trivia, for when one goes to the absurdism that occurs. We'll heal those who are absorbed with it, ultimately, for they will either broaden or they will not try until they must, but they are growing much more rapidly than you can envision.

"My Beloved Children, I Am closer to you than your own thoughts and deeper than your soul."

Session #74
  May 30, 1981
  9:04 P.M. – ?

You will see that the purpose of this book has been to enlarge and enlighten and show that you are so very loved by Me, for you are Life, and that Life is of God and you are ultimately of God. You will understand that I AM All there is, and will do so very soon. You must never fear again the power of what your religions have termed Satan, for Satan is only an illusion within an illusion and like a mist will vanish soon, and you will see that you are Love itself. When you leave the Earth you will be able to deal with the World of Fear, but you will still be within the illusion, like a person walking through a mystical garden created by a holograph. You are reality and your holograph is not on the same level as your reality. Ultimately it is the product of your consciousness. You will see this more clearly in the second book which will follow this book. That book will deal with one of the single most puzzling subjects that you are now consciously dealing with although there are subjects that you are dealing with, unconsciously, that are greater but on the conscious level; this is the subject of sin and repentance, or pain or karmic debt. These are subjects that are very difficult for you to deal with and the book on Karmic Debt will go into that at greater length than this book. As I have said you must understand that this book was not written by Pat and was not the creation of a subconscious mind, and the support given by Barbara was support of Divine Love but this book was written long before Pat and Barbara ever entered this plane and is not to be taken as a divine revelation that you will now pound into the ground with theories and assumption, group discussions and treaties, but rather is, as I have said, to be read and discarded if it is not inspiring. That is all it was ever meant to be, My Children. You will see that you will never be separate from Me in any way under any circumstances at any time, My Beloved Children, for I am closer to you than your own thoughts and deeper than your soul.

SESSION
ON THE SOURCE

Messages from God
PASSAGE FROM FEAR
Armageddon or Renaissance?

and

Messages from God
PASSAGE FROM KARMA
A Coming Release from Sin and Repentance

Channeled through Patricia Grabow
Support given by Barbara McCormick

Questions for the Session on The Source of this material were
posed by Bruce McArthur
March 1982·

SESSION ON THE SOURCE

of the two channeled books:

Messages from God
PASSAGE FROM FEAR
Armageddon or Renaissance?

and

Messages from God
PASSAGE FROM KARMA
A Coming Release from Sin and Repentance

Transcribed Tape #6
Questions–Session on The Source

Sessions were recorded at Trinity Ranch; Hamilton, Montana in February 1982, following the channeling of *Messages from God: Passage from Fear* and *Messages from God: Passage from Karma*. At that time, Barbara McCormick had passed away. Barbara, in addition to Bruce and Charlotte McArthur, had supported Patricia during the origin of the books. Bruce and Charlotte, two of the four people Patricia was led to before the books began, had been, for fourteen years, on the Board of Directors for the A.R.E. (Association for Research and Enlightenment), The Edgar Cayce Foundation. They were practical and spiritual support from the beginning of the channeling process, learned and comfortable with it.

Bruce asked to clarify the source of the books. He expressed the opinion that The Source for *Messages from God: Passage from Fear* and *Messages from God: Passage from Karma* was the purest Source he had known.

Patricia drove to Trinity Ranch with her seven-month-old Robbie, the child she was carrying when channeling the first book. This is a transcription of the first part of the sessions specifically addressing the nature of the source of the material for these books.

Patricia: You may ask the questions, My Son, regarding the source of these books. These are important questions, and you must understand that with the motive of clarity. You may ask questions that Patricia has not been able to ask or was afraid to ask.

Bruce: Thank you. I'm trying to understand from where the source of the material the books are coming from.

Patricia: Yes.

Bruce: The first question is: are you The Ultimate Source of All, and is there no greater awareness than you? Or are you a portion of that with equal awareness?

Patricia: Yes. It is a difficult question to answer. The book on Karmic Debt will clarify some of that question. The language is very difficult to deal with. In your language, you have assumed that partial is separate from a partial adjacent to it, when it is actually all a flowing whole; such as individuals are a flowing whole, and that a partial awareness is intermeshed with all the other 'partial awarenesses,' like salt in the stew is not separate from the stew. You will see that awareness-is-awareness like love-is-love. When it is felt, it is a universal truth. One does not experience a different grade of love from another; when they love, they share the same reality. The events surrounding that reality are different, but the reality is the same and is not measurable. That is, you cannot measure love by saying, "I love three liters or five liters of love." You love. It is a separate state of consciousness from, for example, the state of consciousness you went through when working on your income tax, My Son.

But, to continue with the understanding of the source:

The Source is not Patricia, in any way. She is only a channel for that. She was chosen because her motives were truly pure, and she truly would not abuse it in any way. She has had many opportunities in her lifetime to abuse power and has never chosen to do so. Because of that, she became a channel for a separate state of consciousness from a World of Fear.

The Source, throughout the book, is from what is termed the 'Spiritual Universe.' It is like a ray of sunlight that is energy and is not limited to the interaction on the plant that is produced in photosynthesis. But the photosynthesis is the effect, and so The Source is Universal Light. The photosynthesis that is occurring is the book itself, and the communication is from that Source. Light has its own character and is universal. So you could say that The Source is Universal Light. This does not answer your question. If you wish to go back to the specifics of your question, you may.

Bruce: This Universal Light, which is The Source, could be termed the Ultimate Source?

Patricia: Yes, it could be termed the Ultimate Source, but it is not. There is no Ultimate Source. There is an interplay, even within the earth of life; but each life has its own expression. In this case, you are dealing with the expression of that Light. A tree will express that Light in a separate way from a verbal expression; in this particular case, it is needed for Homo sapiens and verbal communication and on this plane. It is the clearest that can be expressed, given the limitations surrounding you.

You must understand that this is just one plane of existence, and Love is a hint of the nature of God. But this is not the totality of God. You are exploring, at this point, the broad sense of God, which is a hint similar to the analogy of the rock and the mountain. The rock is not the mountain, but it has characteristics of the mountain and is certainly worthy of looking at to study what could conceivably be a mountain. Looking at the rock, you cannot envision the size, shape, depth, breadth and life support system that a mountain truly is. However, it is a very broad attempt to understand the breadth with which you are dealing. Infinity is characteristic of God, but not understandable at this time on this plane.

Bruce: Through this material, are we tapping an aspect of infinity?

Patricia: Yes, you are; and within your Larger Being, you understand that, as those who are ready will understand that as well. This is frightening to Patricia. She can face this as well.

Bruce: Are you then essentially the same Source that channeled through Edgar Casey?

Patricia: Yes, but the perspective is different.

Bruce: And the same Source that channeled the Course in Miracles?

Patricia: Yes, I Am.

Bruce: Would you then be Charlotte's source?

Patricia: Yes, I will.

Bruce: How should we address you?

Patricia: You cannot. You cannot name feelings; this is very important that you not find a name.

Charlotte: A name would place a limitation?

Patricia: Yes, it would. It would also, for those who are living in a
World of Fear, allow them to harm those who are continuing this very
important work. It is important that there be protection for those who
are working on this. It is critical. Casey used terms that he knew
would allow people to slough off The Source comfortably and yet
listen to the work. It is important that you do the same.

Bruce: Al Miner in Florida channels a source which is a grouping
of entities known as 'Lama Sing.' What is the difference between
Lama Sing as a Source and You as a Source?

Patricia: There is no technical difference. If one can use the term
'multiple personalities' as The Source, then it is much more acceptable to a World of Fear. For it is understandable to other individuals
that it is used. Then people are not afraid of that source. The term
'Spiritual Universe' has frequently been used in the automatic writing.
The term that has also been used, within a larger sense, is 'soul mate.'
That is similar to what Lama Sing is using. It is, however, limiting
itself by limiting its source. And that is functional, because if the
source is limited, when one is dealing with a limited reality and fearful, then it is more acceptable to those who listen; you cannot communicate until you are able to communicate with individuals where
they are.
    Lama Sing's motives are pure. You will see that the motives of
the heart are truly all that allows a channel to occur. You still feel that

more information is needed, My Son? You could listen to the tape and then formulate further questions. It is acceptable to formulate questions that would relate to those specifically, dealing with what we have termed a World of Fear and answer the questions from that basis. It is important, in these books, to not limit The Source, within your own minds, to a personality or a grouping of personalities; for that would limit what is being communicated as well. It is very important, at this time, to supersede a sense of personality.

Bruce: I understand.

Patricia: Yes, you do.

Bruce: Is it You of whom Christ spoke when He said we should love God with all our heart, body, mind, and soul, and love our neighbors as ourselves?

Patricia: It is not I; it is within the individual. There is a difficult communication that must take place in this area. It is the Christ within that is to be loved. When the Christ within, as Jesus understood, is loved, there is a direct link with what has been traditionally called God. Then the individual understands all that he or she needs to understand and naturally loves what has been traditionally called God. It is not possible to do so without the use of the White Light, at this point: loving The Christ, within the individual, and not loving a defined sense of God, but more discovering what exists once that link is established.

The idea of loving God, as the Biblical admonition gives, is loving a preconception of God. Like a child learning to walk, the child truly does not understand what walking is at the point that he or she learns to walk. But the child finds delight in the process. When you love the Christ within you—it cannot be emphasized enough that the Christ exists within all life—then you go through the process of learning to walk not knowing where the walking process is leading you. You will discover more and more aspects of My Being, My Son.

This is, again, difficult to answer because few words in this language express the feeling experienced when this occurs. It is not that you should love God. It is that you cannot help doing it. Like a plant processing sunlight, it is not that the plant should process sunlight. It is the life of the plant. And I am your life.

Bruce: Thank you. This is very helpful.

Patricia: Yes, I understand that there are terms that are still needing clarification regarding this sense of source. It is important that the questions continue to be asked regarding The Source. Patricia is frightened by it and asks the same questions frequently relating to her fear.

Bruce: As I understand it, in another analogy: Spiritual Universe might represent, in such terms, a huge reservoir of water that various individuals can tap through a pipe leading to that reservoir. Patricia represents this pipe, and others such as Al Miner do too; so the knowledge becomes available to those who are seeking, to the degree that they can comprehend within their language and dimensional understanding.

Patricia: Yes, to the degree that they can overcome what they have been taught from an introduction into a World of Fear. In time, the pipe will not be needed at all and the reservoir will be tapped by everyone. And that is the goal that the individual understands.

Bruce: Would the transition from the World of Fear to the World of Love be the equivalent of the individual becoming Christ?

Patricia: We will clarify much of that, for that is not clear within the text itself, My Son. This is not yet easy for you to understand. You

293

will need exposure to the process involved and will become comfortable with the readings very soon. Barbara is here and supporting Pat metaphysically, as she was before. Please ask the next question.

Bruce: If all is good and all is God, then why is the "World of Fear" necessary?

Patricia: It is not now. It was a survival system that allowed for an evolution that had its day. It is a difficult concept but can be translated into the terms 'definition by antithesis': that is, understanding what is by its opposite. With the knowledge of what is, there was always a light in the room of darkness, like a crack in the door, or a seam in a wall, or whatever. There is no absolute darkness anywhere, My Son. It will seem difficult for you and Charlotte to initially learn about the use of Pat as a channel; but she will help you in many ways of which you will not be conscious, and she will never hurt you in any way. You may ask the next question.

Bruce: The book discourages the study of concepts in groups. It is my feeling that the concepts would be well worthwhile to study by an individual. Is that okay?

Patricia: It is to be done because you wish to, My Son, and is not a directive. But like all ideas, it is not a limited idea. It is a general feeling that when groups are formed, a social group begins, and one who explores receives ideas from others. In the present time, you are not interacting with social groups. You are with Me. In fact, social groups occur essentially in the past, as does language. This is difficult to understand. From the third book to be written, you will better understand the necessity for not having groups. But, you can do whatever you choose, for you are always being led. If you feel comfortable, you should study. You may ask the next question.

Bruce: You said Barbara is here?

Patricia: Yes, she is My Beloved, Beloved Daughter and will never be hurt, nor will Pat, by her leaving. She will visit Pat when she needs the help to cope with her own transition and will love her through this period of difficulty into a period of great joy, My Children. Barbara will help with the editing. It is not unnatural for Barbara to help edit; she is physically not from this school. One can always return to a classroom without it being unnatural and will return as a support, essentially, guest lecturer to the classroom. She has left, essentially graduated, but can help Pat now much more that she did before. You will all better understand the soul mate concept when the third book is written.

"When there is no need to control others, the male and female is not that important. The only threat of male and female, as with orthodox churches, is the fear of lack of control. But that fear will dissipate for those who are truly ready for it."

Order Form

Messages from God	Unit Price	Qty.	Extension
Passage from Fear	$19.95 $ 25.95 CAN		
Passage from Karma	$15.95 $ 20.95 CAN		
(Set of both books)	$29.95 $ 39.95 CAN		

+   Shipping & Handling   *per book*

within USA ☐ $4.50

Global Priority ☐   _____   X   _____   =   _____

*Call for Rate   no. of books

+   Sales Tax   (WA residents add 8.8%)   _____

Total payment $ _____

Payment Method:

Check/ Money Order ☐   Card # _____

Visa ☐   Expiration Date _____ / _____

     month   year

MasterCard ☐   _____

Cardholder's Signature

Orders via:

*Call in:
1-800-461-1931

Fax (this form):
425-398-1380

Postal:
Hara Publishing
P.O. Box 19732
Seattle, WA 98109

Online:
harapub@foxinternet.net
http://www.harapublishing.com

Deliver to:

name _____

address _____

city _____   state _____   zip _____

phone _____   email _____

Printed in the United States
6187